THE RIGHT TO IDENTITY AND ACCESS TO INFORMATION ON GENETIC ORIGIN AND PARENTAGE

European Family Law Series

Published by the Organising Committee of the
Commission on European Family Law

This book originated within the Scientific Research Network RETHINKIN_, funded by the Research Foundation Flanders (file funding number W000220N).

THE RIGHT TO IDENTITY AND ACCESS TO INFORMATION ON GENETIC ORIGIN AND PARENTAGE

Edited by

Ingrid Boone
Machteld Vonk

INTERSENTIA
Cambridge – Antwerp – Chicago

Intersentia Ltd
8 Wellington Mews
Wellington Street | Cambridge
CB1 1HW | United Kingdom
Tel: +44 1223 736 170
Email: contact@larcier-intersentia.com
www.larcier-intersentia.com

Distribution for the UK and
Rest of the World (incl. Eastern Europe)
NBN International
1 Deltic Avenue, Rooksley
Milton Keynes MK13 8LD
United Kingdom
Tel: +44 1752 202 301 | Fax: +44 1752 202 331
Email: orders@nbninternational.com

Distribution for Europe
Lefebvre Sarrut Belgium NV
Hoogstraat 139/6
1000 Brussels
Belgium
Tel: +32 (0)2 548 07 13
Email: contact@larcier-intersentia.com

Distribution for the USA and Canada
Independent Publishers Group
Order Department
814 North Franklin Street
Chicago, IL 60610
USA
Tel: +1 800 888 4741 (toll free) | Fax: +1 312 337 5985
Email: orders@ipgbook.com

ISBN 978-1-83970-437-6
D/2024/7849/31
NUR 822

British Library Cataloguing in Publication Data. A catalogue record for this book is available from the British Library.

CONTENTS

LIST OF CONTRIBUTORS

Ingrid Boone is a Professor of Family Law at the KU Leuven Faculty of Law and Criminology. Her research focuses on the legal design and consequences of the parent-child relationship in its various family forms. She is a member of the Scientific Research Network RETHINKIN_.

Soraya Bou-Sfia currently works at the academic bureau of the Dutch Supreme Court. In 2021 she successfully defended her PhD thesis at Utrecht University on 'The Meaning of Identity Rights for Children in Dutch Family Law. A Study of Articles 8 UNCRC and 8 ECHR'. Soraya graduated from VU University Amsterdam where she completed the Masters in Private Law and Notarial Law. Her research interest is in family law.

Elodie Decorte is a Master of Laws (2014, magna cum laude), Master of Notarial Law (2015, magna cum laude) at Ghent University and Doctor of Law at KU Leuven (2022). She is a substitute lecturer at KU Leuven (since 2023), a legal assistant in youth and children's law at SAM vzw, guiding social workers through the law (since 2022) and a member of the steering committee of the Descent Centre (since 2021).

Jozef Dorscheidt is an Associate Professor of Health Law at the Faculty of Law, Maastricht University, the Netherlands. He holds a PhD from the University of Groningen. Furthermore, he was an alternate juvenile judge at the District Court Groningen, a member of the Dutch Health Council and of the Central Committee on Medical Research involving Human Subjects (CCMO). His research interests involved children's rights issues in health care, legal matters of medical professionalism, and dilemmas at the beginning and the end of life. In Maastricht, his educational and research activities focus on the area of social medicine, especially in connection to labour law and social security law.

Astrid Indekeu is Master in Clinical Psychology/Sexology (KU Leuven), Doctor in Biomedical Sciences (KU Leuven) and a fellow at the KU Leuven (Centre for Sociological Research). She was awarded a research visit at the Brocher Foundation (Switzerland) and a Marie Curie Fellowship at the Karolinska Institute (Sweden). Astrid has been active in the international field of donor conception as a researcher and clinical psychologist since 2008. In 2023 she launched the Support and Expertise Centre for donor-conceived families (www.astridindekeu.com).

A. Janneke B.M. Maas (PhD) is a Researcher and policy-maker at Fiom, the Netherlands. She is Master in Health Sciences (Maastricht University) and Doctor in Developmental Psychology (Tilburg University). She has contributed to several (international) publications in the field of donor conception, and was part of the supervisory committee of the second evaluation of the Artificial Fertilisation Donor Data Act (WDKB) (2019). At Fiom, she is responsible for the collaboration with the Artificial Fertilisation Donor Data Office (SDKB).

Julie Nekkebroeck works as a psychologist/psychotherapist for Brussels-IVF and the Centre for Medical Genetics of the UZ Brussels. She obtained a Doctoral degree at the Vrije Universiteit Brussel in 2008 on 'The health of children born after Preimplantation Genetic Diagnosis' and gained further expertise in the domain of reproductive psychology resulting in several international peer-reviewed publications. For more than 10 years, she has been a full-time clinician, offering daily counselling to patients applying for fertility treatments, among which are patients considering use of donor gametes.

Machteld Vonk is Full Professor of Family Law at the Law Faculty of Radboud University, Nijmegen. Her research focuses on parent-child relationships in contemporary family law.

Tim Wuyts is an Associate Professor at the Law Faculty of the University of Hasselt, a member of the scientific network RETHINKIN_ and chair of the Dutch-speaking commission on the nomination of notaries. His research focuses on determining the role of social and biological parenthood in law.

INTRODUCTION

Ingrid Boone and Machteld Vonk

Do donor-conceived children have a right to know the identity of their sperm or egg donor or should donors have a choice to remain anonymous? What does relinquishing donor anonymity mean for establishing parentage? Should laws regulating access to donor information have retroactive effect? What are the experiences of children conceived with donor sperm? And how can we prepare prospective parents for raising a donor-conceived child? How can we facilitate contact between children and their donor? These are some of the questions that are discussed in the chapters of this book, which is the result of a multidisciplinary seminar about to the right to identity and access to information about genetic origins and parentage organised by RETHINKIN_.[1]

The book starts with a chapter that places the topic in a broader perspective. In this chapter Bou-Sfia explores the right to identity from an international human rights perspective. On the basis of extensive research on this topic, Bou-Sfia states in the Introduction that 'a right to identity is not one and the same as a right to know your origins' and 'the right to identity in the European Convention on Human Rights (ECHR) does not per se contain the same as rights to identity in other instruments'. The chapter examines case law of the European Court of Human Rights (ECtHR) in which the Court specifically refers to identity in the context of Article 8 ECHR. This provides insight into the scope of the right to identity and the concept of identity within the context of Article 8 ECHR. The chapter discusses the development of the right to identity in the Court's case law, from its first appearance in the Commission's report in the case *Burghartz v. Switzerland*[2] in 1992 to the present day. In order to understand the scope of the right to identity, it is vital to understand how the *concept* of identity is interpreted by the ECtHR. On the basis of the ECtHR's case law, Bou-Sfia concludes that identity is both a broad concept – that covers physical, social and personal identity – and an open concept that can develop over time. The right

1 RETHINKIN_ is a Scientific Research Network (WOG) 2015–2024 of the Research Foundation Flanders. RETHINKIN_ steers the scientific redefinition of family law in the Low Countries and aims at taking up an international leading role from there.

2 Report of the Commission to *Burghartz v. Switzerland* (1992).

to know one's origins is one of the aspects related to identity that has developed over time in the ECtHR's case law and may nowadays be regarded as one of the core aspects of identity.

In the second chapter Decorte discusses how ideas about whether a child should be told about their conception with donated gametes have changed over time. Traditionally parents were advised not to tell children they were donor-conceived, but nowadays it is deemed to be in the child's interest to know the details about their conception. This naturally raises the question whether a donor-conceived child has the right to know the identity of the donor? Decorte takes us on a journey through a number of jurisdictions and discusses how they regulate access to information about genetic origins in the context of medically assisted reproduction and whether the national regulations in place do effectively meet the interests of donor-conceived persons as set out in the international legal norms. Decorte discusses the current state of affairs in France, Germany, Ireland, the Netherlands, Switzerland, the United Kingdom and Victoria (Australia). The main focus is on the question how the national regulations strike a balance between the interests of those who were conceived before the new system was introduced ('old' donor-conceived persons) and those who donated at a time when the law still guaranteed anonymity ('old' donors). Some jurisdictions have gone all the way and have abolished donor anonymity completely and with retro-active effect. This approach ensures that all donor-conceived persons are treated equally, at least theoretically. In practice, whether 'old' donor-conceived persons can actually have access to information about their donor depends on whether the information is still available. Several jurisdictions give 'old' donors some control over the release of their personal information: their prior consent is needed or they can oppose to the release of the information. To be successful these systems must be accompanied by additional measures, e.g. encouraging donors to adopt a more open attitude and active preservation of the remaining information.

In the third chapter Wuyts describes different legal paths to ensure the right of (minor or adult) children to know their origin when raised by others than their biological parents outside of adoption cases. Looking at the latest developments in European countries, the chapter discusses new legal paths for children to discover that they are not genetically related to one or both of their legal parents and to discover the identity of their genetic parents. Some jurisdictions recognise that providing information about the child's parentage is part of the parental responsibilities. In addition, in some legal systems a child could use information proceedings to force a (legal) parent to reveal the child's genetic origins. The chapter also describes different legal paths by which to establish genetic origins, once a child knows or seeks certainty about the identity of their biological parents. Wuyts distinguishes three approaches: monistic, dual and blended. In the monistic approach genetic origin can only be established through parenthood proceedings. This path has been considerably widened since the ECtHR pushed national authorities to revise their laws on parenthood proceedings in light of the right to know one's origins. In the dual approach, parenthood proceedings are not the only way to establish one's genetic origins. Some jurisdictions have specific proceedings to discover and establish parentage without legal consequences or with limited legal consequences. In the blended approach the boundaries of the concept of legal family are expanded to include more than two legal parents. Wuyts argues that states should consider a system of multiple parenthood, in which the contributions of genetic and social parents to the life of the child are given appropriate legal consequences.

Conception with the assistance of a donor challenges Euro-American socio-cultural norms and values about kinship and family ties, that are fundamentally based on a biogenetic connection. Indekeu presents the findings of empirical research on the meaning that (intending) parents, donor-conceived people and donors give to genes and genetic relations, and their experiences. The findings illustrate that the meaning of genes and genetics is multi-layered and changeable, dependent on the context, and can even carry conflicting meanings for one individual. Genes can be simultaneously relevant and irrelevant. The importance given to genes can change over time. In giving meaning to genes and genetic connections, people show great flexibility regarding whether or not particular aspects of 'biological' processes and substances matter in their construction of kinship, and show creativity in relation to how such things are made meaningful. One thing that is common is that all those involved struggle with the deeply rooted socio-cultural ideology of biogenetic kinship. A suitable vocabulary is missing. Indekeu argues that each person involved in this field (personal or professional) should be given flexibility in the vocabulary that they use rather than having a specific vocabulary imposed upon them, or imposing a vocabulary on others. Donor conception creates complex networks. In the last decade more and more services have been set up to facilitate contact between genetic relatives. These services make it possible for same-donor peers to find and contact each other. Indekeu concludes that in the search for information about ancestry, (genetic) networks are created rather than merely connections between two people. As a society, we are only beginning to explore these constantly expanding networks.

Moral standards, public attitudes towards the importance of genetics and kinship in parentage, and legal frameworks also influence the counselling of intending parents by fertility centres. Fertility centres which offer treatment with donor gametes have a responsibility to offer evidence-based counselling on the use of donor gametes, including information provision, assessment of readiness to use donor gametes, guidance of patients on deciding whether to disclose donor conception and psycho-education on the lifelong management of this topic. Nekkebroeck's chapter gives us an insight into the daily practice of counselling parents who consider use of donor gametes in Belgium's largest fertility clinic, Brussels IVF. First the chapter describes the characteristics of the population in need of donor gametes, the types of donation offered at the fertility clinic and what counselling in infertility entails. Only professionally trained mental health professionals can provide infertility counselling. The chapter then goes into the details of counselling intending parents in need of donor gametes in daily practice. How do mental health professionals help intending parents to go through a change (and grief) process, since the initial idea of procreating with own genetic material does not correspond to what is possible? How is the readiness of intending parents – heterosexual couples, lesbian couples or single women – for the use of donor gametes assessed? Nekkebroeck explains that practices in counselling intended parents who consider use of donor gametes have changed significantly over the past few decades, from stressing the need for secrecy, in the past, to more actively promoting openness nowadays. Donor conception is a topic that not only needs to be managed prior to conception but also after conception and eventually for an entire lifetime by parents as well as children. However, once patients achieve pregnancy, they leave the fertility clinic and further follow-up is not offered as standard. Nekkebroeck argues that co-operation of the fertility centres with professional networks should be encouraged to ensure families and donors have access to additional support and long-term follow up.

The last two chapters zoom in on experiences in The Netherlands, which may be relevant for other jurisdictions developing regulations surrounding the knowledge of origins. In 1994 the Dutch Supreme Court ruled that children in principle have a right to know who their parents are.[3] There are circumstances where a biological parent's right to anonymity outweighs the right of the child, but these cases are very rare. In brief, the case concerned was brought by a woman born in 1935 in an institution for unwed mothers. This institution would record the identity of the biological father (if this information was available) in the pregnant woman's file upon her entering the institution. The daughter asked the institution for access to the information about her biological father in her mother's file, but the institution claimed it could not grant access to this information without the mother's consent. The Dutch Supreme Court decided that the institution should provide the child with the information about her biological father despite the mother's refusal to consent because the right of the daughter to know the identity of her father outweighed the mother's right to keep this information secret. The reasoning in this judgment is, amongst other things, based on a general right to personality which forms the basis for many constitutional rights relating to the integrity of the person, Article 7 of the UN Convention on the Rights of the Child and a 1989 judgment by the German *Bundesverfassungsgericht* on a similar question. The 1994 judgment did not cover the right to information about genetic origins for children conceived

3 Hoge Raad 15 April 1994, ECLI:NL:HR:1994:ZC1337.

with donor sperm or eggs, because there was a Bill pending in Parliament on this topic. This Bill, however, was not passed by Parliament until 2003, and came into force on 1 April 2004 as the Artificial insemination Donor Data Act.[4] The Act gives children conceived with donor gametes after 1 June 2004 the option to receive information about their donor (including the identity of the donor). Since 2004 the Act has been evaluated twice, in 2012 and in 2019. Dorscheidt's chapter discusses the second evaluation of the Act which was aimed at establishing whether the Act in its current form is 'children's rights-proof'. There are a number of concerns relating both to the Act itself and to the application of the Act in practice. Since the very beginning there have been problems with the registration of donor data by the providers of fertility services in the central register held by the Artificial Insemination Donor Data Foundation that was set up in 2004. Furthermore, serious concerns were raised in relation to the Act's transitional regime with regard to access to donor data for children conceived before 1 June 2004. The Act gives children conceived with donor gametes after 1 June 2004 the option to receive information at their request from the Foundation about the identity of the donor, but the donor must consent to the dissemination of this information. If the donor refuses to consent, the Foundation must weigh the interests of the donor-conceived child against the donor's interests. The child's interests take precedence unless the donor has substantial interests that outweigh those of the child. It is, as yet, unclear what such substantial interests might be since the donor child must be 16 years old before donor-identifying information can be requested. However, children conceived with donated gametes before 1 June 2004 do not fall under this regime. Whether or not they have access to donor-identifying information depends on the choices made by the donor at the time of donation or the donor's willingness to come forward at a later date.

The possibilities for children conceived before 1 June 2004 to acquire information about their donor are discussed in the final chapter. Indekeu and Maas discuss 10 years of experience with the Fiom KID-DNA database, which is a unique database in the sense that it is 'the only donor conception DNA database that has been under unchanged management (Fiom), in collaboration with the same genetic laboratory (the Canius-Wilhelmina Hospital, Nijmegen) and stable funding for more than 10 years.' The database, which was launched in 2010, is a voluntary register that facilitates the exchange of information and contact between donor-conceived people and donors. The chapter briefly discusses the way the database operates and the psychosocial support that is offered to the registrants, but its focus is on the (growing) number of donors and donor-conceived people who registered with the database, how many of them were linked over the years and their experiences of subsequent contact.

4 Wet donorgegevens kunstmatige bevruchting, *Staatsblad* 2002, 240.

The database is a voluntary database and relies on the willingness of donors to be found and brought into contact with their genetic offspring. Both Dorscheidt and Indekeu and Maas address the consequences of the prospective nature of the Artificial Insemination Donor Data Act, which creates an imbalance in the right to know genetic origins for those conceived before and after 1 June 2004 with donated gametes. The voluntary register will offer this knowledge for some, but the complex question remains whether when push comes to shove the rights of the donor who was promised anonymity should outweigh the child's right to know their genetic origins or vice versa.

A recent case before the European Court of Human Rights shows once more how relevant these topics are.[5] In the case of *Gauvin-Fournis and Silliau v. France* the applicants complained that they were refused permission by the national authorities to obtain information about the identity of their respective donors or non-identifying material about them, pursuant to the principle of anonymity in gamete donations. The applicants were born in 1980 and 1989 respectively through medically assisted reproduction involving a donor, at a time when donor anonymity was the rule in France. The coming into force of the Bioethics Act of 2 August 2021 on 1 September 2022 put an end to this principle of anonymity. Children born from gametes donated prior to that date can apply to a commission which is responsible for contacting the donors in order to obtain their consent to the disclosure of the relevant information. The first applicant had applied to the designated authority in this way but was informed that their request had been refused. At the time when the applicants had applied to the domestic courts and subsequently to the Court, it was absolutely impossible for them to obtain information about their donor. The ECtHR found that France had not breached its positive obligation to ensure effective respect for the applicants' private life. The Court reiterated that Article 8 ECHR protects the right to know one's origins. The Court noted that the claims of persons conceived through gamete donation are increasingly being acknowledged as legitimate, and are supported by the Court's case law to the effect that a mechanism for access to information about one's origins has to allow for balancing of the rights and interests at stake. The Court found that the French legislature had duly weighed the interests and rights at stake after an informed and gradual process of reflection on the need to lift donor anonymity. The Court concluded that the legislature had acted within its wide margin of appreciation, admittedly reduced by the fact that an essential part of the applicants' private life was at issue. This judgment illustrates the overall conclusion of the present book: the decision of a jurisdiction to lift donor anonymity is not the end of the process by far.

---

[5] ECtHR 7 September 2023, *Gauvin-Fournis v. France* and *Silliau v. France* nos. 21424/16 and 45728/17.

THE RIGHT TO IDENTITY IN THE EUROPEAN CONVENTION ON HUMAN RIGHTS

Soraya Bou-Sfia*

* Soraya Bou-Sfia wrote the dissertation 'The Meaning of Identity Rights for Children in Dutch Family Law' at Utrecht University (UCERF), under the supervision of Prof. mr. W.M. Schrama and mr. dr. S.D. Burri. She successfully completed her research on 17 September 2021. The present chapter is an adaptation of the second part of her thesis and written in response to the presentation she gave at the *RETHINKIN expert seminar* on 16 April 2021. The collection and selection of case law of the ECtHR is updated to 1 August 2020. This chapter should therefore serve as a basis for follow-up research.

1. INTRODUCTION

A right to identity for individuals is protected within the European human rights framework on the basis of Article 8 of the European Convention on Human Rights (ECHR). But what does the right to identity amount to? Is it a right for individuals to be themselves and to protect all that is important to their identity, which possibly demands respect for 'who a person is and to whom or what someone belongs'? Does the right require recognition of an individual's existence: a right to be recognised as a person (before the law), which demands respect for the fact 'that someone exists'? Or does the right to identity come down to 'the right to know one's biological/genetic origin', since the right to identity not infrequently comes up in discussions on parentage in the context of adoption, anonymous birth,[1] surrogacy etc. This chapter on the right to identity aims to answer such questions on the basis and meaning of this right as it is given in the case law of the European Court on Human Rights (ECtHR, or the Court). If the right to identity arises in the context of Article 8 ECHR, what are we talking about then? In this chapter it will become clear that: 1) a right to identity is not one and the same as a right to know your origin, and 2) the right to identity in the ECHR does not per se contain the same as rights to identity in other instruments. Research into the meaning and scope of the right to identity as embodied in various instruments clarifies what the possible similarities and differences are. Although the meaning of 'identity rights' in other instruments than the ECHR is hereafter briefly discussed, the focus is on the meaning of the right to identity given by the ECtHR.

What is meant by 'identity rights' requires some explanation. After all, there is no unambiguous explanation available as to what is meant by 'identity rights'. Logically, identity rights can best be seen as rights that relate to the protection of the identity of individuals. Because the term 'identity' itself is not unambiguous either, this author defines 'identity rights' as rights that *explicitly* focus on identity, such as the 'right to identity' based on Article 8 ECHR. The ECHR is, however, not the only instrument that protects the identity of individuals through a right that explicitly connects to identity.

Identity rights can be found in multiple legal instruments, at different levels. They occur at international, regional and national levels and are embodied in binding as well as non-binding legal instruments. A key example of identity rights is undoubtedly Article 8 of the Convention on the Rights of the Child (CRC). This children's right explicitly concerns the preservation of a child's[2]

1 An anonymous birth is a birth where the mother gives birth to a child without disclosing her identity, or where her identity remains unregistered. See, e.g., J. Marshall, 'Secrecy in births, identity rights, care and belonging', (2018) 30(2) *Child and Family Law Quarterly*.

2 Based on Article 1 of the CRC 'a child means every human being below the age of eighteen years unless under the law applicable to the child, majority is attained earlier'.

identity and is part of the CRC since its establishment in 1989: 'States Parties undertake to respect the right of the child to preserve his or her identity ....' Whenever reference is made in literature to identity rights, Article 8 CRC is frequently cited. It is often mentioned that the introduction of Article 8 CRC was the first time that 'the right to identity' was explicitly laid down in a legally binding instrument.

This identity right for children is an important identity right, for several reasons. Not only because it is laid down in the (almost) globally ratified CRC and therefore has worldwide relevance, but also because of its influence on other human rights instruments. This influence is seen both in international and regional instruments. The inclusion of this right to preservation of children's identity in the 1989 convention has inspired later treaty drafters to also include a similar identity right for children. Examples are the 2006 International Convention for the Protection of All Persons from Enforced Disappearance (Article 25(4) CED)[3] and the 2008 Convention on the Rights of Persons with Disabilities (Principle 3(h) CRPD).[4] Also, Article 8 CRC is referred to in other instruments, such as the UNHCR Guidelines on Determining the Best Interests of the Child.[5] The influence of Article 8 CRC can also be seen at a regional level. A recent example can be found in the Brussels II-bis recast in which reference is made to Article 8 CRC.[6]

The protection of identity, however, is not only laid down as a specific right for children, but also as a right for all individuals. For example, the EU's Declaration of Fundamental Rights and Freedoms contains a general right to identity, which

---

3 'Given the need to protect ... their right to preserve, or to have re-established, their identity, including their nationality, name and family relations as recognized by law, States Parties which recognize a system of adoption or other form of placement of children shall have legal procedures in place to review the adoption or placement procedure, and, where appropriate, to annul any adoption or placement of children that originated in an enforced disappearance.'

4 'Respect for the evolving capacities of children with disabilities and respect for the right of children with disabilities to preserve their identities.'

5 'Important factors to be considered when determining the development needs of the child, as defined in the Convention on the Rights of the Child, include: the "right ... to preserve his or her identity, including nationality, name and family relations" (Article 8) ....' *2021 UNHCR Best Interests Guidelines: Assessing and Determining the Best Interests of the Child*, p. 51. https://www.refworld.org/pdfid/5c18d7254.pdf.

6 'Where a decision on the placement of a child in institutional or foster care is being contemplated in the Member State of the habitual residence of the child, the court should consider, at the earliest stage of the proceedings, appropriate measures to ensure respect of the rights of the child, in particular the right to preserve his or her identity and the right to maintain contact with the parents, or, where appropriate, with other relatives, in light of Articles 8, 9 and 20 of the UN Convention on the Rights of the Child.' Council Regulation (EU) 2019/1111 of 25 June 2019 on jurisdiction, the recognition and enforcement of decisions in matrimonial matters and the matters of parental responsibility, and on international child abduction, [2019] OJ L 178/1–115, recital 84.

also dates back to 1989.[7] Protection of identity was included in Article 6, which reads as follows: 'Everyone shall have the right to respect and protection for their identity.' Moreover, and more recently, it has become clear that regional human right instruments, such as the American Convention on Human Rights (ACHR) and the ECHR, contain a right to identity. These instruments contain no explicit right, but the regional human rights courts have 'accepted' such a right through interpretation of the treaties as 'living instruments that develop over time'. Thus, we may say that protection of identity has a broad legal basis and is strongly rooted in human rights, as protected through multiple identity rights.

The follow-up question is of course the question what do identity rights entail. What is protected by these identity rights? The meaning of identity rights is not immediately fathomable. This is first and foremost because no generally accepted definition or description of 'identity' is available, either as a term in daily use or as used in the legal field. Also, the term 'identity' is not easy to understand without a specific context. The legal instruments in which an identity right is laid down do not include a definition of 'identity'. As a consequence, it is not directly clear what is meant by 'identity' and what the various identity rights imply. However, the text of Article 8 CRC gives important direction on the interpretation of children's identity right: identity, according to the treaty provision, relates at least to a child's name, nationality and family relations. This also could, and ideally should, give direction on the interpretation of identity rights in other legal instruments, but the interaction between the different legal instruments cannot be presumed *a priori*. Although it is logical to assume that identity rights are interrelated, if only because all these rights explicitly refer to identity, it cannot be assumed that these rights aim to give the same meaning to and protection of identity. For the record: the fact that 'identity' in the context of Article 8 CRC concerns several personal characteristics of the child, does not mean that the same is true for the content of identity in the right to identity as a European human right. To what extent identity rights are interrelated, and to what extent their meaning and scope are equal, remains to be seen after more research into identity rights from different instruments; such as the following study on the identity right based on the ECHR (hereafter: 'the right to identity'), as used and interpreted by the ECtHR.

2. CASE LAW

It is eminently the Court that, by interpreting the convention's treaty rights, gives substance to these rights and the resulting protection. The interpretation and

7 Adopted by the European Parliament on 12 April 1989.

implications of the convention's treaty rights are not fixed by definition. The ECHR is regarded by the Court as 'a living instrument',[8] which implies that the content of the convention provisions continues to develop over time. And it is because of this development that the right to identity falls within the sphere of the ECHR. After all, the right to identity doesn't follow from the treaty text, which provides merely that 'Everyone has the right to respect for his private and family life, his home and his correspondence.' The Court's case law is therefore the main source for a study on the right to identity in the European human rights framework.[9]

To reflect on what the case law tells us about the right to identity, we need to find out which case law is relevant. So, we open HUDOC, but then what? In selecting relevant cases for the right to identity, the aim is of course to provide as complete an overview as possible. Therefore, no distinction should be made between the different types of documents in the Court's database. All cases could be relevant for the interpretation of the right to identity. Time is also not a relevant factor for selecting possible relevant cases, since of course recent as well as 'old' cases could teach us more about the right to identity. And since case law is published in at least either English or French, searches should be in both languages. So, no filter then, what's next? The search terms themselves. Which search terms will lead us to possible relevant cases? Here the complexity of the study becomes visible. First of all, if we search for 'identity', we get more than 6,000 hits. Needless to say, it is practically impossible to examine the relevance of all case law in which the term identity is used. Also, when we randomly look at the results, we quickly discover that not all cases in which the term 'identity' appears are necessarily relevant. Identity occurs quite frequently in ECtHR case law that is not relevant for the study on the right to identity. For example, there are many cases in which 'identity' only pops up in the context of the identity of the perpetrator, of the victim, of the donor etc. At the same time is it possible that case law in which the term identity is *not* mentioned, may still be of importance for the study on the right to identity. But how do we know? Therefore, I opted to at least connect to case law in which 'identity' is explicitly mentioned, thus leaving out possible relevant case law in which the term 'identity' does not occur.

Multiple searches firstly connected to 'right to identity' were used to systematically search for as much relevant case law as possible. The result is 48 cases addressing the right to identity as a treaty right.[10] It turned out

---

8 The Court notes this for the first time in: *Tyrer v. United Kingdom* (1978), para. 31, as follows: 'The Court must also recall that the Convention is a living instrument which, as the Commission rightly stressed, must be interpreted in the light of present-day conditions.'

9 The case law analysis here covers the published cases in the online database HUDOC.

10 The right to identity first comes up in three cases of the Commission: Report of the Commission in *Burghartz v. Switzerland* (1992); report of the Commission in *Stjerna v.*

that not all of these cases are relevant for the study on the interpretation of the right to identity. In many of these cases 'identity' does not play a visible role. In some of these cases the term 'identity' comes up more often, but for example only in the context of identity cards or the (non-)disclosure of identity of the complainant.[11] In addition, it turns out that there are many more cases in which 'identity' is mentioned in the context of Article 8 ECHR, without mentioning 'the right to identity'; these cases could nevertheless still be relevant for the study on the right to identity. The analysis of the case law on 'the right to identity' revealed considerations on the protection of identity that were not directly linked to 'the right to identity' and where other ECHR case law was cited without explicit reference therein to 'the right to identity'. Therefore, more case law was subsequently collected, selected and examined using various searches in which common terms or considerations related to identity are used. For example, the case law on *physical, social and personal identity*. The starting points for further research were thus determined on the basis of case law that explicitly mentions the right to identity. Unlike the search for case law that explicitly mentions 'the right to identity' where no filter was used, these searches were conducted using the filter '8 ECHR', because the right to identity only pops up in the context of Article 8 ECHR.

3. LEGAL BASIS

The unfiltered search for case law that explicitly mentions the right to identity as a treaty right leads to cases that reveal that this right consistently appears

---

Finland (1993), and in the admissibility decision *K.B. v. The Netherlands* (1993). The right to identity further comes up in 40 cases of the Court. *Bensaid v. United Kingdom* (2001); *P.G. and J.H. v. United Kingdom* (2001); *Odièvre v. France* (2003); *Perry v. United Kingdom* (2003); *Peck v. United Kingdom* (2003); *Morley v. The United Kingdom* (2004); *H.F. v. Slovakia* (2005); *Paramsothy v. The Netherlands* (2005); *Wisse v. France* (2005); *Ebru and Tayfin Colak v. Turkey* (2006); *Jäggi v. Switzerland* (2006); *Karov v. Bulgaria* (2006); *Calmanovici v. Romania* (2008); *Pay v. United Kingdom* (2008); *Reklos and Davourlis v. Greece* (2009); *Menéndez García v. Spain* (2009); *Friend, the Countryside alliance et al. v. United Kingdom* (2009); *Gillan and Quinten v. United Kingdom* (2010); *Uzun v. Germany* (2010); *Güroglu v. Turkey* (2010); *Ciubotaru v. Moldova* (2010); *Pascaud v. France* (2011); *Godelli v. Italy* (2012); *Misick v. United Kingdom* (2012); *Konstantinidis v. Greece* (2014); *Mennesson v. France* (2014); *Labassee v. France* (2014); *Gough v. United Kingdom* (2014); *Gözüm v. Turkey* (2015); *J.S. v. United Kingdom* (2015); *Vukota-Bojic v. Switzerland* (2016); *Bărbulescu v. Romania* (2016); *Vasilica Mocanu v. Romania* (2016); *Ivashchenko v. Russia* (2018); *Benedik v. Slovenië* (2018); *Silliau v. France* (2018); *Gauvin-Fournis v. France* (2018); *Mifsud v. Malta* (2019); *Breyer v. Germany* (2020); *Ghoumid et al. v. France* (2020). The right to identity is also mentioned in five other cases only in an opinion: *Sheffield and Horsham v. United Kingdom* (1998); *Koua Poirrez v. France* (2003); *Vereinigung Bildener Künstler v. Austria* (2007); *N. v. United Kingdom* (2008) and *Ramadan v. Malta* (2016).

11 *Iovcev et al. v. Moldova and Russia* (2019).

in the context of Article 8 ECHR.[12] Almost all cases specifically mention the right to identity as a component of the right to respect for private life under Article 8 ECHR, which is distinguished from the right to respect for family life, one's home and correspondence.[13] In a joint dissenting opinion of several judges in *Odièvre v. France* (2003), it is explained that the right to respect for private life includes aspects that are essential to private life on the one hand and aspects that are peripheral on the other. In the view of these judges, the right to identity belongs to 'the inner core of the right to respect for one's private life'.[14] Subsequent case law shows that the Court has adopted this view.[15] The question arises, however, whether the right to identity is, or should, only be connected to the sphere of private life, and not also to that of family life. It is interesting that in case law where reference is made to the child's right to preserve his or her identity based on Article 8 CRC, this right usually comes up in the sphere of the right to respect for family life. Thus, in the context of Article 8's 'respect for family life', the protection of identity may also come into play. The interrelation between identity and private life, on the one hand,

---

12 *Burghartz v. Switzerland* (1992); *Stjerna v. Finland* (1993); *K.B. v. The Netherlands* (1993); *Sheffield and Horsham v. United Kingdom* (1998); *Bensaid v. United Kingdom* (2001); *P.G. and J.H. v. United Kingdom* (2001); *Odièvre v. France* (2003); *Perry v. United Kingdom* (2003); *Peck v. United Kingdom* (2003); *Koua Poirrez v. France* (2003); *Morley v. United Kingdom* (2004); *H.F. v. Slovakia* (2005); *Paramsothy v. The Netherlands* (2005); *Wisse v. France* (2005); *Ebru and Tayfin Colak v. Turkey* (2006); *Karov v. Bulgaria* (2006); *Jäggi v. Switzerland* (2006); *Vereinigung Bildener Künstler v. Austria* (2007); *Calmanovici v. Romania* (2008); *Pay v. United Kingdom* (2008); *N. v. United Kingdom* (2008); *Menéndez García v. Spain* (2009); *Friend, the Countryside alliance et al. v. United Kingdom* (2009); *Reklos and Davourlis v. Greece* (2009); *Gillan and Quinten v. United Kingdom* (2010); *Uzun v. Germany* (2010); *Güroglu v. Turkey* (2010); *Ciubotaru v. Moldova* (2010); *Pascaud v. France* (2011); *Godelli v. Italy* (2012); *Misick v. United Kingdom* (2012); *Konstantinidis v. Greece* (2014); *Mennesson v. France* (2014); *Labassee v. France* (2014); *Gough v. The United Kingdom* (2014); *Gözüm v. Turkey* (2015); *J.S. v. United Kingdom* (2015); *Vukota-Bojic v. Switzerland* (2016); *Bărbulescu v. Romania* (2016); *Vasilica Mocanu v. Romania* (2016); *Ramadan v. Malta* (2016); *Silliau v. France* (2018); *Gauvin-Fournis v. France* (2018); *Ivashchenko v. Russia* (2018); *Benedik v. Slovenia* (2018); *Mifsud v. Malta* (2019); *Breyer v. Germany* (2020); *Ghoumid et al. v. France* (2020).

13 This isn't the case in *Gözüm v. Turkey* (2015), where it emerged that Article 8 ECHR includes the right to identity. See para. 34 of the French-language decision (not included in the English-language decision): 'Sur ce point, la Cour rappelle que *l'article 8 protège*, entre autres, *un droit à l'identité* et à l'épanouissement personnel ainsi que celui de nouer et de développer des relations avec ses semblables et le monde extérieur (voir Burghartz c. Suisse, 22 février 1994, §24, série A no 280-B) [emphasis added]'. Also in opinions where the right to identity appears, this right is linked to the right to respect for private life under Article 8 ECHR. See the opinions in *Koua Poirrez v. France* (2003) with reference to *Bensaid v. United Kingdom* (2001); joint dissenting opinion in *Odièvre v. France* (2003); *Vereinigung Bildener Künstler v. Austria* (2007) with reference to *Wisse v. France* (2005); *N. v. United Kingdom* (2008) with reference to *Bensaid v. United Kingdom* (2001).

14 Joint dissenting opinion on *Odièvre v. France* (2003), para. 11.

15 *Jäggi v. Switzerland* (2006); *Menéndez García v. Spain* (2009); *Pascaud v. France* (2011); *Godelli v. Italy* (2012); *Konstantinidis v. Greece* (2014); *Mennesson v. France* (2014); *Labassee v. France* (2014).

and family life, on the other, is one that might require further attention and reflection.

4. DEVELOPMENT

The right to identity first appeared in the case law of the European Court in the early 1990s. It was the Commission that introduced this right as a treaty right. In the Commission's report on admissibility in the case of *Burghartz v. Switzerland* in 1992 the Commission considered that the right to respect for private life under Article 8 ECHR ensures a sphere in which everyone can freely develop and realise their personality, and that this right to develop and realise one's personality necessarily entails the right to identity.

> The Commission considers that the right to respect for private life as enshrined in Article 8 para. 1 (Art. 8-1) of the Convention ensures a sphere within which everyone can freely pursue the development and fulfilment of the personality. *The right to develop and fulfil one's personality necessarily comprises the right to identity …* (emphasis added).[16]

This observation by the Commission, which specifically shows the connection between the right to respect for private life, the right to identity and the right to the development and realisation of personality, was not further explained and was apparently taken for granted. A year later, in a report in the case of *Stjerna v. Finland* (1993) and in *K.B. v. The Netherlands* (1993), the Commission again referred to the right to identity and in a similar way as in *Burghartz v. Switzerland* (1992). The Court, however, did not adopt the ruling of the Commission regarding the right to identity in these cases. Years later, in 2001, the Court did refer to the right to identity in its case law, for the first time in the case of *Bensaid v. United Kingdom* (2001). The Court referred to the right to identity as previously introduced by the Commission, explicitly referring to the report of the Commission in the case of *Burghartz v. Switzerland* (1992).

> 'Private life' is a broad term not susceptible to exhaustive definition … *Article 8 protects a right to identity …* (see, for example, *Burghartz*, cited above, opinion of the Commission, p. 37, §47 …) (emphasis added).[17]

---

16 Report of the Commission in *Burghartz v. Switzerland* (1992), para. 47: https://www.stradalex.eu/en/se_src_publ_jur_eur_cedh/document/echr_16213-90_001-45558. See also the report of the Commission in *Stjerna v. Finland* (1993), para. 56 and the admissibility decision *K.B. v. The Netherlands* (1993).

17 *Bensaid v. United Kingdom* (2001), para. 47.

In this paragraph, the Court explains what constitutes private life as protected under Article 8 ECHR, highlighting the right to identity as a component of private life. This is presented by the Court as an established fact. The rationale of the right to identity mentioned by the Commission – namely the link with the development and realisation of personality – is left unmentioned by the Court. Because the Court refers to the Commission's report, it may be assumed that the Court agrees with this view of the Commission.

Since *Bensaid v. United Kingdom* (2001), the right to identity has appeared in several cases of the Court and almost always as a component of the right to respect for private life. Set against the large body of case law relating to Article 8 ECHR, reference to the right to identity could be seen as relatively rare. Nevertheless, the right to identity has recurred with regularity over the past two decades in the case law of the Court (40 cases of the Court and in addition in opinions in four other Court cases).[18] In many of the cases with a reference to the right to identity, this right is mentioned in a similar paragraph as in *Bensaid v. United Kingdom* (2001). Thus, the right to identity, when referred to by the Court, is often part of the standard consideration regarding the explanation of the interpretation of the right to respect for private life under Article 8 ECHR. Therefore, it cannot be said that cases in which the right to identity is mentioned are necessarily about the right to identity.

A year after *Bensaid v. United Kingdom* (2001), in *Mikulić v. Croatia* (2002), the Court referred to 'identity', again in its consideration of private life, albeit in a different way. The Court considers in this case – for the first time – that private life sometimes includes aspects of an individual's physical and social identity: 'Private life, in the Court's view, includes a person's physical and psychological integrity and can sometimes embrace aspects of an individual's physical and social identity ....'[19] The link with the right to identity is obvious, even if the Court itself does not explicitly make this link. Physical, social and personal identity refer to both identity and private life. Precisely because the right to private life includes the right to identity, it is not obvious to assume that this paragraph is *un*connected to the right to identity. This means that these cases, although they do not mention the right to identity explicitly, could give more insight in the

18 *Bensaid v. United Kingdom* (2001); *P.G. and J.H. v. United Kingdom* (2001); *Odièvre v. France* (2003); *Perry v. United Kingdom* (2003); *Peck v. United Kingdom* (2003); *H.F. v. Slovakia* (2005); *Wisse v. France* (2005); *Ebru and Tayfin Colak v. Turkey* (2006); *Jäggi v. Switzerland* (2006); *Calmanovici v. Romania* (2008); *Reklos and Davourlis v. Greece* (2009); *Gillan and Quinten v. United Kingdom* (2010); *Uzun v. Germany* (2010); *Ciubotaru v. Moldova* (2010); *Pascaud v. France* (2011); *Godelli v. Italy* (2012); *Konstantinidis v. Greece* (2014); *Mennesson v. France* (2014); *Labassee v. France* (2014); *Gough v. United Kingdom* (2014); *Gözüm v. Turkey* (2015); *Vukota-Bojic v. Switzerland* (2016); *Bărbulescu v. Romania* (2016); *Vasilica Mocanu v. Romania* (2016); *Ivashchenko v. Russia* (2018); *Benedik v. Slovenia* (2018); *Mifsud v. Malta* (2019); *Breyer v. Germany* (2020); *Ghoumid et al. v. France* (2020).

19 *Mikulić v. Croatia* (2002), para. 53.

meaning of the right to identity. It also means that the right to identity in the Court's jurisprudence is more strongly developed than appears at first glance when looking only at the cases that expressly address the right to identity.

5. THE CONCEPT OF IDENTITY

An important question is how identity, in the context of the right to identity, should be interpreted. After all, insight into the meaning of the concept of identity is essential to better understand this right. It should be noted that none of the cases in which the right to identity appears discuss the concept of identity in general terms. What identity generally entails in the sense of the right to identity is thus open. But in a few cases in which the right to identity is mentioned, the Commission and the Court *do* provide more insight into the concept of identity (section 5.1 below). As already mentioned (section 4 above), the protection of identity in the context of Article 8 ECHR extends at least to one's personal, physical and social identity. Therefore, case law on these 'categories of identity' (personal, physical and social identity) could also give more insight into the concept of identity (section 5.2 below). The collection of case law shows that the concept of identity in the context of the right to identity in Article 8 ECHR in any case relates to at least various personal characteristics and certain ties.

5.1. ASPECTS OF IDENTITY

What can we learn about the concept of identity through cases that explicitly mention the right to identity? From the three cases in which the Commission refers to the right to identity in the early '90s, it is made explicit that the concept of identity includes an individual's name.[20] The Commission considered that 'the right to develop and fulfil one's personality necessarily comprises the right to identity, and therefore to a name.'[21] All of these cases involve the last name of the complainants. However, it stands to reason that the right to identity includes both the first name and the last name of individuals, even if this is not made explicit in the decisions. There are no cogent arguments for the view that a person's surname does, but their first name does not fall under the concept of identity. Moreover, further examination of the case law reveals that the Court

---

[20] Report of the Commission in *Burghartz v. Switzerland* (1992); *Stjerna v. Finland* (1993); *K.B. v. The Netherlands* (1993).

[21] Report of the Commission in *Burghartz v. Switzerland* (1992), para. 47. See also the report of the Commission in *Stjerna v. Finland* (1993), para. 56 and the admissibility decision *K.B. v. The Netherlands* (1993).

considers in some cases that the first name *is* an aspect of identity. In that respect the cases *Bohlen v. Germany* (2015) and *Ernst August Von Hannover v. Germany* (2015) are important. Therein, the Court found that the complainants' first names were also an aspect of their identity.[22] Despite the absence of the right to identity in those cases, the link between identity and the first name makes it clear, in the author's opinion, that *the right* to identity also relates to the first name.

> The Court reiterates that Article 8 of the Convention does not contain any explicit provisions on forenames. However, since they constitute a means of identifying persons within their families and the community, forenames do concern private and family life …[23] The Court reiterates that the concept of 'private life' is a broad term not susceptible to exhaustive definition, which covers the physical and psychological integrity of a person and can therefore embrace multiple aspects of a person's identity, such as his or her name, including the forename.[24]

It can be further derived from a number of cases that the right to identity relates to both biological and legal ties of descent.[25] It follows clearly from *Jäggi v. Switzerland* (2006) that the concept of identity relates to biological and genetic ties, since the right to identity includes the right to know one's parentage:

> … in any event the right to know one's ascendants falls within the scope of the concept of 'private life', which encompasses important aspects of one's personal identity, such as the identity of one's parents (see *Odièvre v. France* [GC], no. 42326/98, §29, ECHR 2003-III, and *Mikulić*, cited above, §53). … The Court considers that the right to an identity, which includes the right to know one's parentage, is an integral part of the notion of private life.[26]

---

22 In the case law of the Court with regard to Article 8 of the ECHR, no other cases were found in which the Court established that the first name is part of the right to a name, and in which the first name is linked to identity by the Court. The search term 'including the forename' with the filter '8 ECHR' does not lead to more results.
In Court cases on changing one's first name, including *Erdagöz v. Turkey* (2008), *Golemanova v. Bulgaria* (2011) and *Taşkin (Kemal) et al. v. Turkey* (2010), the Court does not explicitly address identity. In *Taşkin (Kemal) et al. v. Turkey* (2010), however, the complainants argued that the refusal of the change of their forename constituted an unjustified breach of their cultural and ethnic identity. The Court ruled that the complainants were free to bear the desired surname and that the refusal of the change of first name did not hinder their personal identification. See paras. 65 and 66.

23 *Bohlen v. Germany* (2015), para. 35; *Ernst August Von Hannover v. Germany* (2015), para. 34.

24 *Bohlen v. Germany* (2015), para. 45; *Ernst August Von Hannover v. Germany* (2015), para. 44.

25 *Odièvre v. France* (2003); *Ebru and Tayfin Colak v. Turkey* (2006); *Jäggi v. Switzerland* (2006); *Menendez Garcia v. Spain* (2009); *Pascaud v. France* (2011); *Godelli v. Italy* (2012); *Konstantinidis v. Greece* (2014); *Mennesson v. France* (2014); *Labassee v. France* (2014); *Güroglu v. Turkey* (2010); *Gözum v. Turkey* (2015).

26 *Jäggi v. Switzerland* (2006), paras. 25 and 37.

It also follows from case law that the legal ties between a parent and child concern a crucial aspect of identity. The Court notes that an essential aspect of the identity of individuals is at stake where the legal parent-child relationship is concerned.[27]

In a number of cases, the Court relates nationality explicitly to identity.[28] While the Court does not explain which aspect of nationality is engaged, the cases show that it is about nationality in the sense of citizenship. Ethnicity is also considered by the Court to be an essential aspect of an individual's identity.[29] Furthermore, the right to identity has been related to gender identity in an opinion in *Sheffield and Horsham v. United Kingdom* (1998).[30] While the Court did not do so in that case, the Court refers to 'the right to gender identity' in other cases.[31] In these cases, the Court considered: that the right to gender identity is a fundamental aspect of the right to private life under Article 8 ECHR;[32] that the right to gender identity is one of the most intimate aspects of private life[33] and that the right to gender identity is one of the most important aspects of private life and is an element of personal identity.[34] Also, the Court considered in *A.P., Garçon, and Nicot v. France* (2017) that the case involved 'an essential aspect of individuals' intimate identity' because the issue was about the complainants' gender identity.[35] In addition, the Court indicated that sexual orientation also constitutes an essential aspect of the individual's private life and identity.[36]

Furthermore, the case law offers – albeit with some caution – points of departure for the interpretation that cultural features may fall under the right to identity, such as a certain lifestyle, language, or wishes regarding the appearance of a person.[37] Religion and identity are also obviously linked, although none of

---

27 *Mennesson v. France* (2014), paras. 80 and 96.

28 *Mennesson v. France* (2014), para. 97 and *Labassee v. France*, para. 76; *Ghoumid et al. v. France* (2020).

29 *Ciubotaru v. Moldova* (2010), para. 53. This paragraph was subsequently referred to in the opinion of Judge Pinto De Albuquerque in the case *Ramadan v. Malta* (2016), para. 11, fn. 39. 'In this respect, it should be mentioned that the Court has recently held that an individual's ethnic identity must be regarded as an essential aspect of his or her private life and identity, along with such aspects as name, gender, religion and sexual orientation'.

30 Partly dissenting opinion by Judge Casadevall in *Sheffield and Horsham v. United Kingdom* (1998).

31 *Van Kück v. Germany* (2003); *Y.Y. v. Turkey* (2015); *A.P., Garçon, and Nicot v. France* (2017); *S.V. v. Italy* (2018); *Y.V. v. Bulgaria* (2020).

32 *Van Kück v. Germany* (2003), para. 75; *Y.Y. v. Turkey* (2015), para. 66; *A.P., Garçon, and Nicot v. France* (2017), para. 123.

33 *S.V. v. Italy* (2018), para. 62.

34 *Y.V. v. Bulgaria* (2020), paras. 38 and 63.

35 *A.P., Garçon, and Nicot v. France* (2017), para. 123. The Court considered this again in *Rana v. Hungary* (2020). *Rana v. Hungary* (2020), para. 39.

36 *Ciubotaru v. Moldova* (2010), para. 53.

37 *Friend, the Countryside alliance et al. v. United Kingdom* (2009), para. 44. In *Iovcev et al. v. Moldova and Russia* (2015), under 'case-specific questions', para. 9, the Court refers to a right to cultural identity.

the cases in which the right to identity under Article 8 ECHR explicitly appears involve religion or religious identity. However, religion is mentioned in one case as an essential aspect of private life and identity, namely in *Ciubotaru v. Moldova* (2010).[38] Certainly considering the other aspects that fall under the concept of identity, it is plausible that cultural characteristics and religion are also included. It is precisely the assumption that these aspects would *not* be part of the identity concept of the right to identity that needs substantiation in this author's opinion.

The case law analysis leads, furthermore, to the question to what extent the right to identity relates to external features or appearance.[39] A clear answer does not follow from the case law, but a positive one could be derived from the fact that the Court considers that private life under Article 8 ECHR may include aspects of physical identity (see section 5.2).

It follows from *Benedik v. Slovenia* (2018) that an interest in protecting one's identity in relation to one's online activity falls within the scope of the concept of private life.[40] Thus, it seems that anyone's online identity can fall within the scope of the right to identity, which is also referred to in the case.[41]

What is further noteworthy is that in *Bensaid v. United Kingdom* (2001), the case in which the Court first pointed to the right to identity, the Court also for the first time provided an enumeration of aspects that would be important to the personal sphere of individuals and fall within the scope of the right to respect for private life under Article 8 ECHR, namely: gender identification, name, sexual orientation and sexual life.

> 'Private life' is a broad term not susceptible to exhaustive definition. The Court has already held that elements such as gender identification, name and sexual orientation and sexual life are important elements of the personal sphere protected by Article 8 ....[42]

It is notable that in the French-language version of *Bensaid v. United Kingdom* (2001) the aspect of gender identification is not included in the list but the aspect of sex is.[43] That all these enumerated aspects are linked to the right to identity does not appear explicitly from the relevant paragraph. However, it

---

38 *Ciubotaru v. Moldova* (2010), para. 53. See also opinion by Judge Pinto de Albuquerque in *ee* (2016).

39 *S.A.S. v. France* (2014), para. 107; *Popa v. Romania* (2013), para. 33; *Gough v. United Kingdom* (2014).

40 *Benedik v. Slovenia* (2018), para. 119.

41 For the record, the terms 'online identity' and 'digital identity' do not appear in ECHR case law at the time of research.

42 *Bensaid v. United Kingdom* (2001), para. 47.

43 *Bensaid v. United Kingdom* (2001), para. 47. Also mentioned in *K.A. and A.D. v. Belgium* (2005), para. 79.

does seem logical that identity in the sense of the right to identity relates to these characteristics, since the Court connects the right to identity or at least the concept of identity to these aspects, as described before. It is important to emphasise that this is a non-exhaustive list of aspects. As is also the case for the concept of identity in the context of the right to identity, this leaves room for dynamic interpretation and that makes it possible to bring other personal characteristics or aspects that affect identity within the scope of the concept of identity. More guidance on such other aspects could possibly be found in the designation of 'categories' of identity by the court, namely: personal identity, physical identity and social identity.

5.2. CATEGORIES OF IDENTITY

It follows from *Mikulić v. Croatia* (2002) that the protection of physical, social and personal identity may be of significance in the context of Article 8 ECHR.[44] However, the interpretation of the terms physical, social and personal identity is left open. The jurisprudence with reference to 1) physical, 2) social, or 3) personal identity in the context of Article 8 ECHR is analysed, to assess to which extent case law provides greater insight into these three 'categories of identity', that logically fall under the concept of identity within the context of the right to identity.

5.2.1. Physical Identity

What does the Court tell us about the interpretation of physical identity? The search for cases on 'physical identity' yields only one case in the context of Article 8 ECHR. The term 'physical identity', furthermore, only occurs in combination with 'social identity', as in the standard finding from *Mikulić v. Croatia* (2002). In *J.B. and Others v. Hungary* (2018) the Court relates physical identity specifically to age. The Court indicates that age is obviously an aspect of an individual's physical identity, but at the same time is an objective fact not capable of being influenced by freedom of choice in the sphere of private life.[45] This consideration demonstrates that a certain degree of control for individuals (autonomy) may be required in order to let certain aspects fall within the scope of private life, and more particularly, under the scope of the right to identity.

5.2.2. Social Identity

What does the Court consider to be 'social identity'? A few cases provide further insight into the concept of social identity. The analysis of the case law shows

44 *Mikulić v. Croatia* (2002), paras. 53 and 64.
45 *J.B. et al. v. Hungary* (2018), para. 131.

that the Court regards several aspects as falling under social identity, including: biological and legal ties,[46] being a parent of a child,[47] and certain emotional ties between adults and minors in situations other than the classic situations of kinship.[48] In *Paradiso and Campanelli v. Italy* (2017) the Court considered that there is no valid reason to understand the concept of 'private life' as excluding the emotional bonds created and developed between an adult and a child in situations other than the classic situations of kinship, and indicated that this type of bond also pertains to individuals' life and social identity.[49] The Court also relates other kinds of relational status to social identity. According to the Court there is

> no reason why a State's acknowledgment of the real marital status of a person, be it, inter alia, married, single, divorced, widow or widower, should not form part of his or her personal and social identity ... protected by Article 8.[50]

Furthermore, the Court places social ties, specifically between migrants and a country and community, under social identity.[51] Professional life is also connected by the Court to one's social identity, since it considers that restrictions of an individual's professional life may fall within Article 8 where they have repercussions on the manner in which he or she constructs his or her social identity by developing relationships with others.[52] Furthermore, according to the Court's rulings, social identity appears to relate to nationality

46 *Mikulić v. Croatia* (2002); *A.M.M. v. Romania* (2012), para. 51.

47 *Paulik v. Slovakia* (2006), para. 42. See also *Cutajar v. Malta* (2015).

48 *Paradiso and Campanelli v. Italy* (2017).

49 *Paradiso and Campanelli v. Italy* (2017), para. 161.

50 *Dadouch v. Malta* (2010), para. 48 and *Orlandi et al. v. Italy* (2017), para. 144.

51 *Üner v. The Netherlands* (2006); *Maslov v. Austria* (2008); *Joseph Grant v. The United Kingdom* (2009); *Onur v. United Kingdom* (2009); *Omojudi v. United Kingdom* (2009); *Khan A.W. v. United Kingdom* (2010); *Miah v. United Kingdom* (2010); *Kurić et al. v. Slovenia* (2010); *Gezginci v. Switzerland* (2010); *Anam v. United Kingdom* (2011); *Osman v. Denmark* (2011); *A.A. v. United Kingdom* (2011); *Alim v. Russia* (2011); *Trabelsi v. Germany* (2011); *A.H. Khan v. United Kingdom* (2011); *Balogun v. The United Kingdom* (2012); *Akbulut v. United Kingdom* (2012); *Shakurov v. Russia* (2012); *Samsonnikov v. Estonia* (2012); *Abdi Ibrahim v. United Kingdom* (2012); *Shala v. Switzerland* (2012); *Hasanbasic v. Switzerland* (2013); *M.S. v. United Kingdom* (2012); *Vasquez v. Switzerland* (2013); *Ukaj v. Switzerland* (2014); *Palanci v. Switzerland* (2014); *M.P. et al. v. Switzerland* (2014); *Loy v. Germany* (2014); *Moreno Benavides v. Belgium* (2015); *K.M. v. Switzerland* (2015); *Kerkez v. Germany* (2015); *Khan v. Germany* (2015); *Novruk et al. v. Russia* (2016); *Abuhmaid v. Ukraine* (2017); *Hoti v. Croatia* (2018); *Levakovic v. Denmark* (2018); *Mohammad v. Denmark* (2018); *Saber and Boughassal v. Spain* (2018); *Zakharchuk v. Russia* (2019); *Narjis v. Italy* (2019); *Scherbakov v. Estonia* (2020); *Sudita Keita v. Hungary* (2020).

52 *Fernández Martínez v. Spain* (2012), para. 57. See also in slightly different terms, *Fernández Martínez v. Spain* (2014), para. 110 and *Travaš v. Croatia* (2016), para. 53. See further *Antović and Mirković v. Montenegro* (2017), para. 41.

and citizenship,[53] and further, reputation.[54] Because all of these aspects may be important for social identity or form part of it and fall within the scope of the right to respect for private life pursuant to Article 8 of the ECHR, it may logically be assumed that the concept of identity in the context of the right to identity in particular covers these features.

5.2.3. Personal Identity

How does the Court interpret 'personal identity' as a 'category of identity'? In the case law of the Court there are many cases in which 'personal identity' in the context of Article 8 ECHR comes up. However, many of these do not provide more insight into the concept of personal identity. Sometimes, for example, it is only mentioned that private life under Article 8 ECHR includes personal identity,[55] or it is only emphasised that private life relates to important aspects of an individual's personal identity.[56] In other cases, it is noted that the situation in question conflicts with personal identity.[57] What 'personal identity' entails is then left open. Yet there are also cases that *do* provide insight into the meaning of 'personal identity'. These show that there is sometimes overlap with 'the category' social identity, since the Court classifies some aspects under both personal and social identity, like marital status[58] and reputation.[59] From the cases it can be deduced that parentage, parenthood, contact between biological parents and children, as well as obtaining information about children are, in the view of the Court, issues that relate to an important part of the

---

53 *Ahmadov v. Azerbaijan* (2020), paras. 42 and 46; *Alpeyeva and Dzhalagoniya v. Russia* (2018), para. 125; *Andronic v. Romania* (2016), para. 24; *Genovese v. Malta* (2011), para. 30. See also the Opinion by Judge Pinto de Albuquerque in *Ramadan v. Malta* (2016).

54 *Giorgi Nikolaishvili v. Georgië* (2009), para. 122.

55 *Haas v. The Netherlands* (2004) and *Hofmann v. Germany* (2010): 'private life seen in terms of personal identity'; and *Karako v. Hungary* (2009): 'Private life includes personal identity'.

56 See *Jäggi v. Switzerland* (2006), para. 25; *Backlund v. Finland* (2010), para. 37; *Grönmark v. Finland* (2010), para. 39; *Pascaud v. France* (2011), para. 48; *Godelli v. Italy* (2012), para. 45 (in the French-language decision); *Roman v. Finland* (2013), para. 43; *Laakso v. Finland* (2013), para. 38.

57 *Pretty v. United Kingdom* (2002); *I. v. United Kingdom* (2002); *Goodwin v. United Kingdom* (2002); *Koch v. Germany* (2012); *Gross v. Switzerland* (2013); *Mcdonald v. United Kingdom* (2014); *Y.Y. v. Turkey* (2015); *Mennesson v. France* (2014).

58 *Dadouch v. Malta* (2010), para. 48 and *Orlandi et al. v. Italy* (2017), para. 144.

59 *Pfeifer v. Austria* (2007); *Petrina v. Romania* (2008); *A. v. Norway* (2009); *Petrov v. Bulgaria* (2010); *Polanco Torres and Movilla Polanco v. Spain* (2010); *Roberts and Roberts v. United Kingdom* (2011); *Pauliukiene and Pauliukas v. Lithuania* (2013); *Putistin v. Ukraine* (2013); *Mater v. Turkey* (2013); *Hoon v. United Kingdom* (2014); *Hoffmann v. Germany* (2016); *Sousa Goucha v. Portugal* (2016); *Petrie v. Italy* (2017); *Hun v. Turkey* (2017); *Tarman v. Turkey* (2017); *Denisov v. Ukraine* (2018); *Oktar v. Turkey* (2018); *Seferi Yilmaz v. Turkey* (2018); *Kaboglu and Oran v. Turkey* (2018); *Kwiatkowski v. Poland* (2019); *Taşkaya and Ersoy v. Turkey* (2019); *Khadija Ismayilova v. Azerbaijan (No 3)* (2020).

parent's personal identity and therefore the parent's private life.[60] In particular, the identity of biological parents is also identified as an important aspect of one's personal identity – of the (presumed) biological parent as well as that of the child.[61] Therefore, personal identity relates to the legal and biological bond between parents and children, to knowledge of biological parentage, as well as to the de facto bond between parents and children. The same goes for information about one's personal identity, such as a person's birth status: for example, whether or not one has been adopted.[62] Also, the Court links gender identity[63] and sex[64] to personal identity. In several cases, the Court considered that one's name is an aspect of personal identity.[65] Although the Court does not make it explicit that personal identity involves both first name and surname, this can be inferred since the Court *does* – as mentioned before in section 5.1 – explicitly link one's first name to one's identity in other case law. Furthermore, the Court regards photographs depicting a person ('image', 'picture' or 'photograph') as one of the aspects to which this person's personal identity relates.[66] The attainment of an

60 *Anayo v. Germany* (2010), para. 62 and *Schneider v. Germany* (2011), para. 90.

61 *Odièvre v. France* (2003); *Jäggi v. Switzerland* (2006); *Ebru and Tayfun Colac v. Turkey* (2006); *Phinikaridou v. Cyprus* (2007); *Wulff v. Denmark* (2010); *S.H. et al. v. Austria* (2010); *Backlund v. Finland* (2010); *Godelli v. Italy* (2012); *Kautzor v. Germany* (2012); *Roman v. Finland* (2013); *Laakso v. Finland* (2013); *Călin et al. v. Romania* (2016); *Silva and Mondim Correia v. Portugal* (2017); *Glazer v. Poland* (2018); *Çapin v. Turkey* (2019); *Boljevic v. Serbia* (2020).

62 *Konovalova v. Russia* (2014), para. 39; *Ageyevy v. Russia* (2013), para. 193.

63 *A.P., Garçon and Nicot v. France* (2017), para. 95; *X v. North Macedonia* (2019), para. 38; *Y.V. v. Bulgaria* (2020), para. 38; *Rana v. Hungary* (2020), para. 24.

64 *Emel Boyraz v. Turkey* (2014), para. 44.

65 *Pfeifer v. Austria* (2007), para. 33; *Köpke v. Germany* (2010); *Von Hannover v. Germany (No. 2)* (2012), para. 95; *Rothe v. Austria* (2012), para. 42; *Küchl v. Austria* (2012), para. 58; *Ageyevy v. Russia* (2013), para. 193; *Khmel v. Russia* (2013), para. 40; *Lillo-Stenberg and Sæther v. Norway* (2014), para. 26; *Jelševar et al. v. Slovenia* (2014), para. 29; *Konovalova v. Russia* (2014), para. 39; *Couderc and Hachette Filipacchi Associés v. France* (2015), para. 83; *X. v. San Marino* (2016), para. 24; *Pihl v. Sweden* (2017), para. 23; *Egill Einarsson v. Iceland* (2017), para. 32; *Bogomolova v. Russia* (2017), para. 51; *Kaboglu and Oran v. Turkey* (2018); *Vicent del Campo v. Spain* (2018), paras. 36 and 40; *López Ribalda et al. v. Spain* (Grand Chamber, 2019), para. 87; *Høiness v. Norway* (2019), para. 63; *Vučina v. Croatia* (2019), para. 28; *Rana v. Hungary* (2020), para. 24.

66 *Von Hannover v. Germany* (2004), para. 50; *Anguelov v. Bulgaria* (2004); *Pfeifer v. Austria* (2007), para. 33; *Köpke v. Germany* (2010); *Kaboglu and Oran v. Turkey* (2018); *López Ribalda et al. v. Spain* (2018), para. 55 and *López Ribalda et al. v. Spain* (2019), para. 87; *Høiness v. Norway* (2019), para. 63; *Vučina v. Croatia* (2019), para. 28. See also *Schüssel v. Austria* (2002). In the French-language decision of *Von Hannover v. Germany* (2004), the Court speaks of 'ou son droit à l'image'. Also in English-language decisions, the Court sometimes speaks of 'image', assuming that this concept corresponds in this context to the concept of 'picture'. See *Khmel v. Russia* (2013), para. 40; *Jelševar et al. v. Slovenia* (2014), para. 29; *Bogomolova v. Russia* (2017), para. 51; *Pihl v. Sweden* (2017), para. 23; *Egill Einarsson v. Iceland* (2017), para. 32. See *Vicent del Campo v. Spain* (2018), para. 36: 'elements relating to a person's right to their image'. The Court also sometimes uses the concept 'photo', See *Küchl v. Austria* (2012), para. 58; *Rothe v. Austria* (2012), para. 42; *Von Hannover v. Germany (No. 2)* (2012), para. 95.

academic degree is also a relevant aspect of personal identity, according to the Court.[67]

The collection of case law shows that social and personal identity are in part associated with the same aspects that have also been explicitly brought within the scope of the right to identity, but that there are also aspects to social and personal identity that are not expressly linked to the right to identity. Precisely because these aspects are linked to identity and fall under the notion of private life within Article 8 of the ECHR, it is logical that those aspects – although they are related to identity in different ways – fall in particular under the right to identity. However, it remains unclear *whether*, and if so *to what extent* it matters that an aspect of identity falls within physical, personal or social identity.

6. IMPLICATIONS

The fact that different aspects are part of identity leaves open the question what this means in terms of protection and obligations. For example, what does it mean that an individual's name is covered by the right to identity? And what protection does the right to identity provide for biological and legal ties, gender identity, nationality, etc.? The right to identity could lead to specific obligations regarding the acquisition of certain aspects of identity. The right then possibly implies that certain aspects of identity should be able to be obtained by a person, for reasons connected to the importance of the development or preservation of his or her identity. And it might mean that acquired aspects of identity must in general be respected and thus may not be changed without consent. It could also mean that it should be possible to change certain aspects of identity for reasons of identity perception. What protection can individuals, for example, derive from their right to identity with regard to obtaining or retaining a (double) surname or, alternatively, changing a first or last name, or their registered gender? Also, it is conceivable that certain aspects of identity are more strongly protected because they are considered more important to identity, by the Court, than others. The question is then how and on what basis the Court decides which aspects are (more) important. It is unclear what difference it makes in terms of protection and obligations that certain aspects are considered important to identity by the Court, and other aspects are 'only' linked to identity. Furthermore, specific

---

Or 'photograph', See *Ageyevy v. Russia* (2013), para. 193; *Lillo-Stenberg and Sæther v. Norway* (2014), para. 26; *Konovalova v. Russia* (2014), para. 39; *Couderc and Hachette Filipacchi Associés v. France* (2015), para. 83; *X. v. San Marino* (2016), para. 24; *P.N. v. Germany* (2020), para. 56.

[67] *P.R. v. Austria* (2019), para. 28.

questions regarding the protection of the identity of children (as minors) arise, for example in the context of parental disputes. How do the courts deal with conflicts between parents about specific aspects of the identity of the child (e.g. the child's name, legal ties or religious identity) or about what is important for the preservation or the development of the child's identity? How does one decide what the identity of the child consists of? And what role does the child's view of his own (right to) identity play?

Since, in its case law mentioning the Article 8 ECHR right, the Court leaves open what the right to identity entails for individuals – including children – as well as for state parties, the question of the protection and obligations that (may) arise from the right to identity cannot easily be answered. None of the cases discusses this in a general sense and the Court does not expressly find in a violation of the right to identity in any of them. Moreover, in most cases the right to identity is not discussed during the substantive handling of the complaint, and thus for this reason too it is difficult to deduce from case law what this right could mean *in abstracto* or *in concreto*. Still, there are some general considerations, and identity-specific considerations related to general doctrines, that follow from the Court's case law, which are relevant in the context of fleshing out the implications of the right to identity (section 6.1). Also, there is case law in which the Court shows the importance of the right to identity in general (section 6.2). More insight into the implications of the right to identity could also be found in case law regarding rights that the Court has introduced regarding particular aspects of identity ('sub-rights').

6.1. GENERAL DOCTRINES AND THE RIGHT TO IDENTITY

In the case law that mentions the right to identity, there are some general findings of the Court that contribute to an understanding of the protection and obligations that follow from Article 8 ECHR. These findings concern the general doctrines of effective protection (section 6.1.1) and of negative and positive obligations (section 6.1.2). It is logical to assume that these doctrines are also relevant to the implications of the right to identity, since this right stems from Article 8 ECHR. It also turns out that identity, and therefore the right to identity, is of importance for the 'margin of appreciation' doctrine (section 6.1.3).

6.1.1. Effective Protection

In its jurisprudence, the Court states that the treaty rights of the ECHR are not intended to be merely illusory or theoretical. Rather, the treaty rights should provide practical and effective protection: 'The Court reiterates that it is of crucial importance that the Convention is interpreted and applied in a manner which renders its rights *practical and effective, not theoretical and illusory*' (emphasis added).[68]

The Court may interpret treaty rights dynamically and evolutionarily and 'in light of the present day conditions'.[69] In doing so, the Court may also take into account developments within international and European law as well as the national law and legal practice of the states bound by the Convention.[70] It is hard to see why these basic principles would not apply in the context of the right to identity, since that right is a treaty right. The right to identity should therefore not be only theoretically relevant, but should be understood and applied in such a way that it provides effective protection. This shows the relevance of the question of the (specific) guarantees for individuals and (concrete) obligations on states consequent upon the right to identity.

6.1.2. Negative and Positive Obligations

The obligations that follow from Article 8 ECHR can be both negative and positive in nature.[71] This means that states must not only refrain from interfering with treaty rights, but may also have positive obligations that require actions on their part. This applies both to respect for family life,[72] as well as private life.[73] On the one hand, states must respect the right to identity and in principle refrain from interfering with this right. On the other hand, state action is required to ensure effective protection of the right to identity. Moreover, the obligations of states apply not only in the relationship between citizens and the state (vertical relationship), but also in the relationships among citizens themselves (horizontal relationship).[74] In order to achieve the required effective protection of treaty rights, including the right to identity, states must act, for example, in a certain way or establish certain legal guarantees under national law.[75]

---

68 *Y.Y. v. Turkey* (2015), para. 103; *I. v. United Kingdom* (2002), para. 54; *Christine Goodwin v. United Kingdom* (2002), para. 74. See also e.g. *Călin et al. v. Romania* (2016), para. 101; *Karoussiotis v. Portugal* (2011), para. 84; *Artico v. Italy* (1980), para. 33.

69 *I. v. United Kingdom* (2002), para. 55 with reference to *Tyrer v. United Kingdom* (1978), para. 55; *Goodwin v. United Kingdom* (2002), paras. 74 and 75.

70 *Y.Y. v. Turkey* (2015), para. 104.

71 The Court considered this for the first time in *Marckx v. Belgium* (1979), para. 31.

72 *Marckx v. Belgium* (1979), para. 31.

73 The Court first considered this in *Airey v. Ireland* (1979), para. 32. See further e.g. *Godelli v. Italy* (2012), para. 47.

74 *X and Y v. The Netherlands* (1985), para. 23. 'These obligations may involve the adoption of measures designed to secure respect for private life even in the sphere of the relations of individuals between themselves.'

75 *Marckx v. Belgium* (1979), para. 31.

6.1.3. *Margin of Appreciation*

It follows from settled case law of the Court that there are various ways of ensuring respect for private life.[76] This is also evident from case law in which the right to identity has been mentioned.[77] The way in which states give substance to the various negative and positive obligations arising from Article 8 ECHR is, in principle, up to states themselves.[78] This also applies to the assessment that states will have to make when there are conflicting interests and rights. States must strike a fair balance when weighing them up.[79] States are considered better placed than the Court to make such concrete decisions and balances. The Court thus grants states a certain 'margin of appreciation' in the execution of their obligations. When dealing with complaints, the Court will assess the actions of states in light of their margin of appreciation and will consider whether states have struck a proper balance when weighing up the various interests.

In determining the extent of the margin of appreciation concerning the right to private life, the issue of identity is relevant. In a number of cases in which the right to identity is mentioned, it appears that identity has an impact on the scope of the margin of appreciation that states are entitled to in fulfilling the obligations that follow from Article 8 ECHR.[80] For example, in *Mennesson v. France* (2014) and *Labassee v. France* (2014) the Court considered that the margin afforded to states is limited when the issue concerns an important aspect of identity.

> ... where a particularly important facet of an individual's existence or identity is at stake, the margin allowed to the State will normally be restricted ... regard should also be had to the fact that an essential aspect of the identity of individuals is at stake ... The margin of appreciation afforded to the respondent State in the present case therefore needs to be reduced.[81]

The margin of appreciation of states is also considered in the cases *A.P., Garçon and Nicot v. France* (2017), *S.V. v. Italy* (2018) and *Y.T. v. Bulgaria* (2020). The

---

76 *X and Y v. The Netherlands* (1985), para. 24. 'there are different ways of ensuring "respect for private life" ....'

77 *Jäggi v. Switzerland* (2006); paras. 33 and 36; *Pascaud v. France* (2011), paras. 55 and 59; *Godelli v. Italy* (2012), para. 47; *Konstantinidis v. Greece* (2014), para. 47.

78 *X and Y v. The Netherlands* (1985), para. 24. See also *Godelli v. Italy* (2012), para. 52.

79 See for the first time under Article 8 ECHR *Keegan v. Ireland* (1994), para. 49. 'However, the boundaries between the State's positive and negative obligations under this provision do not lend themselves to precise definition. The applicable principles are, none the less, similar. In both contexts regard must be had to the fair balance that has to be struck between the competing interests of the individual and of the community as a whole ....'

80 *Mennesson v. France* (2014), paras. 77, 79–80; *Labassee v. France* (2014), paras. 56 and 59; *A.P., Garçon and Nicot v. France* (2017), paras. 121–123; *S.V. v. Italy* (2018), para. 62.

81 *Mennesson v. France* (2014), paras. 77 and 80; *Labassee v. France* (2014), paras. 56 and 59.

Court here limited the breadth of the margin of appreciation, because the issues in these cases relate to the right to gender identity.[82] When states have less discretion, treaty protection is stronger, which means the state has less freedom to determine how to give effect to the treaty obligations. The fact that the Court indicates that identity reduces the breadth of states' margin of appreciation is therefore an important point. It is precisely for this reason that it is striking that the influence of identity on that margin emerges only in some cases, and not in other cases in which the right to identity is invoked and which have multiple points of reference to identity.

The influence of identity on the breadth of the margin of appreciation also comes up in case law in which the right to identity is not even mentioned.[83] It follows from the case law analysed that the Court linked the scope of the margin to identity for the first time in 2007, in *Evans v. United Kingdom* (2007). Therein, it explained that identity is regarded as be one of the factors considered that affects the margin of appreciation of states. The Court noted in this case that where the issue affects a particularly important aspect of the identity of individuals, the margin of appreciation afforded to states is restricted. The Court went on to explain that other factors, including whether there is consensus among States Parties on the issue to be assessed, may lead to a wide(r) margin of appreciation.

> A number of factors must be taken into account when determining the breadth of the margin of appreciation to be enjoyed by the State in any case under Article 8. Where a particularly important facet of an individual's existence or identity is at stake, the margin allowed to the State will be restricted. Where, however, there is no consensus within the member States of the Council of Europe, either as to the relative importance of the interest at stake or as to the best means of protecting it, particularly where the case raises sensitive moral or ethical issues, the margin will be wider ... There will also usually be a wide margin if the State is required to strike a balance between competing private and public interests or Convention rights ....[84]

---

82 *A.P., Garçon and Nicot v. France* (2017), para. 123. 'Ensuite, parce que les requêtes ont trait à l'identité sexuelle des individus, la Cour ayant déjà eu l'occasion de souligner que « la notion d'autonomie personnelle reflète un principe important qui sous-tend l'interprétation des garanties de l'article 8 » (voir, précités, *Pretty*, §61, *Van Kück*, §69, et *Schlumpf*, §100) et que le droit à l'identité sexuelle et à l'épanouissement personnel est un aspect fondamental du droit au respect de la vie privée (voir *Van Kück*, précité, §75). Ce constat la conduit à retenir que l'État défendeur ne disposait and l'espèce que d'une marge d'appréciation restreinte.' See also *S.V. v. Italy* (2018), para. 62 and *Y.V. v. Bulgaria* (2020), para. 63.

83 In total, 48 cases and additionally three opinions were selected after several searches. The link between the scope of the margin of appreciation and identity emerges in some opinions. See the opinion of Judges Keller and Spano on *Y.Y. v. Turkey* (2015); the opinion of Judge Ranzoni on *A.P., Garçon and Nicot v. France* (2017) and the opinion of Judge Pinto De Albuquerque on *Babiarz v. Poland* (2017).

84 *Evans v. United Kingdom* (2007), para. 77.

The analysis of case law has shown that the Court does not deal consistently with the influence of identity on the margin of appreciation, even though it is important for the outcome of the case. The Court should eliminate the ambiguity about when identity can result in a (more) narrow margin of appreciation for states. In any case, it can be concluded that the fact that identity has been identified as one of the factors that can influence states' margin of appreciation shows that from a European human rights perspective, states should treat issues about the identity of individuals, and thus the right to identity, with caution.

6.2. RIGHT TO IDENTITY REQUIRES CAREFUL INVESTIGATION

The case law studied indicates that in matters concerning the right to identity, states must carry out an extra careful investigation when weighing the interests involved. The judges giving the joint dissenting opinion in *Odièvre v. France* (2003) observed that the right to identity leads to the fact that in matters in which that right is at stake, states must weigh up the interests most carefully ('the fairest scrutiny was called for when weighing up the competing interests'), because it concerns one of the most important aspects of the right to respect for private life.[85] The Court subsequently adopted this view, albeit in slightly different terms ('particularly rigorous scrutiny is called for when weighing up the competing interests'), as is shown in a number of cases.[86] Therefore, a thorough investigation must take place where the right to identity is concerned. This could be seen as very important in the context of protection and state obligations regarding the right to identity in general, however this specific identity-related consideration comes up only in a few cases and only in the context of parentage.

6.3. MORE DIRECTION IN IMPLICATIONS BY 'SUB-RIGHTS'

It follows from a number of general findings that the right to identity consists, in any case, of a collection of various sub-rights with regard to (certain aspects of) identity. The analysis of case law shows that the Court sometimes refers to a right concerning a specific aspect of identity, such as the right to a name and the right to gender identity. The Court has also mentioned some general rights in relation to identity, such as the right to establish aspects of identity.

---

85 Joint dissenting opinion in *Odièvre v. France* (2003), para. 11.

86 *Jäggi v. Switzerland* (2006); *Pascaud v. France* (2011); *Godelli v. Italy* (2012); *Konstantinidis v. Greece* (2014).

With these various sub-rights, the Court gives at least some direction to what the broader right to identity protects and thus to the obligations that may follow from the right to identity. It appears that at least the following rights follow from the right to identity: the right to a name;[87] the right to know one's parentage;[88] the right to establish legal parentage in biological parents;[89] the right to gender identity;[90] and – albeit very cautiously – the right to cultural identity.[91] The Court also refers to the right of individuals to establish details of their identity as individual human beings in its jurisprudence.[92] It follows from case law that the establishment of aspects of identity should at least relate to obtaining information that is important for one's (personal) identity, such as information about a person's biological parents and early childhood,[93] and the establishment of a legal parent-child relationship, including kinship.[94] Although an expressed direct link to the right to identity is usually lacking, the link seems obvious, since the link between the right to identity with some of these sub-rights has been made, namely to the right to know one's parentage and to establish legal parentage in known biological parents. The Court further identified a right linked to a person's social identity, namely the right to lead a' private social life', through which an individual can develop his or her social identity.[95] The question again arises, however, what a specific 'right' with regard to some aspects of identity implies in terms of protection. The term 'right' as such gives little direction as to the specific obligations. An examination of the case law on the relevant aspects of these sub-rights stemming from the right to identity – for example case law on the right to know one's parentage and to legal

87 Report of the Commission in *Burghartz v. Switzerland* (1992), para. 47. See also the report of the Commission in *Stjerna v. Finland* (1993), para. 56 and the admissibility decision *K.B. v. The Netherlands* (1993).

88 *Jäggi v. Switzerland* (2006).

89 *Pascaud v. France* (2011); *Konstantinidis v. Greece* (2014).

90 *Y.Y. v. Turkey* (2015); *A.P., Garçon, and Nicot v. France* (2017); *S.V. v. Italy* (2018).

91 *Bobeico et al. v. Moldova and Russia* (2015).

92 In *Ciubotaru v. Moldova* (2010), in which the right to identity is also mentioned. The right is further mentioned in *Goodwin v. United Kingdom* (2002) and *I v. United Kingdom* (2002). There is also more case law, including in which the right to identity comes up, wherein the Court refers to 'establishing aspects of identity', without referring to *the right* to establish it. It probably does not matter. After all, what matters is the fact that establishing aspects of identity is protected.

93 Report of the Commission in *Gaskin v. United Kingdom* (1987); *Mikulić v. Croatia* (2002); *Odièvre v. France* (2003); *Phinikaridou v. Cyprus* (2007); *S.H. et al. v. Austria* (2010); *Wulff v. Denmark* (2010); *A.M.M. v. Romania* (2012); *Paradiso and Campanelli v. Italy* (2015); *Silva and Mondim Correia v. Portugal* (2017); *Călin et al. v. Romania* (2016); *Mifsud v. Malta* (2019).

94 *Mennesson v. France* (2014) and *Labassee v. France* (2014).

95 *Fernández Martínez v. Spain* (2012). See also *Khadija Ismayilova v. Azerbaijan (No. 3)* (2020); *López Ribalda et al. v. Spain* (2019); *Altay v. Turkey (No. 2)* (2019); *Cătăniciu v. Romania* (2018); *National Federation of Sportspersons' Associations and Unions (FNASS) et al. v. France* (2018).

establishment of parental ties – should provide more insight into what exactly these rights protect, what guarantees are included, and what obligations this imposes. This might also give more insight into the added value of a right that is connected to the right to identity.

6.4. SPECIFIC OBLIGATIONS

Case law also clearly shows that the right to identity can lead to specific obligations in specific cases. The cases *Mennesson v. France* (2014) and *Labassee v. France* (2014), for example, show that states must take into account the interests surrounding identity, in these cases the interests of children born to surrogate mothers abroad.[96] On the basis of *Mennesson v. France* (2014) and the Court's *Advisory Opinion* (2019)[97] regarding that case, it can be concluded that the right to identity leads to the obligation for states, in the context of international surrogacy, to recognise the legal relationship between a child and his or her genetic 'intended parent' as well as the other intentional parent, regardless of the latter's (lack of) genetic relationship with the child. The Grand Chamber of the Court states that the non-genetic bond between the intended mother and the child is equally important for the identity of the child.[98] States must provide an effective and sufficiently rapid mechanism to establish such parent-child relationships. Further research into the obligations of states formulated by the Court in the specific circumstances where a link with identity is made may contribute to a better understanding of the implications of the right to identity.

7. CLOSING REMARKS

The right to identity under Article 8 ECHR has been examined here by analysis of the ECHR case law in which the Court explicitly refers to identity within the framework of Article 8 ECHR. In order to gain understanding of the right to identity, a larger body of case law is relevant than the case law that explicitly refers to 'the right to identity'. Moreover, it appears that the Court is much more likely to comment on identity without expressly mentioning the 'right to identity', for example, on personal or social identity, than it is to explicitly mention the right to identity. The case law gives no reason to assume that rulings of the Court in which the right to identity is mentioned should be

96 *Mennesson v. France* (2014), para. 101; *Labassee v. France* (2014), para. 80.

97 *Advisory Opinion* (10 April 2019), request no. P16-2018-001.

98 *Advisory Opinion* (10 April 2019), no. P16-2018-001, para. 40.

judged differently than rulings of the Court in which it comments on identity within the framework of Article 8 of the ECHR, but in which the right to identity is not included. This means that case law in which the right to identity is not mentioned in so many words can still provide insight into the content of that right.

The case law in which this right to identity is explicitly mentioned does provide some insight into the meaning and scope of this right. First of all, the Court interprets the right to identity and the concept of identity, without defining them in general terms. It has become clear that the Court sees identity as *a broad concept* that consists of a collection of personal characteristics and ties which, in particular, can be linked to physical, social and personal identity. These 'aspects of identity' do not only comprise aspects that have a strong legal connotation, for instance in relation to the registration of those characteristics by the government, such as name, biological ties and sex. Social bonds, for example the bond between a parent and a child, also fall under the individual's protected identity. Secondly, it appears that identity is *an open concept* that can develop over time through dynamic interpretation. This also fits with the view of the ECHR as a 'living instrument'. Furthermore, the case law shows that so far, it is mainly the concept of identity that is given more meaning by the Court and that there is a lot of space left for determining the implications of the right to identity and thus for the development of the right to identity. The right to identity can at least be regarded as an umbrella that provides a certain protection to various interests, and to rights that can be related to those aspects of identity. It is relevant here that some aspects covered by the protected concept of identity are considered 'essential' to one's identity (e.g. biological ties, gender identity and ethnic identity) and thus form the core of the protected identity. These aspects will probably be protected more strongly than other aspects that generally are less connected or important to identity. In any case, states should treat identity issues with caution, and conduct thorough investigations in matters of identity, since these matters can restrict the state's margin of appreciation.

All in all, it appears that the right to identity under Article 8 of the ECHR is over 20 years old but is still in its infancy. The right to identity is still far from crystallised. With the introduction of that right into the scope of protection of the ECHR, individuals have in any case been handed 'a pearl'. It is up to the practitioners to make use of it so it can develop further.

THE RIGHT TO ACCESS INFORMATION ABOUT ONE'S GENETIC ORIGINS IN THE CONTEXT OF MEDICALLY ASSISTED REPRODUCTION

Time Changes Everything?

Elodie Decorte

1. INTRODUCTION

Medically assisted reproduction has helped many people to fulfil their desire to have children. Nearly 11 million fertility treatments, which have led to the birth of almost three million children, took place in Europe between 1997 and

2018.[1] The figures show an upward trend: from around 35,000 children born in 1997 to over 200,000 children born in 2018.[2]

Medically assisted reproduction can involve the use of gametes (sperm and/or eggs) or embryos from a donor. Although many parents prefer having a genetically related child, the use of donor gametes or embryos is sometimes the only option.[3] Heterosexual couples with fertility or safety problems (e.g. at high risk of transmitting genetic disorders) and same-sex couples or single women with a desire to have children have to turn to donor gametes or embryos.[4] This chapter deals with the question of preserving or abolishing donor anonymity in the field of gamete and embryo donation. To this day, donor anonymity versus access to information about the donor has been a key issue in the debates on medically assisted reproduction.

The next section of this chapter focuses on recent developments that have taken place in the complex field of medically assisted reproduction and the right to know one's genetic origins. The rights of donor-conceived persons to know about their origins have changed for the better in the past 30 years. Traditionally, most jurisdictions favoured anonymous donation. These days, the principle of the absolute anonymity of the donor is called into question both at international and national level.[5]

Section 3 of this chapter provides an analysis of the legislation in different (European) jurisdictions that have already decided to waive donor anonymity. The current situation in France, Germany, Ireland, the Netherlands, Switzerland, the United Kingdom and Victoria (Australia) is discussed. Although these jurisdictions have national laws that provide access to information about donors to donor-conceived persons, this does not necessarily imply that the same rules apply for 'all' donor-conceived persons. By introducing a new system of non-anonymity, these jurisdictions have chosen to balance the interests in favour of donor-conceived persons, since they can access information about the donor. But when a new system is introduced, the question arises of to which cases the old system continues to apply and to which cases the new system applies. Will there be a difference in treatment between future gamete donations and gamete donations from the past, i.e. those where anonymity was promised at the time of the donation? And in particular: how does national law strike a balance between the interests that those conceived before the new system

1 C. Wyns, Ch. De Geyter, C. Calhaz-Jorge, M.S. Kupka, T. Motrenko, J. Smeenk, C. Bergh, A. Tandler-Schneider, I.A. Rugescu and V. Goossens, 'ART in Europe, 2018: results generated from European registries by ESHRE', *Human Reproduction Open* 2022/3, p. 5.

2 Ibid., p. 4.

3 J.C. Kirkman-Brown and M.V. Martins, '"Genes versus children": if the goal is parenthood, are we using the optimal approach?', 35(1) *Human Reproduction* 2020, pp. 5–11.

4 Gay couples will also need a surrogate mother.

5 See below sections 2.2 and 2.3.

was introduced ('old' donor-conceived persons) have in accessing information about their donor and the interests that those who donated before the new system was introduced ('old' donors) have in connection with sharing this information? The jurisdictions mentioned above have been selected because they have various ways of dealing with this question.

The aim of this research is to determine whether these national laws do effectively meet the interests of donor-conceived persons in having access to information about their genetic origins. The main focus here is on the rights and interests of the 'old' donors and donor-conceived persons, or those who donated or were conceived before the new system of non-anonymity was introduced.

2. FROM ANONYMITY TO OPENNESS

2.1. TIMES HAVE CHANGED

The use of donated gametes or embryos creates a tension between genetic and legal conceptions of parenthood. The child's legal parents, at least one of them, will be different from the genetic parents. As the child grows up, the legal parents face tough questions and decisions: will they tell their child about the donor conception? If so: when will they tell? How will they tell? If parents decide to be open about the child's conception, or when the child accidentally discovers the truth, the child might wonder who the donor is and if there is any resemblance with the donor. Many donor-conceived children, especially when they get older, want to discover who their donor is, or at least have the opportunity to access information about their donor.[6]

Traditionally, most countries favoured anonymous donation, meaning that in the past persons conceived through gamete or embryo donation could not obtain any information about their donor.[7] The main concerns of these countries

---

6 Government Committee on the Reassessment of Parenthood, *Child and parents in the 21st century*, December 2016, p. 108, https://www.rijksoverheid.nl/documenten/rapporten/2016/12/07/rapport-van-de-staatsommissie-herijking-ouderschap-kind-en-ouders-in-de-21ste-eeuw; Nuffield Council on Bioethics, *Donor conception: ethical aspects of information sharing*, April 2013, pp. 57–69, http://nuffieldbioethics.org/project/donor-conception; V. Jadva, T. Freeman, W. Kramer and S. Golombok, 'Experiences of offspring searching for and contacting their donor siblings and donor', 20(4) *Reproductive BioMedicine Online* 2010, pp. 523–532; J.E. Scheib, A. Ruby and J. Benward, 'Who requests their sperm donor's identity? The first ten years of information releases to adults with open-identity donors', 107(2) *Fertility and Sterility* 2017, pp. 483–493; O.B.A. Van Den Akker, M.A. Crawshaw, E.D. Blyth and L.J. Frith, 'Expectations and experiences of gamete donors and donor-conceived adults searching for genetic relatives using DNA linking through a voluntary register', 30(1) *Human Reproduction* 2015, pp. 111–121.

7 For more information see S. Allan, *Donor Conception and the Search for Information. From secrecy and anonymity to openness*, London/New York, Routledge, 2017.

were to guarantee respect for the donor's private and family life, to preserve the family peace of the legal parents by avoiding (unwanted) interference from the donor, and to prevent an imminent decline in the number of donors.[8] In addition to guaranteeing donor anonymity, the medical profession advised parents against telling their child about the donor conception. This was dismissed as unnecessary and potentially harmful.[9] Although this chapter will not elaborate on the question whether or not the parents (or the public authorities) have a duty to inform the donor-conceived person about the donor conception, it is important to understand that secrecy about the mode of conception and donor anonymity are inextricably linked to each other.[10] Donor-conceived persons can only ask for information about their donor if they know or suspect that they were donor-conceived.

Today, this traditional model of secrecy about the mode of conception and donor anonymity is challenged both by the evolution of genetic technology and by changes in society. First, genetic testing makes it possible for donor-conceived persons to access their genetic data and hence to find their donor and genetic half-siblings. Access to these tests is very easy via the internet. Secrecy and anonymity can de facto no longer be guaranteed.[11] Secondly, in today's society, the stigma associated with the use of assisted reproduction techniques seems to be decreasing. At the same time there is a growing awareness that hiding the truth about a child's origins constitutes a greater risk for family peace than telling the truth (at the appropriate time). It is also generally recognised that knowledge about one's genetic origins is important for personal development and identity building.[12]

---

8 K.R. Daniels and K. Taylor, 'Secrecy and openness in donor insemination', 12(2) *Politics & the Life Sciences* 1993, pp. 155–170.

9 L. Frith, E. Blyth, M. Crawshaw and O. Van Den Akker, 'Secrets and disclosure in donor conception', 40(1) *Sociology of Health & Illness* 2018, pp. 188–203, p. 190; P. Nordsqvist and C. Smart, *Relative strangers. Family life, genes and donor conception*, New York, Palgrave Macmillan, 2014, pp. 20–21.

10 E. Decorte, 'Donor Conception. From Anonymity to Openness' in K. Boele-Woelki and D. Martiny (eds.), *Plurality and Diversity of Family Relations in Europe*, Antwerp, Intersentia, 2019, p. 155.

11 Committee on Social Affairs, Health and Sustainable Development, *Anonymous donation of sperm and oocytes: balancing the rights of parents, donors and children (Report)*, Strasbourg, Council of Europe, 20 February 2019, Explanatory memorandum, para. 17, https://pace.coe.int/en/files/25439/html; G. Pennings, 'Genetic databases and the future of donor anonymity', 34(5) *Human Reproduction* 2019, pp. 786–790.

12 T. Freeman, 'Gamete donation, information sharing and the best interests of the child: an overview of the psychosocial evidence', 33(1) *Monash Bioethics Review* 2015, pp. 45–63; L. Frith, E. Blyth, M. Crawshaw and O. Van Den Akker, 'Secrets and disclosure in donor conception', 40(1) *Sociology of Health & Illness* 2018, pp. 188–203, p. 191; A. Indekeu, *Anders en toch gewoon. Families na donorconceptie*, Tielt, Lannoo, 2021, pp. 20–21; P. Nordqvist, 'Telling reproductive stories: social scripts, relationality and donor conception', 55(4) *Sociology* 2021, pp. 677–695; J. Readings, L. Blake, P. Casey, V. Jadva and S. Golombok,

Furthermore, the argument that abolishing donor anonymity will lead to an immediate decline in the number of donors is not backed by statistics. No drastic and persistent decrease in gamete donations has been noted in the countries which have already decided to abolish donor anonymity.[13] In Sweden, for example, donor anonymity was abolished in the '80s. This resulted in a decrease in the number of sperm donors, but in the first few years only. Afterwards the donations steadily increased.[14] The same goes for the Netherlands, the United Kingdom and Victoria (Australia).[15] These countries still struggle with a donor shortage[16] – however, this is also true for countries where donor anonymity is still protected, such as Belgium.[17] A donor shortage is therefore not directly or solely due to abolishing donor anonymity. There are other reasons that also have an impact on the number of donors.[18] Donors are, for example, screened rigorously, meaning that not all donor candidates are accepted as a donor.[19] It is possible that some potential donors are deterred

---

'Secrecy, disclosure and everything in-between: decisions of parents of children conceived by donor insemination, egg donation and surrogacy', 22(5) *Reproductive BioMedicine Online* 2011, pp. 485–495, p. 486.

13 At least in the countries that have figures available.

14 K. Daniels and O. Lalos, 'The Swedish Insemination Act and the availability of donors', 10(7) *Human Reproduction* 1995, pp. 1871–1874, pp. 1872–1873.

15 Nuffield Council on Bioethics, *Donor conception: ethical aspects of information sharing*, April 2013, pp. 78–79, http://nuffieldbioethics.org/project/donor-conception; D.H. Adams, S. Ullah and S. De Lacey, 'Does the removal of anonymity reduce sperm donors in Australia?', 23(3) *Journal of Law & Medicine* 2016, pp. 628–636; M. Day, 'Number of sperm donors rises in UK despite removal of anonymity', 334 *British Medical Journal* 2007, p. 971; H.B. Winter, W.J. Dondorp, M.C. Ploem, N.O.M. Woestenburg, C.P.M. Akerboom, J. Legemaate and G.M.W.R. De Wert, *Evaluatie Embryowet en Wet donorgegevens kunstmatige bevruchting*, The Hague, ZonMw, 2012, pp. 111–112, pp. 125–126.

16 L. Culley, N. Hudson, F. Rapport, E. Blyth, W. Norton and A.A. Pacey, 'Crossing borders for fertility treatment: motivations, destinations and outcomes of UK fertility travellers', 26(9) *Human Reproduction* 2011, pp. 2373–2381; E. Ekerhovd and A. Faurskov, 'Swedish sperm donors are driven by altruism, but shortage of sperm donors leads to reproductive travelling', 113(3) *Upsala Journal of Medical Sciences* 2009, pp. 305–314; I. Rodino, S. Goedeke and S. Nowoweiski, 'Motivations and experiences of patients seeking cross-border reproductive care: the Australian and New Zealand context', 102(5) *Fertility & Sterility* 2014, pp. 1422–1431; H.B. Winter, W.J. Dondorp, M.C. Ploem, N.O.M. Woestenburg, C.P.M. Akerboom, J. Legemaate and G.M.W.R. De Wert, *Evaluatie Embryowet en Wet donorgegevens kunstmatige bevruchting*, The Hague, ZonMw, 2012, pp. 13–14.

17 G. Pennings, C. Autin, W. Decleer, A. Delbaere, L. Delbeke, A. Delvigne, D. De Neubourg, P. Devroey, M. Dhont, T. D'hooghe, S. Gordts, B. Lejeune, M. Nijs, P. Pauwels, B. Perrad, C. Pirard and F. Vandekerckhove, 'Cross-border reproductive care in Belgium', 24(12) *Human Reproduction* 2009, pp. 3108–3118; A. Thijssen, N. Dhont, E. Vandormael, A. Cox, E. Klerkx, E. Creemers and W. Ombelet, 'Artificial insemination with donor sperm (AID): heterogeneity in sperm banking facilities in a single country (Belgium)', 6(2) *Facts, Views & Vision in ObGyn* 2014, pp. 57–67.

18 E. Blyth and L. Frith, 'The UK's gamete donor "crisis" – a critical analysis', 28(1) *Critical Social Policy* 2008, pp. 74–95, p. 82.

19 At European Union level, for example, there are directives with selection criteria and laboratory tests for donors of reproductive cells: Directive 2004/23/EC of the European Parliament and

by these tests.[20] Another explanation is that the group of parents who turn to donor gametes in order to fulfil their desire to have children is increasing (e.g. lesbian couples and single women). Finally, a (large) part of demand is not reflected in the official figures. There are always would-be parents who leave the official circuit and go looking for a donor online. Some also travel abroad.[21] This means there often is a hidden shortage.

2.2. DEVELOPMENTS AT THE INTERNATIONAL LEVEL

The traditional model of donor anonymity is not only challenged by the evolution of genetic technology and by changes in society, but also by human rights law. In international and European human rights law the emphasis has gradually shifted from the interests and rights of the donor to remain anonymous to the interests and rights of donor-conceived persons to know their genetic origins. Several international instruments reflect this development.

In 2019 the Parliamentary Assembly of the Council of Europe (PACE) stated in a recommendation that 'anonymity should be waived for all future gamete donations in Council of Europe member States, and the use of anonymously donated sperm and oocytes should be prohibited'.[22] Although this recommendation is not binding on the Member States, it definitely supports the view that international and European human rights law has moved towards recognition of the right to know one's genetic origins.[23] This right can

of the Council of 31 March 2004 on setting standards of quality and safety for the donation, procurement, testing, processing, preservation, storage and distribution of human tissues and cells, *Official Journal of the European Union* 7 April 2004; Commission directive 2006/17/EC of 8 February 2006 implementing Directive 2004/23/EC of the European Parliament and of the Council as regards certain technical requirements for the donation, procurement and testing of human tissues and cells, *Official Journal of the European Union* 9 February 2006.

20 Moreover, egg donation is a rather painful and complicated process.

21 F. Shenfield, J. De Mouzon, G. Pennings, A.P. Ferraretti, A. Nyboe Andersen, G. De Wert and V. Goossens (ESHRE), 'Cross border reproductive care in six European countries', 25(6) *Human Reproduction* 2010, pp. 1361–1368.

22 Parliamentary Assembly, *Recommendation 2156: Anonymous donation of sperm and oocytes: balancing the rights of parents, donors and children*, 12 April 2019, para. 7.1, https://pace.coe.int/en/files/27680/html; The recommendation is based on the report by Petra De Sutter: Committee On Social Affairs, Health and Sustainable Development, *Anonymous donation of sperm and oocytes: balancing the rights of parents, donors and children*, 20 February 2019, https://pace.coe.int/en/files/25439/html.

23 The Committee of Ministers replied to the recommendation and also expressed concern about the fact that some donor conceived persons do not have the right to know the identity of their donor. The Committee subsequently invited the European Committee on Legal Co-operation (CDCJ), in consultation with the Committee on Bioethics (DH-BIO), the Committee on Transplantation of Organs and Tissues (CD-PTO) and the Ad Hoc Committee on the Rights of the Child (CAHENF), to consider the feasibility and desirability of preparing a draft recommendation or other non-binding instrument to assist Member States in protecting

(primarily) be derived from the United Nations Convention on the Rights of the Child (CRC)[24] and the European Convention on Human Rights (ECHR).[25]

The CRC guarantees the right of children to know their parents (Article 7) and the right to (preserve their) identity (Article 8).[26] A key principle of the CRC is that the best interests of the child shall be a primary consideration in all actions concerning children (Article 3). The use of general terms (e.g. 'parents' and 'identity') leaves these articles open to more than one interpretation.[27] Nevertheless, the majority opinion gives a broad interpretation of the legal norms of the CRC.[28] Every child, irrespective of their background, enjoys the same level of protection.[29] With regard to this broad interpretation, Articles 7 and 8 CRC also apply to donor-conceived children in their search for information about their genetic origins.[30] Moreover, the Committee on the Rights of the Child explicitly states in several of its concluding observations that recognising the right of donor-conceived children to access information about their genetic origins is important and that this right falls within the ambit of Articles 7 and 8

---

the rights of donor-conceived persons to know their origins (Committee of Ministers, *'Anonymous donation of sperm and oocytes: balancing the rights of parents, donors and children' PACE Recommendation 2156 (2019). Reply adopted by the Committee of Ministers*, Council of Europe, 9 October 2019). In 2021 DH-BIO sent a questionnaire to Member States on the right to know (DH-BIO, *Replies by the member States to the questionnaire on access to medically assisted procreation (MAP), on the right to know about their origin for children born after MAP and on surrogacy*, Council of Europe, 2022). In 2022 the CDCJ published a report recognising the relevance and added value of elaborating a recommendation on the topic. This is foreseen for 2024–2025. (CDCJ, *Comparative study on access of persons conceived by gamete donation to information on their origins*, Council of Europe, 2022).

24 UN General Assembly, *Convention on the Rights of the Child*, 20 November 1989, United Nations Treaty Series, vol. 1577, p. 3.

25 Council of Europe, *European Convention for the Protection of Human Rights and Fundamental Freedoms*, 4 November 1950, European Treaty Series no. 5.

26 The CRC only applies to children, not to donor-conceived adults who wish to know their genetic origins. Unlike the CRC, the ECHR (see below) applies to all persons, minor or adult.

27 E. Decorte, 'Een kinderrechtenconforme benadering van toegang tot afstammingsinformatie voor donorkinderen', *Tijdschrift Jeugd- en Kinderrechten* 2021/1, 12–15; L. Pluym, *Een familierechtelijk statuut voor draagmoederschap*, Mechelen, Wolters Kluwer Belgium, 2015, p. 394.

28 S. Bou-Sfia, *De betekenis van identiteitsrechten voor kinderen in het Nederlandse familierecht. Een onderzoek naar de artikelen 8 IVRK en 8 EVRM*, Amsterdam, Off Page, 2021, 470; R. Hodgkin and P. Newell, *Implementation Handbook for the Convention on the Rights of the Child for Unicef*, 2007, pp. 105–106, https://www.unicef.org/lac/media/22071/file/Implementation%20Handbook%20for%20the%20CRC.pdf; L. Pluym, Een familierechtelijk statuut voor draagmoederschap, Mechelen, Wolters Kluwer Belgium, 2015, pp. 394–396; J. Tobin and F. Seow, 'Article 7: The Rights to Birth Registration, a Name, Nationality and to Know and Be Cared for by Parents' in J. Tobin (ed.), *The UN Convention on the Rights of the Child: a commentary*, Oxford, Oxford University Press, 2019, p. 237, pp. 241–259.

29 According to Articles 1 and 2 CRC, every child has all the rights in this convention and this convention applies to every child without discrimination of any kind; R. Blauwhoff, *Foundational facts, relative truths. A comparative law study on children's right to know their genetic origins*, Antwerp, Intersentia, 2009, p. 45.

30 See references in n. 28 above.

CRC.[31] The Committee has also expressed concern about the fact that children born in the context of medically assisted reproduction with donor gametes do not have the right to know the identity of their biological parents.[32] Member States are urged to adjust their legislation.[33]

The European Court of Human Rights (ECtHR) considers that the right to an identity and the right to personal development, which includes the right to know one's genetic parentage, are an integral part of the notion of private life. Therefore, it is protected under Article 8 of the ECHR.[34] According to the ECtHR, children, but also adults, have a vital interest in obtaining information about their genetic origins. The interests of individuals in discovering their parentage does not disappear with age, quite the reverse.[35] But the right to know one's genetic origins is not to be regarded as an 'absolute' right, which means that a balancing of interests has to take place to resolve the conflict.[36] In a recent judgment, specifically in the context of donor conception, the ECtHR considers that states enjoy a wide margin of appreciation in weighing up the interests and rights at stake.[37] According to the ECtHR there is no clear consensus on the issue of access to genetic origins, merely a recent trend in favour of lifting donor anonymity (see section 3.3.2.1).[38]

---

31 Concluding Observations on the United Kingdom of Great Britain and Northern Ireland, 2002, CRC/C/ 15/Add.188, paras. 31–32.

32 Concluding Observations on France, 1994, CRC/C/15 /Add.20, para. 14; Concluding Observations on Norway, 1994, CRC/C/15 /Add.23, para. 10; Concluding Observations on Denmark, 1995, CRC/C/15 /Add.33, para. 11; Concluding Observations on Monaco, 2001, CRC/C/15 /Add.158, paras. 24–25.

33 Concluding Observations on Belgium, 2019, CRC/C/BEL/CO/5-6, para. 20.

34 See for example: ECtHR, *Gaskin v. United Kingdom*, 7 July 1989, §39, no. 10454/83; *Mikulić v. Croatia*, 7 February 2002, §54, no. 53176/99; *Odièvre v. France*, 13 February 2003, §29, no. 42326/98; *Jäggi v. Switzerland*, 13 July 2006, §37, no. 58757/00; *Phinikaridou v. Cyprus*, 20 December 2007, §§53, no. 23890/02; *Backlund v. Finland*, 6 July 2010, §§37 and 46, no. 36498/05; *Pascaud v. France*, 16 June 2011, §§48 and 59, no. 19535/08; *Godelli v. Italy*, 25 September 2012, §§50 and 52, no. 33783/09; *Laakso v. Finland*, 15 January 2013, §§38 and 46, no. 7361/05; *Röman v. Finland*, 29 April 2013, §§43 and 51, no. 13072/05; *Calin and Others v. Romania*, 19 July 2016, §§83 and 92, nos. 25057/11, 34739/11 and 20316/12; *Gauvin-Fournis and Silliau v. France*, 7 September 2023, §112, nos. 21424/16 and 45728/17.

35 *Jäggi v. Switzerland*, 13 July 2006, §40, no. 58757/00; *Godelli v. Italy*, 25 September 2012, §56, no. 33783/09; *Gauvin-Fournis and Silliau v. France*, 7 September 2023, §112, nos. 21424/16 and 45728/17.

36 S. Besson, 'Enforcing the child's right to know her origins: contrasting approaches under the Convention on the Rights of the Child and the European Convention on Human Rights', 21(2) *International Journal of Law, Policy and the Family* 2007, pp. 137–159, pp. 150–152.

37 According to the ECtHR the wide margin of appreciation is admittedly reduced because an essential aspect of the private life is at stake, but how far this reduction extends is not further defined (*Gauvin-Fournis and Silliau v. France*, 7 September 2023, §§112, 123, nos. 21424/16 and 45728/17). In previous judgments the ECtHR also stated that there is a wide margin of appreciation in the context of medically assisted reproduction (*X, Y and Z v. United Kingdom*, 22 April 1997, §44, no. 2183/93; *S.H. and others v. Austria*, 3 November 2011, §88, no. 57813/00; *Pejřilová v. Czech Republic*, 8 December 2022, §§43, 45, 46, no. 14889/19).

38 *Gauvin-Fournis and Silliau v. France*, 7 September 2023, §§111, 112, 121, 123, nos. 21424/16 and 45728/17. Three judges expressed a joint dissenting opinion.

2.3. DEVELOPMENTS AT THE NATIONAL LEVEL

This tendency to give priority to the interests and rights of donor-conceived persons to know their genetic origins is also reflected in the legislation of several (European) jurisdictions that have waived the principle of donor anonymity. These jurisdictions grant donor-conceived persons access to information about their donor. Sweden was the first country to abolish donor anonymity in 1985.[39] The Swedish example was then followed by several other countries such as Austria (1992),[40] Switzerland (2001),[41] the Netherlands (2004),[42] Norway (2005),[43] the United Kingdom (2005),[44] Finland (2007),[45] Croatia (2012),[46] Germany (2018),[47] Portugal (2019),[48] Ireland (2020)[49] and France (2021).[50] Outside Europe, Australia and New Zealand, for example, grant donor-conceived persons access to information about their donor.[51] And even in countries that are still holding on to the principle of donor anonymity, this is increasingly being questioned.[52]

---

39 Lag om insemination (Law on Insemination) 1984 (enacted 1985). Replaced by Lag (2006:351) om genetisk integritet (Genetic Integrity Act) 2006.

40 §20 Fortpflanzungsmedizingesetz (Reproductive Medicine Act), 275 *Bundesgesetz*, 1992.

41 Article 27 Loi fédérale sur la procréation médicalement assistée (Federal Law on Medically Assisted Reproduction) 18 December 1998.

42 Article 3 Wet donorgegevens kunstmatige bevruchting (Artificial Insemination Donor Data Act) 2002.

43 §§2–7 Lov om humanmedisinsk bruk av bioteknologi m.m. (bioteknologiloven) (Act on Biotechnology) 2003.

44 The Human Fertilisation and Embryology Authority (Disclosure of Donor Information) Regulations 2004 (SI 2004/1511).

45 Article 23 Lag om assisterad befruktning (1237/2006) (Act on Assisted Fertility Treatments).

46 Article 15(1) Zakon O Medicinski Pomognutoj Oplodnji nr. 71-05-03/1-12-2 (Law on Medically Assisted Reproduction) 2012.

47 Gesetz zur Regelung des Rechts auf Kenntnis der Abstammung bei heterologer Verwendung von Samen vom 17. Juli 2017 (Sperm Donor Register Act).

48 Lei n.º 48/2019 Regime de confidencialidade nas técnicas de procriação medicamente assistida, procedendo à sexta alteração à Lei n.º 32/2006, de 26 de julho (procriação medicamente assistida) (Act on Confidentiality Regime for Medically Assisted Procreation Techniques).

49 Section 35 Children and Family Relationships Act 2015 (No. 9 of 2015).

50 Article 5 Loi n° 2021-1017 du 2 août 2021 relative à la bioéthique (Law on Bioethics).

51 S. Allan, *Donor Conception and the Search for Information. From secrecy and anonymity to openness,* London/New York, Routledge, 2017, pp. 79–80.

52 See for example: Projet de loi (n° 7674) portant organisation de l'accès à la connaissance de ses origines dans le cadre d'une adoption ou d'une procréation médicalement assistée avec tiers donneurs and Ministry of Justice, 'Sam Tanson a présenté le projet de loi sur l'accès aux origines en cas d'adoption ou de PMA', *Le Gouvernement Luxembourgeois*, 7 oktober 2020 (Luxemburg); I. Riano-Galan, C.M. Gonzales and S.G. Riestra, 'Ethical and legal questions of anonymity and confidentiality in gamete donation', *Analaes de Pediatria* 2021, 337.e1-337.e6 (Spain); current proposals to amend the law in Belgium: Proposal to amend the law regarding the foundation of an institution for the storage and control of donor information, Parliamentary documents Chamber 2019–2020, no. 55-0186/001; Proposal

3. TIME TO SAY GOODBYE, BUT (DO NOT) LEAVE THE PAST BEHIND

Ignoring the rights of donor-conceived persons to access information about their genetic origins no longer seems tenable. For reasons set out above, jurisdictions that still retain absolute anonymity, such as Belgium,[53] need to implement a new legal framework that grants donor-conceived persons access to information about their donor.[54]

Although more and more jurisdictions choose to abolish donor anonymity and grant donor-conceived persons access to information, this does not necessarily imply that all donor-conceived persons have the same rights. When a new system is introduced, the question arises of which cases the old system (of donor anonymity) continues to apply to and which cases the new system (of access to information about the donor) applies to.

The next section focuses on the legislation in different (mostly European) jurisdictions, namely France, Germany, Ireland, Switzerland, the Netherlands, the United Kingdom and Victoria (Australia). These jurisdictions have already decided to abolish donor anonymity and regulate access to information about donors for donor-conceived persons. After a brief analysis of the legislation in these jurisdictions concerning the right to know one's genetic origins in the context of medically assisted reproduction, the focus shifts to the scope of the new system: does it apply to future gamete donations only or does it also apply to gamete donations from the past, i.e. those where anonymity was promised at the time of the donation? And in particular: how does national law strike a balance between the interests that 'old' donor-conceived persons have in accessing information about their donor and the interests that 'old' donors have in connection with withholding/sharing this information?

---

to amend the 2007 Act regarding medically assisted reproduction and the destination of supernumerary embryos and gametes concerning the non-anonymous donation of gametes and the advancement of the donor-conceived child's right to an identity, Parliamentary documents Chamber 2019–2020, no. 55-0310/001; Proposal to amend the 2007 Act regarding medically assisted reproduction and the destination of supernumerary embryos and gametes concerning the anonymity of donor gametes, Parliamentary documents Chamber 2020–2021, no. 55-2114/00.

53 Donor anonymity is protected in Belgium in Article 22, section 2 and Article 51, §1, section 1 'Act regarding medically assisted reproduction and the destination of supernumerary embryos and gametes' of 6 July 2007, *Belgian Law Gazette (Belgisch Staatsblad or BS)* 17 July 2007, 38.575.

54 For more information: E. Decorte, *Recht op kennis van afstammingsinformatie bij medisch begeleide voortplanting*, Bruges, die Keure, 2022.

3.1. NEW SYSTEM OF NON-ANONYMITY

The above-mentioned jurisdictions have not simply waived the principle of donor anonymity; they also have set up a system to collect and preserve information about the donor and they have procedures in place to give donor-conceived persons access to information about their donor. In what follows, the system, the type of information and the procedure are briefly discussed.[55]

3.1.1. Central Register

The different jurisdictions have all opted for a central system, meaning they centralise all information about donors, recipient parents and children born as a result of donor procedures in a (often newly-established) central register of information. In France this is the *Commission d'accès aux données non identifiantes et à l'identité du tiers donneur* controlled by the Minister for Health,[56] in Germany, the *Samenspenderregister* controlled by the *Bundesinstitut für Arzneimittel und Medizinprodukte* (BfArM),[57] in Switzerland, the *Office fédéral de l'état civil* controlled by the *Office fédéral de la santé publique*,[58] in Ireland, the National Donor-Conceived Person Register controlled by the Minister for Health,[59] in the Netherlands, the Central government register controlled by the *Stichting Donorgegevens Kunstmatige Bevruchting*,[60] in the United Kingdom, the HFEA register controlled by the Human Fertilisation and Embryology Authority (HFEA)[61] and in Victoria (Australia) the Central Register controlled by the Victorian Assisted Reproductive Treatment Authority (VARTA).[62] It is

55 For more detailed information about the national laws concerning the right to know one's genetic origins in these jurisdictions: Committee on Bioethics, *Replies by the member States to the questionnaire on access to medically assisted procreation (MAP), on the right to know about their origin for children born after MAP and on surrogacy*, Strasburg, Council of Europe, 2021; S. Allan, *Donor Conception and the Search for Information. From secrecy and anonymity to openness*, London/New York, Routledge, 2017, pp. 77–142; European Committee on Legal Co-Operation (CDCJ), *Right of donor-conceived persons to know their origins Access of people conceived by gamete donation to information on their origins Responses received from member States to the Questionnaire*, Strasburg, Council of Europe, 2022; E. Decorte, 'Donor Conception. From Anonymity to Openness' in K. Boele-Woelki and D. Martiny (eds.), *Plurality and Diversity of Family Relations in Europe*, Antwerp, Intersentia, 2019, pp. 154–169; E. Decorte, *Recht op kennis van afstammingsinformatie bij medisch begeleide voortplanting*, Bruges, die Keure, 2022.

56 Article L. 2143-6 Code de la santé publique.

57 https://www.bfarm.de/DE/Das-BfArM/Aufgaben/Samenspender-Register/_node.html.

58 https://www.bj.admin.ch/bj/fr/home/gesellschaft/zivilstand/spenderdatenregister.html.

59 Section 33 Children and Family Relationships Act 2015.

60 https://www.donorgegevens.nl/.

61 https://www.hfea.gov.uk/.

62 https://www.varta.org.au/.

up to the fertility clinics and/or the gamete banks to transfer the details of the donations and fertility treatments to the central register.

3.1.2. Non-Identifying and Identifying Information

The information about the donor can be subdivided into two groups: identifying and non-identifying information.[63] Identifying information is information on the identity of the donor, such as the name, the date of birth, the place of birth and the address of the donor. Non-identifying information about the donor is information that does not directly reveal or indirectly indicate the identity of the donor but that gives the donor-conceived person the possibility to form a picture of the donor, such as the donor's physical description (e.g. height, weight, eye and hair colour) or their motivation for donating the gametes. The list of non-identifying information can vary between very extensive or very limited. In Germany, for example, the registration of non-identifying information about the donor is not mandatory. This information is only stored on a voluntary basis.[64] In the United Kingdom this is obligatory (as in the other jurisdictions) and the list of non-identifying information is very comprehensive: physical description, ethnic group (also of the donor's parents), the number and sex of the children of the donor, occupation, religion, interests, whether the donor was adopted or themselves donor-conceived, marital status, details of any screening tests and medical history, skills, reason for donating, goodwill message and self-description.[65] It is important to note that these non-identifying data are all collected at the time of the donation, so that they represent the donor at that time. The physical characteristics, interests and self-description of the donor are examples of information that can quickly become outdated.

---

63 France: Article L. 2143-3 Code de la santé publique; Germany: §2(2) Sperm Donor Registry Act; Ireland: sections 24(3) and 34 Children and Family Relationships Act 2015; Switzerland: Article 24 Loi fédérale sur la procréation médicalement assistée 18 December 1998; The Netherlands: Article 2 Wet donorgegevens *juncto* Articles 2–3 Besluit van 11 augustus 2003, houdende bepaling van de gegevens en bescheiden als bedoeld in artikel 2, eerste lid, onderscheidenlijk artikel 3, achtste lid, van de Wet donorgegevens kunstmatige bevruchting; The United Kingdom: reg. 2 Human Fertilisation and Embryology Authority (Disclosure of Donor Information) Regulations 2004; Victoria: sections 57–60 Assisted Reproductive Treatment Act 2008.

64 §2(3) Sperm Donor Registry Act.

65 Regulation 2(2) Human Fertilisation and Embryology Authority (Disclosure of Donor Information) Regulations 2004; HFEA, *Code of Practice*. 9th edition, version 4, London, HFEA, October 2023, pp. 118 (para. 11.42) and 218 (para. 20.13) https://portal.hfea.gov.uk/media/za0j5qqr/2023-10-26-code-of-practice-v9-4.pdf.

3.1.3. *Procedure to Access Information*

When a person knows or suspects they are donor-conceived they can ask for non-identifying and/or identifying information about the donor by submitting a request to the central register where all the information is gathered.[66] All these jurisdictions limit the right of access from a certain age.[67] The limit varies between 12 and 18 years, with sometimes a distinction made between non-identifying and identifying information.[68] This is, for example, the case in the Netherlands and the United Kingdom: from the age of 12 (NL) and 16 (UK) onwards, non-identifying information can be released to the child and from the age of 16 (NL) and 18 (UK), identifying information about the donor can be released.[69] The underlying idea is to make the donor-conceived person gradually accustomed to having information about the donor.[70] Before this age,

---

66 France: Article 5 Loi n° 2021-1017 du 2 août 2021 relative à la bioéthique; Germany: §10 Sperm Donor Registry Act; Ireland: section 34 Children and Family Relationships Act 2015; Switzerland: Article 27 *Loi fédérale sur la procréation médicalement assistée* 18 December 1998; The Netherlands: Article 3 Wet donorgegevens; The United Kingdom: section 31ZA Human Fertilisation and Embryology Act 1990; Victoria: sections 57–63 Assisted Reproductive Treatment Act 2008.

67 In Ireland assisted reproductive technology remains largely unregulated by legislation. A Bill on assisted human reproduction is currently pending (https://www.oireachtas.ie/en/bills/bill/2022/29/). It outlines the conditions relating to the donation of gametes and embryos for use in assisted reproduction treatments by others. It also provides for the establishment of an Assisted Human Reproduction Regulatory Authority, an independent body to oversee the fertility sector. The Bill also lowers the current age limit to access information about the donor from 18 to 16 years.

68 Committee on Bioethics, *Replies by the member States to the questionnaire on access to medically assisted procreation (MAP), on the right to know about their origin for children born after MAP and on surrogacy*, Strasburg, Council of Europe, 2021; European Committee on Legal Co-Operation, *Right of donor-conceived persons to know their origins Access of people conceived by gamete donation to information on their origins Responses received from member States to the Questionnaire*, Strasburg, Council of Europe, 2022; S. Allan, *Donor Conception and the Search for Information. From secrecy and anonymity to openness*, London/New York, Routledge, 2017, pp. 77–142; E. Decorte, 'Donor Conception. From Anonymity to Openness' in K. Boele-Woelki and D. Martiny (eds.), *Plurality and Diversity of Family Relations in Europe*, Antwerp, Intersentia, 2019, pp. 154–169.

69 Article 3, section 1, b) and section 2 Wet donorgegevens kunstmatige donorbevruchting; section 31ZA Human Fertilisation and Embryology Act 1990.

70 In the Netherlands there is discussion about the appropriateness of the current age limits: University of Humanistic Studies, Pro Facto and Fiom, *Zorgvuldigheid in de omgang met leeftijdsgrenzen in de Wet donorgegevens kunstmatige bevruchting*, ZonMw, 2023; Government Committee on the Reassessment of Parenthood, *Child and parents in the 21st century*, December 2016, pp. 90–91, pp. 385–386, https://www.rijksoverheid.nl/documenten/rapporten/2016/12/07/rapport-van-de-staatsommissie-herijking-ouderschap-kind-en-ouders-in-de-21ste-eeuw; H.B. Winter, W.J. Dondorp, M.C. Ploem, N.O.M. Woestenburg, C.P.M. Akerboom, J. Legemaate and G.M.W.R. De Wert, *Evaluatie Embryowet en Wet donorgegevens kunstmatige bevruchting*, The Hague, ZonMw, 2012, pp. 173–174.

parents can often already request certain (non-)identifying information about the donor.[71]

The right of donor-conceived persons to access (identifying) information about the donor is not always absolute. The release of identifying information can have serious consequences for the donor's private and family life, since the donor-conceived person might possibly want contact. Although the donor consents to the release of his or her information at the time of donation, many years pass between the time of donation and the time of being confronted with a request by a donor-conceived person to disclose information. A lot might have changed in the donor's private and/or family life. In the Netherlands and in Ireland, when a donor-conceived person files a request for identifying information, the donor is first notified of this request and can then object to the release of this information.[72] But a simple no from the donor will not be sufficient to stop the information from being released. The basic principle remains that the donor-conceived person has a right to access information about the donor, including identifying information. So, the release of this information can only be refused in exceptional circumstances. The burden of proof rests with the donor.[73] At present, it is still unclear what might be considered an acceptable reason for refusing access.[74] Only in 2021 did the first Dutch donor-conceived children to whom the new system introduced in 2004 applies, reach the age of 16.[75] In Ireland it will still take several years before the first donors who donated after the entry into force of the new system (in 2020) may be confronted with a request to disclose their identity.

---

71 In e.g. the Netherlands, Ireland and the UK, parents can request non-identifying information on the donor, and in Germany identifying information too (Art. 3, section 1, c) Wet donorgegevens kunstmatige donorbevruchting and Art. 5 Reglement Stichting donorgegevens kunstmatige bevruchting; section 34(1) Children and Family Relationships Act (CFRA) 2015; HFEA, Code of Practice, 9th edition, version 4, London, HFEA, October 2023, pp. 215 (para. 20.1) and 218 (para. 20.15); §10(3) Gesetz zur Errichtung eines Samenspenderregisters und zur Regelung der Auskunftserteilung über den Spender nach heterologer Verwendung von Samen (SaRegG) (Sperm Donor Register Act).

72 Article 3, section 2 Wet donorgegevens kunstmatige donorbevruchting; section 35(2) Children and Family Relationships Act 2015.

73 Article 3, section 2 Wet donorgegevens kunstmatige donorbevruchting in conjunction with Article 8, section 2 Reglement Stichting donorgegevens kunstmatige bevruchting; Memorandum in reply concerning the Wet donorgegevens kunstmatige donorbevruchting, *Kamerstukken I* 2000/01, 23207, no. 201b, p. 5; section 35(2)–(3) Children and Family Relationships Act 2015; Explanatory memorandum concerning the Children and Family Relationships (Amendment) Bill 2018, p. 9.

74 E. Decorte, 'Donor Conception. From Anonymity to Openness' in K. Boele-Woelki and D. Martiny (eds.), *Plurality and Diversity of Family Relations in Europe*, Antwerp, Intersentia, 2019, p. 158.

75 An Advisory Committee has been set up in the Netherlands. The Committee gives advice if a donor objects to the release of his/her information (Articles 8 and 12a Reglement Stichting donorgegevens kunstmatige bevruchting).

After this short analysis of the current situation in the different jurisdictions, it is time to have a look at the temporal effect of these national laws concerning the right to know one's genetic origins in the context of medically assisted reproduction. And in particular: if (and how) these jurisdictions try to meet the interests of donor-conceived persons conceived before the new system was introduced.

3.2. PRINCIPLE OF NON-RETROACTIVITY

There is no question that law can adapt, evolve, and be reformed to adjust to the (new) needs of society. A new law is deemed to be an improvement. It would therefore seem logical that the new law has the widest possible scope of application. However, some citizens have an interest in ensuring that the previous law, to which they have adapted their behaviour, continues to apply. So, a balance must be sought between innovation and stability.[76]

In general, laws in most jurisdictions operate from the day they were enacted onward and have 'prospective' effect. This means the law is only applicable to cases which arise after its enactment. 'Retroactive' effect refers to laws that relate also to actions undertaken in the past.

Retroactivity in law is strictly scrutinised by the ECtHR.[77] According to the ECtHR the principle of legal certainty is an aspect of the rule of law and is inherent in many of the rights protected by the ECHR.[78] This means that laws must be sufficiently foreseeable, certain and precise, so that citizens know how they will apply in any particular situation. The retroactive application of laws raises an issue concerning the principle of legal certainty as it poses problems for the foreseeability requirement. It can also affect the legitimate expectations of citizens.[79] Further, the fact that the use of a cut-off date – which is inherent in laws with prospective effect – creates a difference in treatment between the 'old' and the 'new' is, in itself, not a problem according to the ECtHR.[80] It is an inevitable consequence of introducing new systems which replace previous and outdated schemes. The choice of such a cut-off date when introducing a new system falls within the margin of appreciation offered to a state when reforming its policies.[81] The ECtHR recently confirmed this in a case against France,

---

76 T. Vancoppernolle, *Intertemporeel recht*, Antwerp, Intersentia, 2019, pp. 188–194.

77 J. Theunis, *De exceptie van onwettigheid*, Bruges, die Keure, 2011, p. 116.

78 ECtHR, *Marckx v. Belgium*, 13 June 1979, §58, no. 6833/74; *Amuur v. France*, 25 June 1996, §50, no. 19776/92; *Baranowski v. Poland*, 28 March 2000, §56, no. 28358/95; *Vrbica v. Croatia*, 1 April 2010, §55, no. 32540/05.

79 ECtHR, *Pijevschi v. Portugal*, 13 November 2008, §42, no. 6830/05; *Mirolubovs v. Latvia*, 15 September 2009, §86, no. 798/05.

80 ECtHR, *Amato Gauci v. Malta*, 15 December 2009, §71, no. 47045/06.

81 ECtHR, *Amato Gauci v. Malta*, 15 December 2009, §71, no. 47045/06.

specifically in the context of access to information and donor conception (see section 3.3.2.1).[82]

In line with the above, many jurisdictions that have decided to waive donor anonymity and provide donor-conceived persons with the right to access information about their genetic parents, draw a (clear) line in time.[83] This means that donors who donated their gametes anonymously before the new system came into force have the right to remain anonymous and that persons conceived with donor gametes before the new system came into force are prevented from obtaining information about their donor. This is also supported at the international level. The previously mentioned recommendation of PACE explicitly states that: 'Anonymity should be waived for all future gamete donations in Council of Europe member States, … The anonymity of gamete donors should not be lifted retrospectively where anonymity was promised at the time of the donation.'[84]

3.3. MEETING THE INTERESTS OF 'OLD' DONOR-CONCEIVED PERSONS

Worldwide, we are increasingly seeing that donor-conceived persons are making their voices heard, for example through the media or in court. They also have joined together in support groups, such as *Stichting Donorkind* (the Netherlands),[85] Donor Conceived Register (the United Kingdom),[86] *Spenderkinder* (Germany),[87] *Procréation médicalement Anonyme* (France),[88] Donor Offspring Europe (DOE)[89] or Donorchildren (worldwide).[90] These vocal donor-conceived persons were often conceived during a period where donor anonymity was still protected in their country. There are also many donor-conceived persons who have yet to discover that they are donor-conceived or donor-conceived persons who are conceived in jurisdictions that do not (yet)

---

82 ECtHR, *Gauvin-Fournis and Silliau v. France*, 7 September 2023, nos. 21424/16 and 45728/17.

83 For a more detailed overview: S. Allan, *Donor Conception and the Search for Information. From secrecy and anonymity to openness*, London/New York, Routledge, 2017, pp. 77–142.

84 PACE, *Anonymous donation of sperm and oocytes: balancing the rights of parents, donors and children (Recommendation 2156)*, 2019, para. 7.4. Legal doctrine is also reluctant to accept (absolute) retroactivity: G. Pennings, 'How to kill gamete donation: Retrospective legislation and donor anonymity', 27(10) *Human Reproduction* 2012, pp. 2881–2885; J. Tobin and F. Seow, 'Article 7: The Rights to Birth Registration, a Name, Nationality and to Know and Be Cared for by Parents' in J. Tobin (ed.), *The UN Convention on the Rights of the Child: a commentary*, Oxford, Oxford University Press, 2019, pp. 268–269.

85 https://donorkind.eu/.

86 https://www.donorconceivedregister.co.uk/.

87 http://www.spenderkinder.de/.

88 https://pmanonyme.asso.fr/.

89 https://donoroffspring.eu/.

90 http://www.donorchildren.com/.

have legislation that grants them access to information and who may in the future request information about their donor. Are they all left out in the cold?

From a human rights perspective, there is a need to find a balance between the rights and interests of all parties concerned, in particular the legitimate expectations of the 'old donors' that their anonymity will be preserved – connected with the interest of society in preserving legal certainty – and the interest of the old donor-conceived persons to access information about the donor. After all, many (European) states have been bound by the CRC since the early 1990s (and from the 1950s onward by the ECHR) and have the duty to fulfil their international obligations, such as respecting the rights of (donor-conceived) persons to access information about their genetic parentage. In what follows, we seek existing and/or new solutions in order to achieve a fair balance between the different rights and interests.

3.3.1. *All the Way*

The most far-reaching way to meet the interests of old donor-conceived persons is to give them the same rights as donor-conceived persons who are conceived under the new system. However, this would seriously undermine the principle of legal certainty and the legitimate expectations of old donors. These donors legitimately assumed at the time of their donation that they would never become known to the donor-conceived person.

Nevertheless, the State of Victoria in Australia (since 2017)[91] and Switzerland (since 2001)[92] have abolished donor anonymity completely and with retroactive effect. Donor-conceived persons have the right to access identifying and non-identifying information about their donor regardless of when the donation occurred and regardless of when the donor conception took place. The change in the law in these jurisdictions ensures that all donor-conceived persons are treated equally. At least theoretically, in practice it depends on whether the information is still available.[93]

---

91 Assisted Reproductive Treatment Amendment Act 2016 (Vic.); S. Allan, *Donor Conception and the Search for Information. From secrecy and anonymity to openness*, London/New York, Routledge, 2017, pp. 91–92.

92 Arts. 18–27 and 41 *Loi fédérale sur la procréation médicalement assistée*; D. Manai, 'Assisted reproduction under Swiss law: The truth about the conception and the identity of the gamete donor' in T. Callus, B. Feuillet-Liger and K. Orfali (eds.), *Who is my genetic parent*, Brussels, Bruylant, 2011, pp. 259–271; L. Margot, 'Le droit à la connaissance des origins de l'enfant né de procréation médicalement assistée' in A. Büchler, M. Cottier and I. Schwenzer (eds.), *La pratique du droit de la famille*, Bern, Stämpfli Verlag AG, 2017, pp. 696–724; T. Stegmüller, *Procréation médicalement assistée transfrontière et filiation de l'enfant*, Zurich, Schulthess Médias Juridiques, 2020, p. 141.

93 S. Allan, *Donor Conception and the Search for Information. From secrecy and anonymity to openness*, London/New York, Routledge, 2017, pp. 106, 139; F. Kelly, D. Dempsey, J. Power,

To protect the privacy of old donors the State of Victoria gives them the possibility to lodge a contact preference form when a donor-conceived person requests identifying information.[94] Contact preference forms imply that the donor can choose different contact options, from not wanting any contact at all to wanting contact, and if desired, in a specified way (such as by email by phone or through support services).[95] Penalties may apply if a contact preference is breached.[96] So this means that old Victorian donors cannot object to the release of their identifying information but they can control the level of contact. With this system Victoria tries to find a proper balance between the privacy of donors who do not want to be contacted and the rights of donor-conceived persons by still providing them with information about their donor.

3.3.2. *Half Way*

There are alternatives to abolishing donor anonymity completely with retroactive effect to meet the interests of old donor-conceived persons. Different degrees of 'retroactivity' are conceivable. Several combinations are possible, depending on the type of information that is accessible to the donor-conceived person, how the information can be accessed by the donor-conceived person and how the information is collected by the state. With regard to the type of information, a distinction can be made between non-identifying and identifying information. With regard to how the different types of information can be accessed, there is information release with the consent of the donor and information release without the consent of the donor. With regard to how the information is collected, there is a difference between collecting the information actively and passively. These different combinations are detected in different jurisdictions, as set out below. On the one hand these jurisdictions want to recognise the needs of donor-conceived persons who are searching for information. On the other hand they still require donor-conceived persons to respect the donor's privacy.

3.3.2.1. Release of Information with the Consent of the Donor

The donor's attitude towards anonymity may change over time. It is not inconceivable that donors will be influenced by the recent developments and

K. Bourne, K. Hammarberg and L. Johnson, 'From stranger to family or something in between: donor linking in an era of retrospective access to anonymous sperm donor records in Victoria, Australia', 33(3) *International Journal of Law, Policy and The Family* 2019, pp. 277–297, p. 278.

94 Sections 63–63H Assisted Reproductive Treatment Act 2008.

95 Section 63C Assisted Reproductive Treatment Act 2008.

96 Sections 63(3) and 63G(2) Assisted Reproductive Treatment Act 2008.

by the increased acknowledgement of the right to know one's genetic origins. Some donors actually wonder about the children they helped to conceive and are willing to share (and receive) information about their past donations.[97] So a first alternative is to provide old donor-conceived persons access to information after contacting the donor and asking for his or her consent. This information release does not interfere with the donor's right to privacy because it relies on consent; or it will at least not lead to an unfair balance in the particular case. This is also supported at the international level. The previously mentioned recommendation of PACE, that supports non-retroactivity, makes an exception for 'where the donor has consented to the lifting of the anonymity'.[98] Moreover, it is possible to limit the consent requirement to identifying information. Unlike the release of identifying information, the release of non-identifying information will in principle not lead to contact.[99] It is especially the possibility of contact that can imply far-reaching interference in the donor's privacy.

Furthermore, when giving old donors (some) control over the release of their personal (identifying and/or non-identifying) information, two possible regimes can be distinguished: an 'opt-in' regime and an 'opt-out' regime. In an opt-in regime the explicit and prior consent of the donor is needed for release of information, with possible exceptions in the case of death or unavailability of the donor. In an opt-out regime the explicit and prior consent of the donor is not required, or there is presumed consent of the donor, but with the possibility for the donor to expressly oppose the release of his or her personal information. In the first situation it is a no, as long as the donor does not say yes. In the second situation it is a yes, as long as the donor does not say no. The second situation clearly demands a more active approach from donors who wish to retain their anonymity.

This consent approach is adopted in the Netherlands, the United Kingdom and France. A specific effort was also made in Germany, to accommodate the rights of old donor-conceived persons. The solutions provided by these jurisdictions are discussed below.

The Netherlands

Since the day the *Wet donorgegevens* came into force in the Netherlands, all performers of medically assisted reproduction with donated gametes are

97 A. Indekeu, J. Maas, E. Mccormick, J. Benward and J.E. Scheib, 'Factors associated with searching for people related through donor conception among donor-conceived people, parents, and donors: a systematic review', 2(2) *F&S Review* 2021, pp. 93–119.

98 PACE, *Anonymous donation of sperm and oocytes: balancing the rights of parents, donors and children (Recommendation 2156)*, 2019, para. 7.4.

99 'In principle' because certain non-identifying information about the donor (e.g. personal letter, occupation, hobbies) can (when combined) provide a very detailed view of the donor, and can thus reveal the donor's identity.

obliged to give all information that they hold about past donors to the newly established central government register, created by the *Wet donorgegevens*, to record and store all information regarding past and future donations.[100] In the two years before the *Wet donorgegevens* became operational (2002–2004), old donors could actively indicate whether they wanted to remain anonymous or not.[101] However, even donors who during this two-year period did not actively declare that they wanted to remain anonymous still preserve their absolute right of veto.[102] This means that two systems exist side by side in the Netherlands at the moment. On the one hand identifying information about post-2004 donors is always released to the donor-conceived person, unless the donor can give a plausible argument as to why his or her interests are of such importance that the release of his or her personal details is not appropriate and that his or her interests take precedence over the consequences that not providing this information would have for the child (see section 3.1.3).[103] On the other hand identifying information about pre-2004 donors is never released, unless the donor gives his or her explicit consent. The pre-2004 donor-conceived person cannot lodge an objection or appeal against the decision of the donor. The main aim of the Dutch legislator in making this cut-off point in time was to preserve legal certainty. In contrast with identifying information, non-identifying information about the donor can always be released in accordance with the procedure laid down in the *Wet donorgegevens*, even without the donor's consent.[104] This means the same rules apply for persons conceived before and after the coming into force of the *Wet donorgegevens* when it comes down to the non-identifying information.[105]

---

100 Article 12, section 1 Wet donorgegevens in conjunction with Article 2, section 5 Reglement Stichting.

101 Article 12, sections 2 and 3 Wet donorgegevens; Article 8, 1) Reglement Stichting. Until anonymity was abolished in 2004, a dual system was in action, giving parents a choice between anonymous donors (A-donors) and open-identity donors (B-donors). B-donors agreed with the release of identifying information. Nevertheless, during this transitional period (2002–2004) some B-donors also changed their status to A-donor. This caused a great deal of consternation among parents and donor-conceived children. After two court cases (Court Gelderland 24 March 2021, no. 361950; Court The Hague 2 June 2021, no. C/09/573982 / HA ZA 19-542 C/09/584962 / HA ZA 19-1261), a change in the law is now foreseen to treat B-donors the same as post-2004 donors.

102 Memorandum in reply concerning the Wet donorgegevens, *Kamerstukken I* 2000/2001, 23207, no. 201b, p. 9.

103 Article 3, section 2 Wet donorgegevens; Article 8 Reglement Stichting donorgegevens kunstmatige bevruchting.

104 If this information is still available. Although clinics are obliged to give all information about old donors to the Foundation on Donor Information relating to Artificial Insemination, a great deal of this information is incorrect, destroyed or lost: Evaluation of the Embryowet, *Kamerstukken II* 2017/2018, 30486, no. 17, p. 1.

105 Article 12, section 4 Wet donorgegevens.

However, in recent years, it has become clear that several fertility clinics have applied this transitional regime incorrectly or negligently, in the sense that they have not all (yet) provided the information about their old donors to the central register.[106] The challenges that have arisen in the Netherlands are a good example of how important it is to secure the proper preservation of the remaining information about old donors as soon as possible. This is necessary to guarantee old donor-conceived persons easy and effective access to information about the donor. Otherwise a great deal of this information might get destroyed or lost. States need to take an active role in preserving and releasing the (remaining) information, meaning that a well-functioning and reliable system has to be established. Then, when a donor-conceived person submits a request for information about the donor, the information can be easily traced and the donor can be easily contacted in order to obtain his or her consent.

Germany

To further illustrate the importance of the proper preservation of information, it is worth mentioning the current situation in Germany. Back in 1989, the *Bundesverfassungsgericht* (German Constitutional Court) decided that individuals should have the right to know their genetic identity.[107] This was further confirmed by later jurisprudence.[108] Fertility doctors were obliged to share identifying information about the donor, despite any prior agreement to maintain anonymity with the donor and the parents.[109] Since there was no legislation regulating the exercise and scope of this right, it was very difficult in practice for donor-conceived persons to obtain information.[110] A comprehensive legal framework was needed. In July 2018 the Sperm Donor Registry Act entered into force. Since that date, the personal details of all donors are stored in a central government register (*Samenspenderregister*) controlled by the German BfArM. The *Samenspenderregister* only retains data about sperm donations made from

106 Evaluation of the Embryowet, *Kamerstukken II* 2017/2018, 30486, no. 17, p. 1.

107 Bundesverfassungsgericht 31 January 1989, BVerfGE 79, 256–274 and JZ 1989, p. 335; R. Blauwhoff, *Foundational facts, relative truths. A comparative law study on children's right to know their genetic origins*, Antwerp, Intersentia, 2009, pp. 110–113.

108 Bundesgerichtshof 28 January 2015, *NJW* 2015, p. 1098; Oberlandesgericht Hamm 6 February 2013, *NJW* 2013, pp. 1167–1171; Supreme Court of Germany decision XII ZR 201/13, https://legallibrary.crin.org/supreme-court-of-germany-decision-xii-zr-201-13/.

109 S. Allan, *Donor Conception and the Search for Information. From secrecy and anonymity to openness*, London/New York, Routledge, 2017, pp. 136–137.

110 J. Taupitz and A. Theodoridis, 'Das Gesetz zur Regelung des Rechts auf Kenntnis der eigenen Abstammung bei heterologer Verwendung von Samen', 36 *Medizinrecht* 2018, pp. 457–466, pp. 457–458; A. Spickhoff, 'Vaterschaftsfestllung, Vaterschaft sanfechtung und das Recht auf Kenntnis der Abstammung nach heterologer Insemination', 3(3) *ZfPW* 2017, pp. 257–285, pp. 270–271.

1 July 2018 onwards.[111] Only persons conceived with gametes donated after the coming into force of this new Act can address the BfArM to access information about their donor. So nothing changes for the old donor-conceived persons. They still need to approach the individual sperm banks or fertility clinics in their search for information. However, there is one alternative for the benefit of these pre-2018 donor-conceived persons. To secure their right to access information about their donor – they have this right by virtue of the above-mentioned case law of the *Bundesverfassungsgericht* – the Sperm Donor Registry Act stipulates that all data prior to 2018 have to be stored by these institutions for a period equal to that in the *Samenspenderregistergesetz* (110 years).[112]

The United Kingdom

The central government register in the United Kingdom, operated by the statutory regulatory agency, HFEA, was already set up in the '90s, but donor anonymity was protected until 2005.[113] This means that both non-identifying and identifying information about persons who donated from August 1991 onward can be found in this central register.[114] But this also means that information about these donors cannot be released under the same conditions as under the 2005 law, since all pre-2005 donors donated anonymously. Nevertheless, on reaching the age of 16 these donor-conceived persons can access non-identifying information about their donor. Identifying information about the donor also can be released, but only to adult donor-conceived children and only if the donor re-registers with the HFEA as identifiable.[115] All donors who donated at a UK licensed clinic between 1991 and 2005 have had the opportunity to remove their anonymity and become identifiable to adults conceived from their donation(s). Re-registering means that the donor agrees to his or her identifying information being shared with the children that were born out of his or her donation. The decision to re-register is irreversible.[116]

---

111 E. Decorte, 'Donor Conception. From Anonymity to Openness' in K. Boele-Woelki and D. Martiny (eds.), *Plurality and Diversity of Family Relations in Europe*, Antwerp, Intersentia, 2019, pp. 167–168.

112 Article 1, §13(3) and (4) Sperm Donor Registry Act.

113 The right of the donor-conceived child to access identifying information about the donor was recognised by the Human Fertilisation and Embryology Authority (Disclosure of Donor Information) Regulations 2004. The Disclosure of Donor Information Regulations 2004 only apply to children conceived after 31 March 2005 with gametes donated after this date (reg. 2(3)).

114 HFEA, 'Donor-conceived people and their parents', https://www.hfea.gov.uk/donation/donor-conceived-people-and-their-parents/.

115 HFEA, 'Remove your donor anonymity', https://www.hfea.gov.uk/donation/donors/remove-your-donor-anonymity/.

116 HFEA, 'Remove your donor anonymity', https://www.hfea.gov.uk/donation/donors/remove-your-donor-anonymity/.

France

In France the preservation of donor anonymity has long been a subject of debate, and donor anonymity has only recently been waived.[117] The bioethics law of 1 August 2021 grants all donor-conceived persons aged 18 or older access to identifying and non-identifying information about their donor.[118] This new system only applies to persons conceived with donor gametes after 1 September 2022 and has no retroactive effect, meaning donors who donated their gametes before 1 September 2022 have the absolute right to remain anonymous.[119] But the French legislator also considered the rights of pre-2022 donor-conceived persons. These donor-conceived persons can submit a request for information to the newly established *Commission d'accès aux données non identifiantes et à l'identité du tiers donneur*. This commission is responsible for dealing with information requests from pre-2022 donor-conceived persons as well as post-2022 ones. However, in the case of old donor-conceived persons, both non-identifying and identifying information about the donor will only be released if the donor gives his or her explicit and prior consent.[120] Old donors can actively contact the commission to give their consent. Otherwise, they will be contacted by the commission when a donor-conceived person files a request to obtain their consent.[121]

According to two old donor-conceived persons, this new legal system, although better than before, still does not sufficiently meet their privacy rights. The release of identifying and non-identifying information about the donor is subject to the explicit consent of the donor, even if the donor has already passed away and his or her consent is no longer possible. Also, the reform process took a very long time. Their case was brought before the ECtHR.[122] Although the ECtHR did not underestimate the suffering of these old donor-conceived persons, the ECtHR concluded that there had been no violation of Article 8.[123] The French legislature struck a fair balance between the competing interests at stake and did not overstep its margin of appreciation. In the Court's opinion, the consent of the donor is necessary to respect the situations created under

117 Loi n° 2021-1017 du 2 août 2021 relative à la bioéthique.

118 Arts. L. 2143-2 and L. 2143-5 Code de la santé publique.

119 Art. 5, VII and VIII, Loi n° 2021-1017 du 2 août 2021 relative à la bioéthique.

120 Art. 5, VIII, B-E, Loi n° 2021-1017 relative à la bioéthique; Agence de la biomédecine, *Guide d'accès aux origines.*, https://www.agence-biomedecine.fr/IMG/pdf/guide_patients_acce_s_aux_origines_011221.pdf.

121 Agence de la biomédecine, *Guide d'accès aux origines*, https://www.agence-biomedecine.fr/IMG/pdf/guide_patients_acce_s_aux_origines_011221.pdf.

122 *Gauvin-Fournis and Silliau v. France*, 7 September 2023, nos. 21424/16 and 45728/17. The applicants lodged their applications in 2016 and at that time they had no means to access information about their donor. The ECtHR awaited the result of the third review of the bioethics law (2021) before ruling.

123 Three judges expressed a joint dissenting opinion.

the previous legislation and the slow pace of the reform process was due to the fact that the legislature took its time to organise very detailed debates to a high standard. Abolishing donor anonymity in France was an informed and gradual process of reflection, which cannot be criticised.[124]

3.3.2.2. Voluntary Registers

Unfortunately, the above-mentioned compromise, namely the release of information with the consent of the donor, will come too late for many donor-conceived persons and will lead to little or no information at all. Some records have been lost, destroyed or tampered with. To support these donor-conceived persons in finding out more about their genetic origins some jurisdictions have established a (voluntary) donor register. Through DNA testing, genetic links between donors and donor-conceived persons (and their genetically related siblings) can be found.

National Registers

In 2010 the Netherlands created a voluntary register, 'Fiom KID-DNA Database', for those conceived with donated gametes before donor anonymity was abolished in 2004 and for those for whom no information is available in the central register. The Fiom KID-DNA Database is operated by an independent agency known as Fiom.[125] Almost 3,000 donor-conceived persons and over 900 donors have already signed up for the Fiom KID-DNA Database (up to and including 30 November 2023). Some 300 donors have been matched with one or more donor-conceived persons and 882 donor-conceived persons have been matched with their donor.[126]

For persons conceived prior to 1991, the central register in the United Kingdom keeps no records. To support these donor-conceived persons in finding out more about their genetic origins, a voluntary register, the 'UK DonorLink', was created in 2004. The register has been intended for anyone who donated in a UK clinic or was conceived following treatment in a UK clinic before 1991.[127] In 2013, the UK DonorLink had its name changed to the UK Donor Conceived Register (DCR).

---

124 For a more thorough assessment of the judgment: E. Decorte, 'De tijd heelt niet altijd alle wonden (annotatie bij Gauvin-Fournis en Silliau t. Frankrijk (EHRM, nrs. 21424/16 en 45728/17))', *ECHR updates 16 November 2023*, https://www.ehrc-updates.nl/commentaar/212651?skip_boomportal_auth=1.

125 Fiom is a Dutch foundation specialising in helping women with unwanted pregnancies and questions about one's genetic origins, for more information: https://fiom.nl/.

126 Fiom, *Cijfers en feiten*, https://fiom.nl/kenniscollectie/kid-dna/cijfers-feiten.

127 Section 31ZF Human Fertilisation and Embryology Act 1990.

These kinds of donor registers are not only established by jurisdictions that have already decided to waive donor anonymity, but also by jurisdictions that still preserve donor anonymity, such as Belgium.[128] Although the Belgian legislator gives absolute priority to the interest of the donor to preserve his or her anonymity and disregards the interest of children in knowing their genetic origins, there is one recent success for donor-conceived persons in Belgium: the foundation of a 'Descent Centre' (in Dutch: Vlaams Afstammingscentrum), which includes a DNA database.[129] The database was created to enable parents to be reunited with children they were forced to give up for adoption in the past. It is now aimed at a larger group: all children whose legal parents, or at least one of them, are different from their biological and/or genetic parents. This includes donor-conceived persons. A donor-conceived person must be 12 years of age to join the DNA database. Children under the age of 12 are not precluded, but their participation will depend on their level of maturity, which is assessed by the staff of the centre.[130] The matching process is limited to finding relatives in the first degree. Donor-conceived persons cannot find their genetic (half-)siblings through this DNA database.[131]

The Fiom KID-DNA Database is also mainly aimed at linking donor and donor-conceived persons. Due to the DNA-matching technique, it is not always possible to demonstrate a (direct) relationship between donor-conceived persons. However, when there *is* a match, information can be disclosed. In the UK, donor-conceived persons can join a voluntary register, Donor Sibling.[132]

Commercial Registers

Donor registers are not only set up by law: due to the evolution of biogenetic technology, (commercial) private DNA databases are also mushrooming. US companies, such as 23andMe, Family Tree DNA, AncestryDNA and MyHeritage, sell DNA tests directly to citizen-consumers. The old donor-conceived persons in Ireland, for example, have to turn to these commercial databases, since the

128 The donation of gametes or of embryos should be anonymous: Article 22, section 2 and Article 51, §1, section 1 'Act regarding medically assisted reproduction and the destination of supernumerary embryos and gametes' of 6 July 2007, *Belgian Law Gazette (Belgisch Staatsblad or BS)* 17 July 2007, 38.575.

129 Decree which foresees the foundation of a centre of filiation and DNA database of 26 April 2019, *Belgian Law Gazette (Belgisch Staatsblad or BS)* 17 June 2019, 61.545.

130 Arts. 15–16 Decree of 26 April 2019.

131 Art. 24 Decree of 26 April 2019.

132 Sections 31ZA(2)(b) and 31ZE Human Fertilisation and Embryology Act 1990.

Irish government has not taken any specific measures (yet) to support these donor-conceived persons in their search for their genetic origins.

Unfortunately, there often is a lack of guidance and information. The added value of a database that is established by the government is that it is possible to manage the manner in which the information is communicated to donor-conceived persons and to donors. It is important to ensure that the rights of all parties are fully understood, that parties are made aware of some of the issues that may arise in their search, and that information release happens in a supported and guided way. Nevertheless, these commercial databases are often alluring because of the low(er) joining fee and the faster matching outcomes, since they are not confined to finding relatives in the first degree, but also relatives in the second or even third and fourth degrees.

Limitations

All these voluntary donor registers are created in order to exchange information and to facilitate contact by mutual consent between donor-conceived persons and their donors. However, it must be underlined that these registers only meet the interests of the donor-conceived persons in a limited way. There is no guarantee for donor-conceived persons that they will *ever* receive information about their donor. These registers operate on the basis of voluntariness and reciprocity, meaning that the matching process will take place in a somewhat more passive manner. A donor-conceived person and a donor will only receive information about each other if both parties are actively willing to cooperate. Both the donor and the donor-conceived person need to apply to the register for there to be a match.[133]

Voluntariness may be further hindered if donors have to pay a large sum to become members. The fee for joining the UK DNA database is, for example, £95. However, there is a possibility to discuss payment and payment methods when experiencing financial difficulties.[134] The fee for joining the Descent Centre in the Netherlands is 85 euros.[135] It is not inconceivable that these fees will scare

133 This needs to be nuanced. When someone has their genetic data stored in a (commercial) database, data about their family is also stored indirectly. It is therefore not impossible for an anonymous donor to be found without having ever donated his or her DNA to a database, see for example M. Crawshaw, 'Direct-to-consumer DNA testing: the fallout for individuals and their families unexpectedly learning of their donor conception origins', 21(4) *Human Fertility* 2017, pp. 225–228; A. Motluk, 'Tracing dad online', 188(2524) *New Scientist* 2005, pp. 6–7.

134 NHS, *DCR FAQs: Is there a reduced rate for people on low income?*, https://www.liverpoolwomens.nhs.uk/our-services/donor-conceived-register-dcr/faqs/.

135 Ministerial Order to determine the fee for collecting and processing the DNA sample and for matching the DNA profile, *Belgian Law Gazette (Belgisch Staatsblad or BS)* 21 June 2021, 64.256.

off some donors. Not only financial incentives, but also sensitisation is needed to encourage donors. It is important to attract the attention of the anonymous donors. The more donors that join the database, the greater the chance of finding genetic matches. This is only possible if states invest in publicity and in awareness campaigns, so that donors and donor-conceived persons find their way to these registers.

To support pre-2004 donor-conceived persons in discovering more information about their donor, the Dutch Ministry of Health, Welfare and Sport has, for example, made several public appeals for donors to join the Fiom KID-DNA Database and has exempted pre-2004 donors and pre-2004 donor-conceived persons from the enrolment fee for joining the Fiom KID-DNA Database.[136]

4. CONCLUSION

Today, donor anonymity is being challenged. It is challenged by the evolution of genetic technology and by changes in society, but also by international and European human rights law. The emphasis has gradually shifted from the interests and rights of the donors to remain anonymous to the interests and rights of the donor-conceived persons to know their genetic origins. Over the last decade more and more jurisdictions have abolished anonymity and granted donor-conceived persons access to information about their donor. These jurisdictions have chosen to tip the balance of the competing interests in favour of the donor-conceived person. This can only be welcomed. But this does not necessarily imply that all donor-conceived persons have the same rights.

On the one hand, laws in most jurisdictions only operate from the day they were enacted onward. The law is thus only applicable to cases which arise after its enactment. This means that persons conceived with donor gametes before the new system entered into force are excluded. On the other hand, we are increasingly seeing that these donor-conceived persons are making their voices heard.

From a human rights perspective, there is a need to find a balance between the rights and interests of all parties concerned, in particular the legitimate expectations of the old donors that their anonymity is preserved, connected with the interest of wider society in preserving legal certainty, and the interest of the old donor-conceived persons to access information about their donor. These

136 Fiom, *Kosten van inschrijving*, https://fiom.nl/afstammingsvragen/donorconceptie/fiom-kid-dna-databank/kosten-inschrijving; Fiom, *Demissionair minister de Jonge roept anonieme donoren op zich bekend te maken*, 15 March 2021.

jurisdictions, although they have already decided to abolish donor anonymity for the future, are now confronted with the (maybe even more) difficult search for balance between innovation and stability.

Having discussed the issue of donor anonymity of old donors and how it is approached in a number of (mostly European) jurisdictions, it is obvious that important differences exist between the various national laws concerning donor conception and the rights of old donor-conceived persons to access information about their genetic origins. The approach followed depends on which interests are preponderant according to the national legislator. Putting the emphasis mainly on the interests of the old donor-conceived persons by granting them the same rights as persons conceived under the new system ('full retroactivity') is still the exception. Many jurisdictions make a clear cut-off point in time. This means that donors who donated their gametes anonymously before the new system came into force have the right to remain anonymous and that persons conceived with donor gametes before the new system came into force are prevented from obtaining information about their donor. These jurisdictions concentrate more on the interests of the donor and the interests of society (e.g. the principle of legal certainty).

Nevertheless, more and more jurisdictions are tempering this cut-off by also granting old donor-conceived persons access to information about their donor, but only under certain conditions. Important conditions are often reciprocity and voluntariness. These jurisdictions try to find a fair balance by guaranteeing the freedom of choice for old donors. This was also recently confirmed by the ECtHR. Moreover, the experiences of these jurisdictions show that, to be successful, this must be accompanied by additional measures, e.g. sensitisation to encourage donors to adopt a more open attitude, and active preservation of the remaining information. Although this is the end of this chapter, the decision of a jurisdiction to end donor anonymity is not the end of the process by far.

NEW LEGAL PATHS TO DISCOVER AND ESTABLISH GENETIC ORIGINS?

Tim Wuyts

1. INTRODUCTION

Society evolves due to scientific advances in assisted reproductive techniques (ART),[1] allowing couples and single parents to form their families.[2] Nowadays, children can have more people playing different roles in their lives besides

---

1 At the time of the redaction of this article, researchers announced that a healthy baby boy had been born who had DNA from three people: https://www.biospace.com/article/child-born-with-the-dna-of-3-parents; See also: T.C. De Campos and C. Milo, 'Mitochondrial Donations and the Right to Know and Trace One's Genetic Origins: an Ethical and Legal Challenge', 32(2) *International Journal of Law, Policy and The Family* 2018, 170–179.

2 N.M. Alfonso Aleman, 'Children conceived through assisted reproduction: the extent and limits of their right to know their genetic origins. A comparative legal approach among the

their biological parents. For instance, parents can raise children conceived through surrogacy or gamete donation to whom they have no genetic link, or polyamorous parents can choose to raise children with two or more other people.[3] The modern family has different elements (emotional, functional, social) that may complement and conflict with each other.[4] While reproductive medicine and gamete donation help couples have offspring when they cannot conceive naturally, in legal terms, it raises the question of whether these children have the right to know their genetic origins.[5] Both Articles 7 and 8 of the United Nations Convention on the Rights of the Child (CRC)[6] and the case law on Article 8 of the European Convention on Human Rights (ECHR)[7] recognise this right.[8] This new reality invites legislators worldwide to rethink traditional legal concepts such as legal parentage and parental responsibilities.

During this process of rethinking, legislators face the same challenges: for instance, how to deal with questions of genetic origin, and how does this relate to protecting family life and parental responsibilities? And how to deal with (conflicting) rights of the child, the gamete donor and non-biological parents?

The approach to the issue of conflicting rights varies in the different legal systems, depending on how a legal system balances all the rights and interests at stake in their legislation.[9] Even in Europe, we are still far from a consensus on how to protect the right of every child to know the identity of their genetic parent. The European Court of Human Rights (ECtHR) considers that each member

---

jurisdictions of United Kingdom, Sweden, Netherlands, United States, Spain, and Argentina', 25(3) *ILSA Journal of International & Comparative Law* 2019, 435, 435–437.

3 S. Davies, 'Queering America's Heteronormative Family Law through "Well-Conceived" Legislation (Or, Genetic Parents Exist and Sometimes Your Kid Might Want to Know Them)', 46(1) *American Journal of Law & Medicine* 2020, 89, 89–90.

4 S. Ann Kamei, 'Partitioning Paternity: The German Approach to a Disjuncture Between Genetic and Legal Paternity With Implications for American Courts', 11 *San Diego International Law Journal* 2010, 509, 511–512.

5 B. Preloznjak, 'Modern challenges in the implementation of the child's right to know his origin', *EU and Comparative Law Issues and Challenges Series* vol. 4 *EU 2020: Lessons from the Past and Solutions for the Future* 2020, 1175, 1176.

6 D. Lyons, 'Domestic Implementation of the Donor-Conceived Child's Right to Identity in Light of the Requirements of the UN Convention on the Rights of the Child', 32(1) *International Journal of Law, Policy and The Family* 2018, 1, 22–23.

7 See, for example, ECtHR (Grant Chamber) 7 July 1989, n° 10454/83 (*Gaskin v. U.K.*); ECtHR 13 July 2006, n° 58757/00 (*Jäggi v. Switzerland*).

8 B. Preloznjak, 'Modern challenges in the implementation of the child's right to know his origin', *EU and Comparative Law Issues and Challenges Series*, vol. 4, *EU 2020: Lessons from the Past and Solutions for the Future* 2020, 1175, 1177–1182.

9 See, for the importance to find the balance between confronted rights and interest: B. Preloznjak, 'Modern challenges in the implementation of the child's right to know his origin', *EU and Comparative Law Issues and Challenges Series*, vol. 4, *EU 2020: Lessons from the Past and Solutions for the Future* 2020, 1175, 1198; See also in paternity proceedings: S. Ann Kamei, 'Partitioning Paternity: The German Approach to a Disjuncture Between Genetic and Legal Paternity With Implications for American Courts', 11 *San Diego International Law Journal* 2010, 509, 523–526.

state has quite a wide margin of appreciation in regulating such rights, as there is no 'consensus amongst member states, regarding the relative importance of the issue at stake or the best ways to protect it, especially when it comes to moral questions or delicate ethical issues'.[10] According to the case-law of the ECtHR, the state's margin in principle extends both to its decision to intervene in the area and, once it has intervened, to the detailed rules it lays down in order to achieve a balance between the competing public and private interests. However, the ECtHR is of the opinion that it falls within its duty to carefully examine the arguments taken into consideration during the legislative process and leading to the choices that the legislature has made and to determine whether a fair balance has been struck between the competing interests of the state and those persons directly affected by those legislative choices.[11]

Although we follow the same path in Europe in the slipstream of ECtHR jurisprudence in implementing the right to know one's origin as part of the right to private life, states are travelling at different speeds.[12] New paths are often created on an *ad hoc* basis after a constitutional court has declared legislation contrary to the constitution or the jurisprudence of the ECtHR.[13] A legislator may create a new legal path but keep another path explicitly closed at the same time. Some legislatures seem to move forward with the handbrake on, afraid of the consequences of going too fast. One of the reasons for this may be the belief that such legal recognition would have a destabilising effect on (traditional) family structures.[14] Another reason may be that an end to donor anonymity might scare off potential donors and/or interfere with their right to private life. The most common argument in this context is that unless their anonymity is guaranteed, it will become difficult to find gamete donors.[15] A global approach is missing and neither the ECtHR nor the CRC provide universally accepted guidance on how to accomplish a balance between the competing rights

---

10 ECtHR (Great Chamber) 24 January 2017, n° 25358/12, *Paradiso and Campanelli v. Italy*, §184.

11 ECtHR 5 May 2022, n° 8709/20, *Lia v. Malta*, §§60–61.

12 See, for example, the evolution from secrecy to openness in numerous countries, recognising the rights of people born as a result of donor-conception to information: R. Lukasiewicz, 'The Scope of Donor-Conceived Person's Rights to Access Information About the Gamete Donor in Europe – A Comparative Review', 13(4) *Journal of Politics and Law* 2020, 88; D. Lyons, 'The Constitutionality of Extending the Right to Identity Provisions in the Children and Family Relationships Act 2015 to Donor-Conceived Children', 16 *Hibernian Law Journal* 2017, 63, 64.

13 See, for instance, BVerfG 13 February 2007, *FamRZ* 2007, 441 in *NJW* 2007, 753, case of Herrn S. (Vaterschaftstests).

14 S. Ann Kamei, 'Partitioning Paternity: The German Approach to a Disjuncture Between Genetic and Legal Paternity With Implications for American Courts', 11 *San Diego International Law Journal* 2010, 509, 527–528 and 558.

15 E. Decorte, 'Een kinderrechtenconforme benadering van toegang tot afstammingsinformatie voor donorkinderen', *Tijdschrift voor Jeugd- en Kinderrechten* 2021/1, 7, 10.

implicated.[16] As a result, an effective way to protect a person's right to know their genetic origin is still not guaranteed in all cases.

This chapter will focus on how the right of children to know their origin when raised by persons other than their biological parent(s) outside of adoption can be inserted into the Belgian legal framework. It will not deal with the recognition of this right in the national legal framework as such, but will describe different possible legal paths to ensure this right. Therefore, the chapter will look at the issue through the eyes of the children.[17] The first question to be discussed is how children can know that they are not genetically related to one or both legal parents? This will be called 'discovering'. Once they are informed, the next question will be identifying their (potential) genetic parent. This will be termed 'exploring'. Finally, the question remains how they can establish genetic origins. This will be called 'establishing'. The focus here will be on rethinking the legal framework to reinforce the right to know one's origins. What are the possible legal paths? What are the strengths and weaknesses of each path? To answer these questions, the sections below will look at the latest developments in the legal framework of (mostly) European countries and add some proposals from legal scholars and law reform commissions.

2. NEW LEGAL PATHS TO DISCOVER THE TRUTH ABOUT YOUR CONCEPTION

2.1. KNOWLEDGE THAT YOUR LEGAL PARENTS ARE NOT YOUR GENETIC PARENTS

The first issue is how children discover that they are not genetically related to one or both of their legal parents. An essential question in this regard is whether parents have a legal duty to inform their children about how they were conceived, especially in cases where they are not biological or genetic parents. If parents do not inform their children, they might believe their entire life that their legal parents are also their genetic parents. However, in some cases, inevitably, questions will arise about the genetic origin, for instance, in single- and dual-parent lesbian families.

Legal systems treat this issue very differently. One notices an evolution towards more openness in ART cases, following in the footsteps of adoption

16 S. Ann Kamei, 'Partitioning Paternity: The German Approach to a Disjuncture Between Genetic and Legal Paternity With Implications for American Courts', 11 *San Diego International Law Journal* 2010, 509, 532.

17 The term 'children' is used here not in the sense of 'minors' but simply as offspring.

cases, where more openness was accepted at the end of the twentieth century.[18] For instance, clinics and doctors in the USA formerly recommended that heterosexual parents not inform their children that they used a gamete donor (due to stigma associated with infertility). However, times have changed, and even the American Society for Reproductive Medicine now recommends that parents tell their children about their genetic origins.[19] In the same way, the Dutch Government Committee on the Reassessment of Parenthood stresses the importance of creating openness about one's origins through general practitioners and midwives but also civil service officials.[20] This openness is not always explicitly included in the legal framework as a duty. It is sometimes encouraged indirectly, as I will show in the following examples of proposals and measures to improve this openness.

Some legal systems encourage openness about identity issues in adoption cases but remain silent in other cases. For example, according to Belgium law, a parent has, in general, no legal obligation to tell the child about their genetic origins. However, sometimes it is immediately apparent that one of the legal parents is not the genetic parent: for instance, children in single- and dual-parent lesbian families. In other cases, it may depend on the parents' attitude since they decide, in principle, what is in the child's best interest.[21] On the other hand, in adoption cases, parents receive training on genetic origin issues as a precondition for starting adoption proceedings.[22] Adoptive parents are encouraged to talk about this subject with their children in due time.[23]

---

18 S. Davies, 'Queering America's Heteronormative Family Law through "Well-Conceived" Legislation (Or, Genetic Parents Exist and Sometimes Your Kid Might Want to Know Them)', 46(1) *American Journal of Law & Medicine* 2020, 89, 102; See also: N. Cahn, 'No secrets: openness and donor-conceived "half-siblings"', 39(2) *Capital University Law Review* 2011, 313, 314–315; L. Gilman and P. Nordqvist, 'Organizing Openness: How UK Policy Defines the Significance of Information and Information Sharing about Gamete Donation', 32(3) *International Journal of Law, Policy and The Family* 2018, 316, 316–319. The authors raise the question about the information pathways available to those affected by donations, as well as the way these are framed and whether this might be done in ways which enable multiple 'truths' about the kind of act gamete donation is and the connections it creates (at 330).

19 S. Davies, 'Queering America's Heteronormative Family Law through "Well-Conceived" Legislation (Or, Genetic Parents Exist and Sometimes Your Kid Might Want to Know Them)', 46(1) *American Journal of Law & Medicine* 2020, 89, 102–103; See also by extension: F. Darroch and I. Smith, 'Establishing identity: how direct-to-consumer genetic testing challenges the assumption of donor anonymity', 59 *Family Court Review* 2021, 103, 107.

20 Recommendation n° 9, Rapport van de staatscommissie herijking ouderschap, 'Kind en ouders in de 21ste eeuw', https://www.rijksoverheid.nl/documenten/rapporten/2016/12/07/rapport-van-de-staatsommissie-herijking-ouderschap-kind-en-ouders-in-de-21ste-eeuw, 383–386.

21 T. Wuyts, *Ouderlijk gezag. Een coherente gezagsregeling voor minderjarigen*, Antwerpen, Intersentia, 2013, 595, paras. 816 and 660, para. 914.

22 Art. 346-2 old Civil Code.

23 For example, Art. 6(9) Decision of the Flemish Government concerning the preparation of an adoption, *Belgisch Staatsblad* 24 maart 2016.

Other legal systems encourage parents indirectly to inform their children about their conception. For example, in Irish law, all entries on the National Donor-Conceived Person Register are, at the same time, noted in the Register of Births. A donor-conceived person who has attained the age of 18 and applies for a copy of their birth certificate will be informed that further information is available from the Register regarding the donor conception.[24] The Irish legislator wants to encourage legal parents to disclose the existence of the donor conception before donor-conceived people have the opportunity to discover their status independently.[25] Following legal scholars, the right to information is largely illusory in the case of donor-conceived children unless they know that they are donor-conceived. Therefore, the maintenance of a Register would not be enough. It is arguable that a corresponding duty exists to tell children that they have an interest in accessing that very information.[26]

In addition, the Dutch Government Committee on the Reassessment of Parenthood advises establishing the right to information about one's origins as an integral part of the duties and rights of those exercising custody of a child.[27]

Children can also get confirmation about their legal parents' genetic parenthood by using genetic testing voluntarily. However, in some legal systems, voluntary genetic testing is forbidden or strongly discouraged. In French law, a genetic test can only be ordered by a court.[28] In German law, the legislator established so-called 'clarification proceedings'.[29] The German parliament has decided to allow private testing only with the consent of both legal parents. This approach is closely connected to the principle that the mother is the sole custodian of the rights of a non-marital child (§1626a Civil Code) and decides whether genetic testing is allowed. The German Act Concerning Genetic Testing of Humans[30] prohibits secret testing by a father (§26) and determines the conditions for testing (§17). It has been criticised as infringing the individual's right to control the use of their own genetic information.[31] The requirement of the free and informed consent of the test subject makes a balancing exercise

---

24 Section 39(4) Children and Family Relationships Act 2015.

25 D. Lyons, 'The Constitutionality of Extending the Right to Identity Provisions in the Children and Family Relationship Act 2015 to Donor-Conceived Children', 16 *Hibernian Law Journal* 2017, 63, 67.

26 L. Bracken, 'In the Best Interests of the Child? The Regulation of DAHR in Ireland', 23(4) *European Journal of Health Law* 2016, 391, 400.

27 Recommendation n° 6, Rapport van de staatscommissie herijking ouderschap, 'Kind en ouders in de 21ste eeuw', https://www.rijksoverheid.nl/documenten/rapporten/2016/12/07/rapport-van-de-staatsommissie-herijking-ouderschap-kind-en-ouders-in-de-21ste-eeuw, 386.

28 Art. 16-11, §1 Civil Code.

29 §1598a Civil Code; See for further detail, section 4.2.1 below.

30 Gesetz über genetische Untersuchungen beim Menschen – Gendianostikgesetz GenDG.

31 B.P. Harbuck, 'Lessons for Germany's Gendiagnostikgesetz from Europe's Protocol on Genetic Testing for health purposes', 10(2) *Washington University Global Studies Law Review* 2011, 371, 371–372.

between a person's interest in knowing their father's identity and the possible father's privacy interests impossible.[32] Anyway, what is forbidden by the law does not in practice prevent parents and children from finding ways to get certainty about genetic descent.

2.2. DISCOVERING THE IDENTITY OF YOUR GENETIC PARENTS

Another aspect of the right to know your genetic origins is the right to know the identity of your genetic parents. How can children find out who their genetic parents are? This right is in some legal systems explicitly recognised. However, there are differences between the legal systems on how it is ensured.

In some legal systems, the duty of parents to inform their children about the identity of their genetic parents is explicitly recognised by case law. For example, the Dutch Supreme Court has recognised since 1994 that a child has the right to know the identity of their biological parents.[33] This right is not absolute, though the right of an adult child to know who conceived them takes precedence over the right of the mother to conceal this from her child. The same court ruled in 2016 that providing information about the child's parentage is one of the duties of parental authority.[34] According to the Dutch Civil Code[35] parental authority includes the right and the duty of a parent to care for and educate their minor child. The care and responsibility for the child's mental well-being and personal development include providing information about their ancestry.[36] It should be mentioned that some lower courts, like the Court of Appeal of Arnhem, decided earlier that the interest of the child in knowing who the biological parents are, include the right to information but also the right to renounce this knowledge.[37]

In addition, in some legal systems, a child could also use information proceedings to force a parent to reveal their genetic origin. For example, under German law, the right to know one's genetic origin is fundamental but not absolute. It is a firmly held right that must always be balanced against other rights. The child's rights do not always win but must always be considered and given great weight. In a case where a child filed a claim to force her genetic

---

32 Ibid 393–394.

33 HR 15 April 1994, *NJ* 1994, 608, case note W.C.E. Hammerstein-Schoonderwoerd.

34 HR 18 March 2016, *NJB* 2016, 645; *NJ* 2016/210, case note S.F.M. Wortmann.

35 Article 1:247, §1 Dutch Civil Code.

36 See, for example, Court of Den Haag 15 January 2020, ECLI:NL:GHDHA:2020:55, paras. 5.6–5.8. In this case, the Court even ordered the identity of the biological father to be revealed to the child ('statusvoorlichting') under compulsion.

37 Court of Arnhem 13 September 2012, ECLI:NL:GHARN:2012:BX7942, paras. 31–35.

mother to reveal the names of her potential genetic fathers, the court weighed the mother's right to keep her sexual history private against the right of the child to know her genetic heritage. While the child's right was not absolute, the mother's privacy right was also not absolute. Courts must carefully balance both parties' rights and interests.[38]

Finally, the same remark about voluntary genetic testing (see section 2.1) can be made in cases where a child knows that their legal parents are not their genetic parents and wants to discover the identity of their genetic parents. Websites like *23andme.com*, which enable families of all kinds to find unexpected connections, may do even more to speed up this process.[39] So even when a legal system prohibits clarification on a voluntary basis, legal questions may arise. Even anonymity agreements promising donors' privacy cannot prevent this.[40]

3. NEW LEGAL PATHS TO EXPLORE GENETIC ORIGINS

Once a donor-conceived person has discovered that their legal parent is not their genetic parent, how can they discover the (potential) identity of their biological or genetic parent if the identity is not known to the legal parents? This question has already been addressed partly by Decorte who, in her chapter, discusses the registration of the donor's identity and access to this information. The question remains whether there are other paths by which to explore genetic origins, for instance, when no Medically Assisted Reproduction (MAR) was used.

Some legal systems protect the traditional family structure in order to avoid issues related to genetic origin. For example, France does not allow surrogacy.[41] MAR was until recently restricted to stable heterosexual couples of reproductive age, and at least one of the members of the couple had to be a genetic parent (old L 2141-2 Public Health Code). In 2021 the French Parliament, after a long debate,[42] approved a new Bill that opens the road to MAR for more couples

---

38 Constitutional Court 6 May 1997, 96, *Entscheidungen des Bundesverfassungsgericht* (BVerfGE) 56 (268–269); S. Ann Kamei, 'Partitioning Paternity: The German Approach to a Disjuncture Between Genetic and Legal Paternity With Implications for American Courts', 11 *San Diego International Law Journal* 2010, 509, 533.

39 See in extension: F. Darroch and I. Smith, 'Establishing identity: how direct-to-consumer genetic testing challenges the assumption of donor anonymity', 59 *Family Court Review* 2021, 103.

40 M.C. York, 'I Just Took a DNA Test – Turns Out, I'm 100% Breaching My Donor Anonymity Contract: Direct-to-Consumer DNA Testing and Parental Medical-Decision-Making', 28(2) *Indiana Journal of Global Legal Studies* 2021, 293.

41 Art. 16-7 Civil Code.

42 See for the discussion between both chambers of the French Parliament: Projet de loi n° 3833 modifié par le Sénat en deuxième lecture, relatif à la bioéthique; Rapport n° 3891 fait au nom de la commission mixte paritaire chargée de proposer un texte sur les dispositions restant en discussion du projet de loi relatif à la bioéthique, p. 7 en 11.

(including same-sex) and single mothers.[43] German law similarly protects the 'traditional view' of the family in its law governing reproductive rights. It strongly discourages assisted reproduction.[44] Furthermore, surrogacy mediation is still forbidden under a recently (22 November 2019) adopted Act.[45]

Other legal systems in contrast, consider expanding the registration of genetic origin to encompass cases outside MAR. For instance, the Dutch Government committee on the Reassessment of Parenthood recommends replacing the words 'parentage information' with the words 'information about the origin'.[46] Furthermore, the committee recommends creating a register of origin in which information other than the donor data already registered is included.[47] The committee proposes a system where as much information about genetic origin as possible is registered, including information submitted by the legal parents and, with the permission of the legal parents or a judge, third parties. Access to this information should be regulated in the same way as in cases of MAR.

4. NEW LEGAL PATHS TO ESTABLISH GENETIC ORIGINS

Once a child knows or seeks certainty about the identity of their biological parents, the last question will be how they can formally establish their genetic origin. Different paths exist depending on the approach of the legal system. Two questions are decisive: first, whether the legal system is willing to rethink the notion of what a family can be; second, whether there are any legal consequences attached to the formal establishment of origin. Based on the answers to these two questions, three approaches can be distinguished: monistic, dual and blended.

---

43 Art. 1 Loi n° 2021-1017 du 2 août 2021 relative à la bioéthique, *Journal officiel de la République Française* 3 août 2021, replacing L 2141-2 CSP with a new public health code.

44 Embryonenschutzgesetz – EschG.

45 Gesetz über die Vermittlung und Begleitung der Adoption und über das Verbot der Vermittlung von Ersatzmüttern (Adoptionsvermittlungsgesetz AdVermiG).

46 Recommendation n° 4, Rapport van de staatscommissie herijking ouderschap, 'Kind en ouders in de 21ste eeuw', https://www.rijksoverheid.nl/documenten/rapporten/2016/12/07/rapport-van-de-staatsommissie-herijking-ouderschap-kind-en-ouders-in-de-21ste-eeuw, 382.

47 Recommendation n° 7, Rapport van de staatscommissie herijking ouderschap, 'Kind en ouders in de 21ste eeuw', https://www.rijksoverheid.nl/documenten/rapporten/2016/12/07/rapport-van-de-staatsommissie-herijking-ouderschap-kind-en-ouders-in-de-21ste-eeuw, 386.

4.1. EXPANSION OF OLD PATHS (MONISTIC APPROACH)

I want to start with the most common path followed by legal systems today: expanding the old paths. Old paths are existing ways to establish genetic origin by using legal status proceedings. In countries where specific proceedings to discover and formally establish one's genetic origin are missing, the only remaining path to follow is that of parentage proceedings.

Since the turn of the twenty-first century, a remarkable evolution has taken place towards a broader use of parentage proceedings. Stability of legal ties, legal certainty and the protection of the legal family are no longer legal aims that can prevent parentage proceedings in an absolute way. According to well-established case law of the ECtHR, the situation in which a legal presumption is allowed to prevail over biological and social reality, without regard to both established facts and the wishes of those concerned and without actually benefiting anyone, is not compatible, even having regard to the margin of appreciation left to the state, with the obligation to secure effective 'respect' for private and family law.[48] The ECtHR applies this principle in all cases where a child or a parent seeks through legal proceedings to establish their legal relationship with a person by confirming or denying the biological truth. The ECtHR urges national authorities in Europe to revise their law on parentage proceedings in light of the right to respect for private life, which encompasses important aspects of one's personal identity, such as the identity of one's parents.[49] Consequently, Member States have to abolish all legal obstacles[50] to discovering and establishing one's parentage and make sure a fair balance of interests is struck between the competing interests,[51] particularly in this kind of case where a thorough balancing of interests is required.[52] Courts must attach special weight to the right to know one's parentage.[53] A person seeking to establish the identity of their ascendants has a vital interest, protected by the ECHR, in receiving the information necessary to uncover the truth about an important aspect of their

48 ECtHR 27 October 1994, n° 18535/91, *Kroon and others. v. The Netherlands*, §40; ECtHR 24 November 2005, n° 74826/01, *Shofman v. Russia*, §44; ECtHR 12 January 2006, n° 26111/02, *Mizzi v. Malta*, §113; ECtHR 10 October 2006, n° 10699/05, *Paulik v. Slovakia*, §46; ECtHR 9 November 2006, n° 11449/02, *Tavli v. Turkey*, §35; ECtHR 20 December 2007, n° 23890/02, *Phinikaridou v. Cyprus*, §63.

49 ECtHR 13 February 2003 (Grand Chamber), n° 42326/98, *Odièvre v. France*, §29.

50 For example, a time-limit for instituting paternity proceedings. The Court ascertained whether the nature of the time-limit in question, and/or the manner in which it was applied, was compatible with the ECHR (ECtHR 6 July 2010, n° 36498/05, *Backlund v. Finland*, §44; ECtHR 19 October 2021, n° 69997/17, *Lavanchy v. Switzerland*, §33).

51 ECtHR 6 July 2010, n° 36498/05, *Backlund v. Finland*, §46.

52 ECtHR 13 July 2006, n° 58757/00, *Jäggi v. Switzerland*, §37; ECtHR 16 June 2011, n° 19535/08, *Pascaud v. France*, §59.

53 ECtHR 7 February 2002, n° 53176/99, *Mikulic v. Croatia*, §64; ECtHR 13 July 2006, n° 58757/00, *Jäggi v. Switzerland*, §38.

personal identity.[54] In proceedings for establishment of paternity, where a careful balancing exercise is required, the best interest of the child should be given priority.[55] In this connection, the Court also emphasises that the interest of persons in receiving the information necessary to eliminate any uncertainty regarding their personal identity does not disappear with age; in fact, quite the reverse.[56]

In Belgium, for example, the Constitutional Court, inspired by the case law of the ECtHR, declared unconstitutional a legislative bar on challenges to paternity where the child in question has been treated as the child of his legal father (*possession d'etat*)[57] (which is comparable with family life), and further deemed various time-limits imposed for actions to challenge[58] paternity or recognise[59] paternity unconstitutional. The case law of Belgium's Constitutional Court was crucial to the success of the paternity claim by (the newly recognised) Princess Delphine van Saksen-Coburg.[60]

Another interesting issue is whether DNA testing can be imposed by court order. Again, the case law of the ECtHR is evolving in the direction toward more acceptance. In the opinion of the Court, the protection of third persons may preclude them from being compelled to make themselves available for medical testing of any kind, including DNA testing. The Court has examined whether a fair balance was struck between the competing interests in those cases.[61] A system that has no means of compelling the alleged father to comply with a court order for DNA tests to be carried out can nevertheless be compatible with the obligations deriving from Article 8, taking into account the state's margin of appreciation. However, such a system must also secure the interests of the individual seeking the establishment of paternity when paternity cannot be established using DNA testing. In the Court's opinion, the lack of any procedural measure to compel the alleged father to comply with the court order is only in conformity with the principle of proportionality if the state provides alternative means enabling an independent authority to determine the paternity claim speedily.[62]

---

54 ECtHR 13 July 2006, n° 58757/00, *Jäggi v. Switzerland*, §38.

55 ECtHR 15 October 2019, n° 44690/09, *Çapin v. Turkey*, §77.

56 ECtHR 13 July 2006, n° 58757/00, *Jäggi v. Switzerland*, §§38 and 40; ECtHR 15 October 2019, n° 44690/09, *Çapin v. Turkey*, §77.

57 Constitutional Court 3 February 2016, n° 18/2016.

58 Constitutional Court 3 February 2016, n° 18/2016.

59 Constitutional Court 17 October 2019, n° 142/2019.

60 Court of Appeal Brussels 1 October 2020, *Tijdschrift voor Jeugd en Kinderrechten* 2021, 251, case note T. Wuyts.

61 ECtHR 29 January 2019, n° 62257/15, *Mifsud v. Malta*, §77.

62 ECtHR 7 February 2002, n° 53176/99, *Mikulic v. Kroatië*, §64; ECtHR 29 January 2019, n° 62257/15, *Mifsud v. Malta*, §§54–60.

Many legal systems provide for genetic testing by court order within parentage proceedings. This is the case, for example, in Belgium,[63] France,[64] Germany,[65] the Netherlands,[66] and England & Wales.[67] In some legal systems, such as the Netherlands[68] and Germany,[69] genetic testing can also be ordered outside of parentage proceedings, as will be explained in the next sub-section. A court can only decide otherwise for legitimate reasons. In Germany, a DNA sample can even be taken under compulsion.[70] In other legal systems like the Netherlands[71] or Belgium,[72] compulsion is indirectly possible using penalty payments. The Dutch Supreme Court recently ruled that the child's interest in receiving information about their origin prevails over the interest of a presumed father, even if this information must be revealed through DNA testing that violates the physical integrity of the presumed biological father.[73]

In some legal systems like Belgium,[74] the Netherlands[75] and England & Wales,[76] a father's unjustified refusal can be interpreted as an implied confession or, together with other facts pointing in the same direction, as a presumption of parenthood.

4.2. CREATION OF NEW LEGAL PATHS (DUALISTIC APPROACH)

The question arises whether parentage proceedings are always the right path to follow. Many rights and interests are involved in parentage proceedings.

---

63 Art. 331*octies* Civil Code.

64 Art. 16(2) Civil Code.

65 §26 Family Proceeding Act ('FamFG').

66 Art. 194 Judicial Code ('Wetboek van Burgerlijke Rechtsvordering').

67 Section 20(1) Family Law Reform Act 1969.

68 See, for example: Supreme Court of the Netherlands 11 March 2022, ECLI:NL:HR:2022:349, paras. 3.1.2.–3.1.5.

69 §1598a Civil Code.

70 §372*a* Judicial Code ('Zivilprozessordnung').

71 The case law shows that the courts can order a DNA test under compulsion when a penalty payment is not enough. See, for example: Court of Appeal of Arnhem-Leeuwarden 2 March 2021, ECLI:NL:GHARL:2021:1927; Court of Limburg 15 August 2017, ECLI:NL:RBLIM:2017:8202.

72 On this point see Court of Appeal Brussels 16 May 2019, *Tijdschrift voor Jeugd en Kinderrechten* 2021/3, 231, case note T. Wuyts and Y.-H. Leleu, *Droit des personnes et des familles*, Larcier, Brussels 2020, p. 139, para. 115 and p. 598, para. 623; *Contra*: P. Senaeve, 'De rechtspleging inzake afstammingsvorderingen' in P. Senaeve (ed.), *Handboek familieprocesrecht*, die Keure, Mechelen 2020, pp. 848–849, para. 1380.

73 Supreme Court of the Netherlands 11 March 2022, ECLI:NL:HR:2022:349, paras. 3.1.2.–3.1.5.

74 Court of Cassation 17 December 1998, *Rechtskundig Weekblad* 1998–99, 1144, case note F. Swennen.

75 Supreme Court of the Netherlands 9 December 2005, ECLI:NL:HR:2005:AU3262.

76 Section 23 Family Law Reform Act; See, for example: *Re A (Paternity: refusal of blood test)* [1994] 2 FLR 463, CA.

Therefore, one could ask whether it is required to commence parentage proceedings to safeguard the right to know one's origin?

According to the case law of the European Court of Human Rights, parentage proceedings are not the only way to guarantee the right to identity as included in Article 8 ECHR, in particular under the umbrella of the right to private life. It should be possible to determine the identity of one's parents outside the context of parentage proceedings.[77] For example, in *Jäggi v. Switzerland*, the state acknowledged that recognition of biological paternity would not affect the register of births, deaths, and marriages.[78]

4.2.1. *Creation of Specific Legal Paths Besides Status Proceedings and without Legal Consequences*

Like Germany and England & Wales, some legal systems have specific legal proceedings to discover and establish one's genetic origin without other legal consequences.

The German Parliament in 2008, following a decision of the German Constitutional Court,[79] created clarification proceedings ('*Abstammungsklärung*'). If a person wants to pursue clarification of genetic paternity, they can do so without putting their *legal* paternity (or their rights to challenge legal paternity) in jeopardy. According to the German Civil Code (Article 1598*a*), clarification proceedings can be brought by (1) the father against the mother and child, (2) the mother against the father and child, or (3) the child against both parents. If the other parties do not consent, the family court can order that individuals submit to testing. The court can only order testing after considering any potential harm to the child.

The German law is subject to criticism in legal doctrine.[80] It leaves open unresolved rights and interests, such as the child's right to remain in ignorance and the rights of men who suspect they are genetic fathers but have no legal relationship to the child, particularly where there is a legally recognised father. According to the German Constitutional Court, the legislator need not provide a separate procedure to determine parentage vis-à-vis a putative biological yet not

---

77 *Cp.* ECtHR 16 June 2011, n° 19535/08, *Pascaud v. France*, §§48–49; ECtHR 6 July 2010, n° 17038/04, *Grönmark v. Finland*, §39; ECtHR 6 July 2010, n° 36498/05, *Backlund v. Finland*, §37; F. Swennen, *Het personen- en familierecht. Een benadering in context*, Intersentia, Antwerp 2021, pp. 420–421.

78 ECtHR 13 July 2006, n° 58757/00, *Jäggi v. Switzerland*, §43; See also: ECtHR 7 April 2009, n° 4914/03, *Turnali v. Turkey*, §§34–35 and 45; ECtHR 21 December 2010, n° 20578/07, *Anayo v. Germany*, §62; ECtHR 15 September 2011, n° 17080/07, *Schneider v. Germany*, §§79–90.

79 Constitutional Court 13 February 2007, *Zeitschrift für das gesamte Familienrecht* 2007, 441 and *NJW* 2007, 753.

80 S. Ann Kamei, 'Partitioning Paternity: The German Approach to a Disjuncture Between Genetic and Legal Paternity With Implications for American Courts', 11 *San Diego International Law Journal* 2010, 509, 543–548.

legal father without changing the legal status of persons involved.[81] Following the Constitutional Court the legislator has a margin of appreciation, since he has to accommodate a multipolar fundamental rights relationship.

There exists a bridge between clarification proceedings and paternity proceedings. Once clarification proceedings are started, the deadline for proceedings to challenge paternity is suspended (§1600b(5) BGB). German legal doctrine criticises this bridge as it undermines the stability of family relationships and social parentage.[82] Furthermore, the protection offered by the proof of reasonable doubt as to paternity in challenge proceedings[83] is completely lifted.

In Belgium's legal doctrine, a growing number of scholars argue for introducing specific proceedings to discover and establish genetic origins without legal consequences.[84] No bridge has to exist between these proceeding and parentage proceedings. Both proceedings should exist along side one another. As a result, parentage proceedings may be subject to restrictions protecting the stability of legal ties and the existing family life since another procedure protects the right to know one's genetic origin.[85]

Perhaps the creation of two separate proceedings can simplify the balance of interests, protect existing family life more effectively and create more legal certainty while guaranteeing at the same time an effective path to establishing genetic origin.

4.2.2. *Creation of Specific Legal Paths for the Purpose of Some Legal Consequences*

There is also another solution conceivable. For example, linking a limited number of legal consequences to the established genetic origin in general and/or on a case-by-case basis.

This idea is not new. For instance, in Belgium (Article 336 old Civil Code), the Netherlands (Article 1:394 Civil Code), and France (Article 342

---

81 Constitutional Court 19 April 2016, 1 BvR 3309/13.

82 R. Frank and T. Helms, 'Kritische Bemerkungen zum Regierungsentwurf eines "Gesetzes zur Klärung der Vaterschaft unabhängig vom Anfechtungsverfahren"', *Zeitschrift für das gesamte Familienrecht* 2007, 1277, 1279; D. Schwab, 'Abstammungsklärung – leicht gemacht. Order: Neuer Dialog in der Familie', *Zeitschrift für das gesamte Familienrecht* 2008, 23, 26; cp. B. Heiderhoff, 'Die Vaterschaftsklärung und ihre Folgen – von der Vaterschapfsanfechtung zur Vaterschaftsbeendigung?', *Zeitschrift für das gesamte Familienrecht* 2010, 8 11.

83 See §171(2) Gesetz über das Verfahren in Familiensachen und in den Angelegenheiten der freiwilligen Gerichtsbarkeit (FamFG).

84 F. Swennen and S. Eggermont, 'Koekoekskinderen in het familierecht' in R. Barbaix et al., *Koekoekskinderen*, Gent, Larcier 2009, 19, para. 36; P. Senaeve, 'Hoe het recht op identiteit wettelijk verankeren?', *Tijdschrift voor Familierecht* 2020/5, 122, 123.

85 P. Senaeve, 'Hoe het recht op identiteit wettelijk verankeren?', *Tijdschrift voor Familierecht* 2020/5, 122, 123–124.

Civil Code), clarification proceedings can be used to obtain maintenance payments from a genetic father. Still, this is only if no legal paternity has been established.

According to the case law of the European Court of Human Rights, Article 8 of the ECHR can be interpreted as imposing on the States Parties an obligation to examine whether it is in the child's best interest to allow the biological father to establish a relationship with his child, in particular by granting contact rights.[86]

Another interesting legal path might be to allow the establishment of the parentage of a third party (for example, a donor) even when the child already has two legal parents, without adverse legal consequences for the established parentage. For example, according to Belgium's law, the establishment of legal parentage of a third party after adoption is possible without adverse legal consequences contrary for the adoption.[87] This approach allows a child to have more than two legal parents simultaneously, but each plays a specific role in the child's life.[88]

4.3. EXPANDING THE BOUNDS OF WHAT A FAMILY CAN BE (BLENDED APPROACH)

Creating new legal paths is not the only answer to reconciling the law with a complex reality. The legislator could simultaneously extend the notion of 'legal family' to more than two legal parents. This adaptation can lead to multiple parenthood, with more than two legal parents on an equal footing parents in the front and back seat or shared parenting for some legal purposes, for example, the exercise of parental responsibilities. Some authors stress the need to use scientific terminology in conjunction with legal definitions to avoid confusing labels.[89]

4.3.1. Multiple Parenthood

The first path to follow is to recognise more than two persons as a parent. The legal consequences can be allocated to all parents or distributed between

86 ECtHR 21 December 2010, n° 20578/07, *Anayo v. Germany*, §71; ECtHR 15 September 2011, n° 17080/07, *Schneider v. Germany*, §104; See, for example: Supreme Court of the Netherlands 11 March 2022, ECLI:NL:HR:2022:349, para. 3.5; Court of Arnhem-Leeuwarden 23 November 2021, ECLI:NL:GHARL:2021:10825, paras. 5.5–5.7.

87 Art. 350 (2) old Civil Code.

88 See also: T. Wuyts, 'Heeft sociaal ouderschap nog een toekomst?', *Tijdschrift voor Familierecht* 2016, 182–183.

89 F. Darroch and I. Smith, 'Establishing identity: how direct-to-consumer genetic testing challenges the assumption of donor anonymity', 59(1) *Family Court Review* 2021, 103, 114.

them. The Dutch Government committee on the Reassessment of Parenthood recommends the legal facilitation of multiple parenthood under certain conditions, for example: voluntarily; limited to four legal parents and two households; only for the mother, genetic parents, and their life companions; with a formal agreement ratified by a court, etc.[90] The committee believes that a child can experience more than two persons as their factual parents, and advises the legislator to provide those children with protection equal to that of children from a family with one or two parents.[91] This is an example of how legal consequences may be allocated to all parents equally.

A remarkable development in adoption cases is that some legal systems explicitly no longer cut all the legal ties between the child and their original family after the adoption.[92] For instance, in English law, the court has to investigate possible contact arrangements after adoption.[93] In French law, adoption does not prevent the right to contact with members of the original family if this serves the child's best interest.[94] In Belgian law, two different types of adoption exist: simple adoption[95] and full adoption.[96] A simple adoption does not cut off a child from their genetic parents, and creates only a legal relationship between the child and the adoptive parent. For example, the child retains inheritance and maintenance rights in the original family.[97] This approach might shed new light on the approach of parenting limited to two legal parents. However, this approach leads to a distinction between parents in the front and back seat.

The US Uniform Parentage Act[98] (2017) left open the option that a court may rule that a child has more than two parents under this Act.[99] This provision

90 Recommendation n° 4, Rapport van de staatscommissie herijking ouderschap, 'Kind en ouders in de 21ste eeuw', https://www.rijksoverheid.nl/documenten/rapporten/2016/12/07/rapport-van-de-staatsommissie-herijking-ouderschap-kind-en-ouders-in-de-21ste-eeuw, 428–434.

91 Rapport van de staatscommissie herijking ouderschap, 'Kind en ouders in de 21ste eeuw', https://www.rijksoverheid.nl/documenten/rapporten/2016/12/07/rapport-van-de-staatsommissie-herijking-ouderschap-kind-en-ouders-in-de-21ste-eeuw, 428.

92 See also: ECtHR (Grand Chamber) 10 December 2021, n° 15379/16, *Abdi Ibrahim v. Norway*, §162. According to the ECtHR the reasons advanced in support of the foster parents' decision to adopt were not sufficient to demonstrate that the circumstances of the case were so exceptional as to justify a complete and definitive severance of the ties between the child and her original mother; nor did they show that their decision was motivated by an overriding requirement pertaining to the child's best interests.

93 Art. 46(6) Adoption and Children Act 2002.

94 Art. 371-4 (2) Civil Code.

95 Art. 353-1 et seq old Civil Code.

96 Art. 355 et seq old Civil Code.

97 Art. 353-15 old Civil Code.

98 https://www.uniformlaws.org/committees/community-home?CommunityKey=c4f37d2d-4d20-4be0-8256-22dd73af068f#:~:text=The%20Uniform%20Parentage%20Act%20(2017,UPA%2C%20last%20revised%20in%202002.

99 Ibid. §613, alternative B.

addresses situations in which multiple individuals have a claim to the parentage of a child. According to the commentary on this article, this alternative is consistent with an emerging trend permitting courts to recognise more than two people as a child's parents. When the Act was drafted, four US States had already expressly allowed a court to find that a child has more than two legal parents. Besides, courts in several other States have reached that conclusion as a matter of common law. According to the commentary, courts in some States have concluded that a child had two legal parents and one equitable parent entitled to at least some rights and duties of a parent.[100]

4.3.2. Sharing Parental Responsibilities

Another approach is to allow the exercise of specific parental responsibilities by third parties in the same way as biological parents without recognising them as legal parents. This approach is not new. For example, some legal systems, like Germany, acknowledge the importance of stepparents and grant them some rights even though the legal parent still holds a full complement of legal rights in relation to the child.[101]

According to English law, in general, a child can have more than two persons exercising parental responsibilities either under a parental responsibility agreement or by court order.[102] English law is complex. Nevertheless, since we live in a complex society, legal scholars experience this as a positive evolution. The question is not whether to prefer the genetic or social parent but how to accommodate both, on the assumption that they both have distinctive contributions to make to the child's life.[103]

At the same time, it is important to rethink the right to parent without fear that a court might grant parental rights to a third-party genetic donor or surrogate. This means protecting non-biological parents from the interference of other adults who might have a biological claim.[104] Therefore, in some legal

---

[100] Comment under §613 US Uniform Parentage Act (2017), https://higherlogicdownload.s3-external-1.amazonaws.com/UNIFORMLAWS/ccec4a4f-cf66-e428-04ba-2d5bd1b97c7b_file.pdf?AWSAccessKeyId=AKIAVRDO7IEREB57R7MT&Expires=1700168957&Signature=opT5QPl5%2FUsDn1mIKoC9K0WcbIo%3D, pp. 56–57.

[101] §1687b Civil Code; D. Schwab, P. Gottwald and S. Lettmaier, *Family and Succession Law in Germany*, Kluwer, The Netherlands 2017, 93, para. 216.

[102] See, for example, s. 4A (1) Children Act 1989: by agreement with the stepparent, both parents may provide for the stepparent to have parental responsibility for the child, or the court may, on the application of the stepparent, order that the stepparent shall have parental responsibility for the child.

[103] S. Harris-Short and J. Miles, *Family law. Text, cases, and materials*, 2nd edn., Oxford University Press, Oxford 2011, 713; In the same sense: M. Freeman, *Understanding Family Law*, 1st edn., Sweet & Maxwell, London 2007, 164.

[104] S. Davies, 'Queering America's Heteronormative Family Law through "Well-Conceived" Legislation (Or, Genetic Parents Exist and Sometimes Your Kid Might Want to Know Them), 46(1) *American Journal of Law & Medicine* 2020, 89, 107.

systems, for instance, in Belgium,[105] France[106] and Ireland,[107] the law regulating medically-assisted reproduction expressly stipulates that a donor has neither legal rights nor legal responsibilities to their offspring.

5. CONCLUSION

We are living in a complex society. A complex society requires tailor-made answers in law. Until now European legislators have only acted if required to protect a specific right and interest. This approach does not provide comprehensive protection of the rights and interests of all parties.

This author believes that children dealing with the same questions about genetic origin should be treated equally. Can it be justified that children are treated differently depending on whether they were adopted or conceived with donor gametes? One can argue that adoption cases are not (entirely) comparable with other cases, but it seems doubtful that the questions about one's genetic origin are very different in adoption cases.[108] It appears that there exist meaningful similarities on this topic.[109] It would therefore be best to the same approach as in adoption cases,[110] where a shift in mindset already has occurred. The European legislation is evolving in that direction.

The law should follow the changes in society and reflect – and, to as great an extent as possible, enable – this new reality by recognising that all children have compatible, equally compelling rights to self-determination and access to information that would allow them to pursue relationships with their missing genetic relatives, should they choose to do so.[111]

---

105 Arts. 27 and 56 Act of 6 July 2007 on assisted reproduction and destination of supernumerary embryos and gametes, *Belgisch Staatsblad* 17 July 2007.

106 Art. 311-19 Civil Code.

107 Section 5(5) Children and Family Relationships Act 2015.

108 T. Wuyts, 'Het recht op identiteit in de Belgische rechtsorde', *Tijdschrift voor Familierecht* 2015, 60, 64–65.

109 *Compare* with: S. Davies, 'Queering America's Heteronormative Family Law through "Well-Conceived" Legislation (Or, Genetic Parents Exist and Sometimes Your Kid Might Want to Know Them)', 46(1) *American Journal of Law & Medicine* 2020, 89, 103; F. Darroch and I. Smith, 'Establishing identity: how direct-to-consumer genetic testing challenges the assumption of donor anonymity', 59 *Family Court Review* 2021, 103, 107; N. Cahn, 'No secrets: openness and donor-conceived "half-siblings"', 39(2) *Capital University Law Review* 2011, 313, 313–315.

110 See for the old approach and the suggested paths in case of adoption: H.A. Schneider, 'Adoption Contracts and the Adult Adoptee's Right to Identity', 6(2) *Minnesota Journal of Law and Inequality* 1988, 185.

111 *Compare* with: S. Davies, 'Queering America's Heteronormative Family Law through "Well-Conceived" Legislation (Or, Genetic Parents Exist and Sometimes Your Kid Might Want to Know Them)', 46(1) *American Journal of Law & Medicine* 2020, 89, 90 and 109–110.

At the level of discovering, it is clearly vital to create openness about one's origin, as the Dutch Government committee and the American Society for Reproductive Medicine have already advised. To that end, it is essential to organise awareness campaigns and to inform legal parents.[112] In Belgium, an adoptive parent must even undertake a course before starting the adoption process.[113] Why not ask the same of persons who want to conceive a child by using donor gametes?

At the level of exploring, this author believes that donor children should be treated the same as adopted children. The same data should be registered. A state should organise access to this register similarly to the access given in adoption cases. I think the UK and the Netherlands are good examples. Besides, creating a clarification process may be necessary when no information is available.

Finally, at the level of establishing genetic origins, a blended approach is required. The main question is how to accommodate genetic and social parents to assume they have distinctive contributions to the child's life. Neither a monistic approach nor a purely dualistic approach can deliver an appropriate answer to this question. Both approaches ignore the complex reality. Hence, one should consider a system of multiple parenthood. This approach exists already in Belgium and France in cases of simple adoption. Integration into a social family does not require cutting all ties with the child's genetic origins. A state could recognise genetic origin in a separate register, as the Dutch Government committee recommended. This registration could generate specific legal consequences without disrupting the legal ties with the social parents. For example, it could allow the biological parent to claim visitation rights in the best interests of the child, or it could facilitate inheritance rights (for example, at the level of taxes).[114] Depending on the agreement made before conception, it could also exclude some legal consequences. For instance, no maintenance claims are possible when a donor donated gametes upon condition that this would be the case.

---

112 *Compare* with: F. Darroch and I. Smith, 'Establishing identity: how direct-to-consumer genetic testing challenges the assumption of donor anonymity', 59 *Family Court Review* 2021, 103, 116.

113 Art. 346-2 old Civil Code; art. 1231-1/2, 2° Judicial Code.

114 *Compare* with: F. Darroch and I. Smith, 'Establishing identity: how direct-to-consumer genetic testing challenges the assumption of donor anonymity', 59 *Family Court Review* 2021, 103, 116: 'Support diverse parenting arrangements that facilitate and promote the child's relationships with both genetic and non-genetic family members.'

THE MEANING OF GENES AND GENETIC RELATIONS FOR (INTENDING) PARENTS, SPERM DONOR-CONCEIVED PEOPLE AND DONORS, AND THEIR EXPERIENCES

Astrid INDEKEU

1. INTRODUCTION

The *right to genetic ancestry* and the *right to identity* as discussed in the previous chapters are closely linked to the concept of 'genes'. Biologically speaking, a gene is a basic unit of heredity, made up of DNA.[1] Every human being starts out with genetic material from a sperm and an egg cell. Not only are genes essential, basic elements of an individual, but the sharing of genes also creates genetic connections between people.

Despite the precise biological definition of what genes are, genes are not just a biological given: they are also a social construct. Over the years, the significance and meaning given to genes and genetic relations have been extensively reviewed in philosophical, psychological, educational, sociological, and legal discourses as well as by lay people. In particular, the significance of genes to the development of identity (in the nature-nurture debate) and in kinship has often been discussed. Sometimes more significance was given to nature, and at other times to nurture.

The last few decades have seen an increased interest in genes within various fields. In the medical world, interest was raised by the Human Genome Project (HGP), an international, collaborative research programme whose goal was the complete mapping and understanding of all the genes of human beings. This 'new genetics' has led to an enhanced emphasis on the importance of genes in the field of health, focusing on genetic predisposition and inheritance. Furthermore, it has also generated revived interest amongst sociologists, anthropologists and psychologists in 'the kin in the gene': genetic kinship and genetic families.[2] More generally, increased interest in ancestry and genetic health information in society can be seen in the exponential increase of the use of direct-to-consumer genetic testing in the last decade, which promises users information about their DNA and genetic relatives.

Although the political environment is relatively liberal and there is a trend towards enhanced acceptance of a diversity of family structures (e.g. adoptive, single parent, gay/lesbian, multiracial, multicultural and donor-conceived family structures), at the same time the dominant Western societal discourse assumes that kinship and family ties should be based on a biological or genetic

1 'What is a gene?: MedlinePlus Genetics', *MedlinePlus*, 22 March 2021. https://medlineplus.gov/genetics/understanding/basics/gene/ (accessed February 2022 – National Library of Medicine).

2 M. Strathern, *After Nature: English Kinship in the Late Twentieth Century*, Cambridge University Press, Cambridge 1992; M. Strathern, *Reproducing the Future: Essays on Anthropology, Kinship and the New Reproductive Technologies*, Manchester University Press, Manchester 1992; K. Finkler, *Experiencing the New Genetics Family and Kinship on the Medical Frontier*, University of Pennsylvania Press, Philadelphia 2000; K. Finkler, 'The kin in the gene: The medicalization of kinship and family in American society', 42(2) *Current Anthropology* 2001, 235–263.

connection. In such a culture, the traditional family – being a nuclear family unit consisting of a heterosexual couple and their genetic children – is presented as a touchstone against which all other forms of families are measured. Consequently, family ties based on biogenetic connections continue to be more highly valued than those based on social ties.[3] These norms and values can make themselves apparent in various ways: in daily conversation, media representation, or national policies.[4] This can also be seen in research and clinical practice, for example the continuous developments of assisted reproductive technologies (ARTs) such as in vitro fertilisation (IVF), intracytoplasmic sperm injection (ICSI), uterus transplants, and artificial gametes to support the human drive for a genetically related child, a child of one's 'own'. To fulfil this wish people will endure costly and invasive treatments. Specifically in relation to Belgium, the Belgian Federal Advisory Committee on Bioethics stated that 'in our society the opinion that the biological parent is the "real" parent is still too prevalent'.[5] A second common prejudice, noted by the Committee and stemming from the development of genetics, is the idea that a human being is determined by their genes. Genes are perceived as the essence of an individual's identity.

Conception with the assistance of a donor has, more than anything else, called into question socio-cultural norms and values about kinship, family, parenthood and identity. This can be seen in the various discourses by medics, lawyers, ethicists, psychologists and sociologists regarding genes, stemming from the early days of donor conception, that have shaped the practice of donor conception.[6] The meaning-making process of (intending) parents, donor-conceived people and donors is therefore not only shaped by personal

---

3 K. Finkler, above n. 2.

4 G. Becker, A. Butler and R.D. Nachtigall, 'Resemblance talk: A challenge for parents whose children were conceived with donor gametes in the US', 61(6) *Social Science & Medicine* 2005, 1300–1309; S.W. Adrian, 'Sperm Stories: Policies and Practices of Sperm Banking in Denmark and Sweden', *European Journal of Women's Studies* 2010, 393–411; S. Crabb and M. Augoustinos, 'Genes and families in the media: Implications of genetic discourse for constructions of the "family"', 17(3) *Health Sociology Review* 2008, 303–312; D. Birenbaum-Carmeli, 'Genetic relatedness and family formation in Israel: Lay perceptions in the light of state policy', 29(1) *New Genetics & Society* 2010, 73–85.

5 Belgian Advisory Committee on Bioethics, 2004. Recommendation n° 27 regarding the donation of sperm and oocytes.

6 See for example: N. Cahn, *The New Kinship. Constructing Donor-Conceived Families*, New York University Press, New York 2013; T. Freeman, S. Graham, F. Ebtehaj and M. Richards (eds.), *Relatedness in Assisted Reproduction. Families, Origins and Identities*, Cambridge University Press, Cambridge 2014; P. Nordqvist and C. Smart, *Relative Strangers: Family Life, Genes and Donor Conception*, Palgrave Macmillan, London 2014; R. Hertz and M.K. Nelson, *Random families. Genetic Strangers, Sperm Donor Siblings, and the Creation of New Kin*, Oxford University Press, New York 2018; J. Gunnarsson Payne, 'Grammars of kinship: biological motherhood and assisted reproduction in the age of epigenetics', 41(3) *Signs: Journal of Women in Culture & Society* 2016, 483–506; L. Mamo, 'Biomedicalizing kinship. Sperm banks and the creation of affinity-ties', 14(3) *Science as Culture* 2005, 237–264.

experiences but also by this wider socio-cultural, legal and regulatory landscape. Such a process always involves a complex interplay between concepts and experiences as people negotiate the ideals and realities of genetics.[7]

This chapter will discuss how (intending) parents, donor-conceived people and donors experience and give meaning to genes and genetics in relation to identity and genetic relatedness within a Euro-American kinship framework, where specific social meanings are assigned to biogenetic connections. The societal, professional, legal and political discourses that frame the practice of donor conception will also be considered. Although the presentation format of three distinct groups – (intending) parents, donor-conceived people and donors – might suggest that these groups are homogenous, the reader should keep in mind that each group includes a variety of situations (e.g. conception by sperm, egg or embryo donation; anonymous, identity-release, known or online donors; one-parent or two-parent households; men/women; parents of young or adult children; young donor-conceived children and adult donor-conceived people, etc.) that might influence the meaning-making of genes and genetic relatedness. In addition to presenting shared experiences and meanings, emphasis is laid here on the diversity and flexibility of people's experiences and meaning-making.

The findings presented in this chapter are based on the author's own research, as well as national and international empirical research. Data available from Belgian or Dutch studies have been included as much as possible.

2. (INTENDING) PARENTS: THEIR MEANING AND EXPERIENCES

2.1. GENES IN RELATION TO PARENTAL IDENTITY

According to Euro-American socio-cultural norms, kinship and family ties are fundamentally based on a biogenetic connection. Ties between parents and children are assumed to emerge from the 'natural facts' of procreation.[8] In such a culture, genetic parents are seen as the 'real' parents. This ideology of biological relatedness is deep-rooted. Some also consider procreating a genetically related child to be a basic human drive.[9] Whether conceptualised as internalised

---

7 T. Freeman, 'Introduction' in T. Freeman, S. Graham, F. Ebtehaj and M. Richards (eds.), *Relatedness in Assisted Reproduction. Families, Origins and Identities*, Cambridge University Press, Cambridge 2014, pp. 1–18.

8 K. Hargreaves, 'Constructing families and kinship through donor insemination', 28(3) *Sociology of Health & Illness* 2006, 261–283.

9 O. van den Akker, 'The acceptable face of parenthood. The relative status of biological and cultural interpretations of offspring in infertility treatment', 3(2) *Psychology Evolution & Gender* 2001, 137–153.

socio-cultural norms or as a human drive, genes play a dominant role in parental identity. Our ideal images of the nature of reproduction, families and relatedness against which we define our real experiences are shaped by this point of view.

The significance and meaning that (intending) parents give to genes become even clearer in the absence of a genetic connection between parent and child, when several (often implicit) assumptions become more explicit. (Intending) Parents perceive a genetic connection between parent and child as automatic and enduring; it creates unconditional and unbreakable bonds and is accompanied by parental authority.[10] When a genetic tie is lacking, as in the case of donor conception, (intending) parents tend to describe the love for their child as insecure and conditional.[11] There is uncertainty about whether a bond will develop ('Will I love the child?', 'Maybe the child will not like me'), and a social bond is imagined as something breakable (e.g. potential offspring leaving the social parent for the donor). Effort is seen as necessary to establish that bond, while in the case of a genetic connection the expectation is that this bond will develop spontaneously from birth. Infertile partners also frequently express doubts about claims to parental rights in the absence of a genetic connection. Additionally, fear exists about possible interference from the donor in the parent-child bond, as if the genetic connection between the donor and the child would automatically bestow parental authority. This does not mean that genetic parents do not have the same doubts ('Will I bond with the child?', 'What will the child be like?', 'What will my influence be on the child's development?'), but non-genetic parents by donor conception frame their doubts in terms of genetics. This emphasis on genetic connection can be seen to be influenced by the context people are living in, a context that has been described as 'the age of genetic essentialism'.[12] Moreover, similar values and norms are seen in other kin-relationships, for example in relation to sibling relationships. Parents are confronted with people asking if siblings have the same donor enabling them to be *real* siblings, and therefore parents prefer the same donor for multiple children. (Intending) Parents can believe that sharing genetics would create stronger siblingship ('They will argue less') and

---

10 J. Carsten, '"Knowing where you've come from": Ruptures and continuities of time and kinship in narratives of adoption reunions', 6(4) *Journal of the Royal Anthropological Institute* 2000, 687–703.

11 A. Indekeu, P. Rober, P. Schotsmans, K. Daniels, K.R. Dierickx and T. D'Hooghe, 'How couples' experiences prior to the start of infertility treatment with donor gametes influence the disclosure decision', 76(2) *Gynecologic & Obstetric Investigation* 2013, 125–132; S. Imrie, V. Jadva and S. Golombok, '"Making the child mine": Mothers' thoughts and feelings about the mother-infant relationship in egg donation families', 34(4) *Journal of Family Psychology* 2020, 469–479.

12 T. Freeman, above n. 7, p. 13.

enhance the feeling of being family for the children.[13] Also, (intending) parents express concerns about whether their own parents would accept their child as 'a real' grandchild, or whether genetically related grand-children would be favoured.

How deep-rooted the significance of a genetic connection is in relation to parental identity can be seen in the existence of these insecurities despite various findings that prove otherwise. For example, there are no accounts known of donors intentionally intruding on the parent-child or partner relationship.[14] Moreover, research has shown over the years that the absence of shared genes does not affect the parent-child relationship and that children conceived by sperm or egg donation are not necessarily confused over who their father/mother is, nor do they reject the parent due to the lack of a genetic connection.[15] Furthermore, the fact that the parental position of those who rely on donor conception to build their family is legally protected does not seem to take away (intending) parents' insecurity.[16] In the case of sperm donation, Belgian law clearly states that parental rights do not extend to the man who donated the semen, and the mother's life partner is assigned parenthood if he/she is married to the mother or if he/she recognises the child.[17] In other words, fatherhood or co-motherhood is legally assigned to a man/woman who has no biogenetic connection with the child. Legally, donors have very limited power but, in a culture that is used to framing 'biological' relatedness as 'real' relatedness, the donor has a symbolic status which can be perceived as threatening to (intending) parents because of the idea that the donor – having provided genetic material – has 'a claim' over the child.[18]

In the context of donor conception, the experience of (intending) parents deviates from internalised values and socio-cultural ideals about what is 'normal' and 'natural'. People who become parents through donor conception are often seen to continue to frame their lack of genetic relatedness as something 'missing'.[19] In managing this divergence, (intending) parents show creativity and flexibility in the way they include biological elements into their definition

---

13 S. Somers, V. Provoost, A. Ravelingien, A. Buysse, G. Pennings and P. De Sutter, 'The last vial. What it means to (aspiring) parents to use the same sperm donor for siblings', 41(1) *Journal of Psychosomatic Obstetrics & Gynaecology* 2020, 62–68.

14 L. Gilman, 'Tracing pathways of relatedness: how identity-release gamete donors negotiate biological (non-)parenthood', 9(2) *Families, Relationships & Societies* 2020, 235–251.

15 L. Blake, S. Zadeh, H. Statham and T. Freeman, 'Families created by assisted reproduction: children's perspectives' in T. Freeman, S. Graham, F. Ebtehaj and M. Richards (eds.), *Relatedness in Assisted Reproduction. Families, Origins and Identities*, Cambridge University Press, Cambridge 2014, pp. 251–269.

16 As long as donor conception takes place within the context of a fertility clinic.

17 Belgian Act of 6 July 2007. Law on assisted reproduction and the use of surplus embryos and gametes [Wet betreffende de medisch begeleide voortplanting en de bestemming van de overtallige embryo's en de gameten], *Belgian Gazette*. 17 July 2007, 38575.

18 S. Imrie, V. Jadva and S. Golombok, above n. 11.

19 K. Hargreaves, above n. 8.

and practice of family.[20] They will try to get as close to prevailing norms as possible, develop or find new norms or normalise diversity of families. For example, (intending) parents will emphasise biological similarities with natural conception (e.g. pregnancy, birth) or how they physically contributed to the baby's development while in the womb,[21] or may make use of the 'grammar of epigenetics' (for example 'I just received a few cells, and it is my body that determines how she will develop, which cells are picked up, and the environment influences a lot, not only the environment on the outside [but also my uterus]').[22] The practice of 'matching' – by which a donor is chosen on the basis of the least discrepancy with the partner of the woman, so that the child can 'pass' for a genetic child of both parents – reinforces the focus on similarities.[23] Some (intending) parents will de-emphasise the importance of genetics in relation to parenthood and their own family relationship ('genes still need to be shaped'), and limit the importance of genetics to health issues (for example, only inform healthcare professionals). Genes can thus be perceived as relevant and irrelevant at the same time. Others highlight their effort and active input in parenthood in an effort to 'make up for' the lack of genetic ties by using words referring to an active role (carrying, giving, done), being a particularly involved father/parent, or by pointing out that commitment and effort matter more than genetics.[24]

By making the transition from intending parent to parent who can actually fulfil their parental role, the confidence of a lot of parents grows; they feel more secure in their parental identity, and the significance and meaning of genetics recedes to the background.[25] This process continues throughout their family life, though for many it will continue to oscillate and there can be times when they feel threatened again in their parental identity. For example, when the child starts asking questions about the donor this can re-activate insecurities about their position as a parent. To be able to retain parental identity, parents also

---

20 P. Nordqvist, 'Bringing kinship into being: Connectedness, donor conception and lesbian parenthood', 48(2) *Sociology* 2014, 268–283.

21 A. Indekeu, P. Rober, P. Schotsmans, K. Daniels, K.R. Dierickx and T. D'Hooghe, above n. 11; S. Imrie, V. Jadva and S. Golombok, above n. 11.

22 J. Gunnarsson Payne, 'Mattering Kinship: Inheritance, biology and egg donation, between genetics and epigenetics' in C. Krolokke, L. Myong, S.W. Adrian and T. Tine Tjornhoj-Thomsen (eds.), *Critical Kinship Studies*, Rowman & Littlefield Publishers, London 2016, pp. 33–47, 41.

23 A. Indekeu, 'Parents' expectations and experiences of resemblance through donor conception', 34(4) *New Genetics & Society* 2015, 398–416.

24 V.M. Grace and K.R. Daniels, 'The (ir)relevance of genetics: engendering parallel worlds of procreation and reproduction', 29(5) *Sociology of Health & Illness* 2007, 692–710; P. Nordqvist, 'Genetic thinking and everyday living: On family practices and family imaginaries', 64(4) *The Sociological Review* 2017, 865–881; A. Indekeu, T. D'Hooghe, K.R. Daniels, K.R. Dierickx and P. Rober, '"Of course he's our child": transitions in social parenthood in donor sperm recipient families', 28(1) *Reproductive Biomedicine Online* 2014, 106–115; S. Imrie, V. Jadva and S. Golombok, above n. 11.

25 A. Indekeu, T. D'Hooghe, K.R. Daniels, K.R. Dierickx and P. Rober, above n. 24.

actively negotiate parental identities, biogenetic relationships and the meaning of conception by disentangling old meanings and creating new ones. Some do this by disentangling the meaning of 'origins' from the meaning of 'originator' in the context of procreation.[26] Origin (being the donation of the genes needed for procreation) is uncoupled from the individual's intention to create a child. It is this intention that makes it possible for parents to see themselves as the originators of the child and thus to be able to claim parenthood.

2.2. GENES AND RELATEDNESS

2.2.1. *Genetic Ties between the Child and the Donor*

Without the donor, there would not have been a family. Parents owe the existence of their family to the donor. This means that the donor, whether anonymous/unknown, 'known', or 'identity-release', is part of the family's story. Parents display a huge variation in the space given to the donor and the meaning given to the genetic tie between the donor and their child. In a society in which prevailing societal values regard the genetic parent as the real parent, the donor is often seen as the 'real father/mother'. Within such a framework, the donor is (at least at the outset) perceived as threatening to the non-genetic (intending) parent and his/her parental position.[27] In trying to find a psychological place for the donor with which the parents feel comfortable, the donor's contribution ('just material we needed') as well as the genetic element ('it is like blood') may be minimised. Alternatively, the donor can be de-personalised ('we needed cells'). Some prefer to think of the donor as someone who helped *them* to become parents. Others acknowledge the donor as 'a person' who contributed to *their child* but still see the donor more as 'a source of information' than in the sense of a kin-relationship. Parents can be curious to know what the donor looks like in order to possibly envisage the child's traits, or to have medical information.[28] In solo-mother families by sperm donation, when there is no threat to a non-genetic parent, mothers can also find it difficult to place the donor within their family-story.[29]

---

26 P. Nordqvist, 'Origins and originators: lesbian couples negotiating parental identities and sperm donor conception', 14(3) *Culture, Health & Sexuality* 2012, 297–311.

27 M. Kirkman, 'Saviours and satyrs: ambivalence in narrative meanings of sperm provision', 6(4) *Culture, Health & Sexuality* 2004, 319–334.

28 A. Indekeu, T. D'Hooghe, K.R. Daniels, K. Dierickx and P. Rober, 'When "sperm" becomes "donor": Transitions in parents' views of the sperm donor', 17(4) *Human Fertility* 2014, 269–277; M.I. Jociles, A.M. Rivas and C. Alvarez, 'Strategies to personalise and to depersonalise donors in parental narratives of children's genetic/gestational origins (Spain)', 42(4) *Suomen Antropologi* 2017, 25–50; S. Imrie, V. Jadva and S. Golombok, above n. 11.

29 S. Zadeh, T. Freeman and S. Golombok, 'Absence or presence? Complexities in the donor narratives of single mothers using sperm donation', 31(1) *Human Reproduction* 2016, 117–124.

Besides giving meaning to the donor or the donor's contribution, (intending) parents also actively negotiate what distance they want to establish from the donor and how they want to manage family boundaries. How parents set the boundaries differs between families. Some (intending) parents prefer to keep family boundaries tight, positioning the donor clearly outside the family (e.g. preferring an anonymous donor, keeping the donor at a distance, not talking about the donor, etc.). Others try to find a balance between acknowledging the donor and establishing distance.[30] There are also parents who consciously include the donor in their family, by choosing a family member as donor. Intra-familial donation can be chosen to enhance the sense of belonging 'inside' the family through the presence of shared characteristics and physical similarities.[31] On the other hand, there are also parents who use a family member as donor and do not disclose the identity of the donor. Moreover, parents can change how they feel about family boundaries and loosen or tighten them (to 'kin' or 'de-kin' the donor), for example in response to their child's actual or potential needs.[32]

Despite (intending) parents' efforts to manage family boundaries, a donor can still slowly invade daily family life in unwanted ways, for example through 'resemblance remarks' or lack of physical or personality trait resemblance to the parents.[33] Resemblance remarks can include short conversations or commentaries about the resemblance of physical and/or personality characteristics between parents and their children. These remarks, especially when referring to the lack of resemblance, have the power to call the boundaries of the family into question, as children are assumed to resemble their parents through the sharing of genes ('Well, where did he get his height from?'). Conversely, parents themselves also often discuss the extent to which the child resembles family members. This can be done in two ways: either resemblance emphasises that the child 'belongs' in the family or a (potential) lack of resemblance can be a source of anxiety, marking them out as different.[34]

---

30 A. Widbom, S. Isaksson, G. Sydsjö, A. Skoog Svanberg and C. Lampic, 'Positioning the donor in a new landscape – mothers' and fathers' experiences as their adult children obtained information about the identity-release sperm donor', 36(8) *Human Reproduction* 2021, 2181–2188.

31 S. Imrie, V. Jadva and S. Golmbok, above n. 11.

32 A. Indekeu, T. D'Hooghe, K.R. Daniels, K. Dierickx and P. Rober, above n. 28.

33 G. Becker, A. Butler and R.D. Nachtigall, 'Resemblance talk: A challenge for parents whose children were conceived with donor gametes in the US', 61(6) *Social Science & Medicine* 2005, 1300–1309.

34 G. Becker, A. Butler and R.D. Nachtigall, above n. 33; P. Nordqvist, 'Out of sight, out of mind: Family resemblances in lesbian donor conception', 44(6) *Sociology* 2010, 1128–1144; S. Isaksson, G. Sydsjö, A.S Svanberg and C. Lampic, 'Managing absence and presence of child-parent resemblance: a challenge for heterosexual couples following sperm donation', 23(8) *Reproductive Biomedicine & Society Online* 2019, 38–46; S. Imrie, V. Jadva and S. Golombok, above n. 11.

Giving meaning is not static; experiences can change, as well as meanings and values. Birth can be a transformative experience: being able to actually take up the parental role, and experiencing an emerging bond and feelings of attachment between the child and the non-genetic parent can enhance parental confidence.[35] This can lead to a more relaxed attitude towards the donor's contribution. Parents have been seen to change their perception of the donor, from a non-person to someone who contributed to their child's existence. Others begin to prioritise the child's needs regarding the donor above their own insecurities as a parent, and they become more interested in information about the donor in order to be able to answer potential questions from their child in the future. Little is yet known about how parents experience (ongoing) contact between the child and the donor, and how this might make them rethink the meaning of genes and genetic connections.

2.2.2. *Genetic Ties between the Child and Other Children Conceived by the Same Donor*

Forming a family with the assistance of a donor not only creates a genetic tie between the parents' child and the donor, but also between their child and other donor-conceived children of the same donor. Parents (from all kinds of families, with both anonymous and identity-release donors) have shown interest in and searched for same-donor peers of their child. Interestingly, parents' interest in the donor and their interest in same donor-offspring seem to be underpinned by different reasons. Research points out that knowing *about* the donor is deemed to be more important than knowing the donor.[36] Parents see the donor as a provider of information rather than someone who will become a part of the family. Conversely, an interest in and searching for same-donor peers or same-donor families often seems to stem from a motivation to create an extended family.[37] Moreover, parents feel less threatened by possible relationships between their child and genetic relatives at a sibling-level than at an ancestor level (the donor), even when both types of relationship might have a positive outcome.

Parents are mainly interested in their child's same-donor peers out of 'curiosity', to obtain information for their 'child's identity development', and

---

35 A. Indekeu, T. D'Hooghe, K.R. Daniels, K. Dierickx and P. Rober, above n. 24.

36 T. Freeman, V. Jadva, W. Kramer and S. Golombok, 'Gamete donation: parents' experiences of searching for their child's donor siblings and donor', 24(3) *Human Reproduction* 2009, 505–516.

37 A. Indekeu, A.J.B.M. Maas, E. McCormick, J. Benward and J. Scheib, 'Factors associated with searching for people related through donor conception among donor-conceived people, parents and donors: a systematic review', 2(2) *F & S Reviews* 2021, 93–119.

'to create kin'.[38] They are curious about possible similarities in physical traits, personality, and interests between their child and same-donor peers. Parents think that this information and/or contact with same donor-offspring might strengthen their child in their sense of identity. Meeting same-donor families raises the possibility of giving their child 'a sense of kinship' and creating a larger extended family or even sometimes providing their child with 'a sibling'. The word 'sibling' (half-sibling, donor-siblings) is often used by parents to refer to these new relationships. Parents feel that the genetic connection is important, or may become important to their children in the future. As the children in these studies were still very young, parents mainly *anticipated* their child's interest rather than responding to an *actual* interest expressed by their child.

Parents, their children, same-donor peers, and the parents of these same-donor peers form wider networks where direct and indirect genetic connections intertwine. Sometimes shared genetics was sufficient to describe these relationships in terms of 'kin', and often shared understandings of donor conception and shared experiences further strengthened the feeling of kinship.[39] While parents describe the relationships between their child and donor-conceived half-siblings as kinship, they describe their own relationships with linked families as significant but not necessarily in traditional family terms.[40]

The fact that parents intentionally search for genetic relatives of their child (such as same-donor peers), and relationships are created, raises questions for research, practice and policy in the field of donor conception. Questions raised by parents include 'How many siblings can my child have?', 'How do I tell him he has so many siblings?', and 'How will this affect my child?'. One key issue is whether we should incorporate psycho-social implications in addition to the risk of consanguinity in determining a maximum number of donor offspring that may be conceived using one donor.[41]

2.3. INFLUENCING FACTORS

In a Belgian context, the Belgian Federal Advisory Committee on Bioethics stated in 2004 that the belief that 'the biological parent is the "real" parent is

38 A. Indekeu, A.J.B.M. Maas, J. Benward, E. McCormick and J.E. Scheib, above n. 37.

39 T. Freeman, V. Jadva, W. Kramer and S. Golombok, above n. 36.

40 A.E. Goldberg and J.E. Scheib, 'Female-partnered women conceiving kinship: Does sharing a sperm donor mean we are family?', 20(3/4) *Journal of Lesbian Studies* 2016, 427–441; R. Hertz, M.K. Nelson and W. Kramer, 'Donor sibling networks as a vehicle for expanding kinship', 38(2) *Journal of Family Issues* 2017, 248–284.

41 J.E. Scheib and A. Ruby, 'Beyond consanguinity risk: developing donor birth limits that consider psychosocial risk factors', 91(5) *Fertility & Sterility* 2009, 33–34.

even more explicit in relation to the role of the man than the woman'.[42] This is because culturally and socio-legally fatherhood is more associated with conception (male genetic material equates with fatherhood) while motherhood is more associated with pregnancy and birth (women are nurturers and carers).[43] However, research findings show that women who become mothers by egg donation can also experience a lot of insecurity about their parental identity as mother due to the lack of a genetic tie with their child.[44] Lesbian couples too can struggle with the imbalance of genetic contribution to their child and need to actively negotiate their parental identity in the absence of a genetic tie (negotiating 'the origins and originators').[45] Sometimes lesbian couples will choose for one partner to donate her eggs to the second partner who carries the pregnancy, to find a biological balance.

3. DONOR-CONCEIVED PEOPLE: THEIR MEANING AND EXPERIENCES

Living in a context described as 'the age of genetic essentialism' where genes are given an important role in the definition of kinship and where the assumption reigns that 'a human is determined by its genes',[46] it is not surprising that donor-conceived people also reflect on the meaning of genes and genetic connections. Genes are experienced as part of daily life: they come up in remarks about resemblance to family members, during doctors' visits if asked about one's medical family history, and in school during classes on biology, sociology, ethics, etc. Donor-conceived people state that even if they do not want to highlight genes per se it is difficult to avoid them as they are so omnipresent in society.[47] Genes are a self-evident part of being donor-conceived. Because donor-conceived people's conception history diverges from the socio-cultural norm where children are assumed to emerge from the 'natural facts of procreation',[48]

---

42 Belgian Advisory Committee of Bioethics, above n. 5.

43 T. Freeman, above n. 7; S. Imrie, V. Jadva and S. Golombok, above n. 11.

44 A. Indekeu and K. Daniels, 'The illusion of normal fertility: women's experiences of pregnancy and birth after oocyte donation' in E. Stevenson and P. Hershberger (eds.), *Fertility and Assisted Reproductive Technology (ART): Theory, research, policy, and practice for health care practitioners*, Springer Publishing Company, New York 2016, pp. 87–102; S. Imrie, V. Jadva and S. Golombok, above n. 11.

45 P. Nordqvist, 'Choreographies of sperm donations: Dilemmas of intimacy in lesbian couple donor conception', 73(11) *Social Science & Medicine* 2011, 1661–1668, P. Nordqvist, above n. 34.

46 Belgian Advisory Committee on Bioethics, above n. 5.

47 A. Indekeu and K. Hens, 'Part of my story. The meaning and experiences of genes and genetics for sperm donor-conceived offspring', 38(1) *New Genetics & Society* 2019, 18–37.

48 K. Hargreaves, above n. 8.

they are triggered to think about the meaning and importance of genes and genetic relatives.

3.1. GENES AND IDENTITY

Donor-conceived people perceive genes as 'building blocks' or 'a starting package' of who they are.[49] These 'building blocks' are different from blood, as they form a unique code.[50] The donor is one of the people who contributed to the genetic basis of their existence: 'their starting package'.

Donor-conceived people are interested in information about the donor, as it might give them some information about 'their building blocks'.[51] However, the weight attributed to the importance of genes or genetics in terms of establishing 'who they are' or 'can become' varies greatly.[52] In relation to some elements (e.g. character traits), this may reflect an inaccurate understanding of or false assumptions about genetic heritance, much like the genetic understanding and assumptions of other, non-donor-conceived people, in looking at one's parents or other family members 'to see what you got from whom'. Donor-conceived people want to know where some physical and character traits come from to better understand themselves, especially when the traits are not shared with their family.[53] By comparing similarities and differences with the donor, they hope for an expanded sense of identity. They want to know what the donor looks like, the kind of person he/she is, his/her occupation, interests, hobbies, motivation for donating, etc. They also search for medical information, wanting to know about potential hereditary diseases, which medical risks to avoid, or to explain a previously experienced illness. This information is perceived as helpful in learning something about themselves and not always because they feel they lack something. Sometimes donor-conceived people search for information to discover and/or assess their defining characteristics and abilities better. Genes are sometimes seen as a kind of reference point, containing information about their potential.[54] Perhaps especially when they feel different from their family, this information could guide them in their identity development. Furthermore, genetic information is not only seen as important to themselves and their own

---

49 A. Indekeu and K. Hens, above n. 47.

50 As genes are perceived as a unique combination, the discovery of multiple same-donor offspring can collide with the feeling of uniqueness.

51 A. Indekeu and K. Hens, above n. 47.

52 A. Ravelingien, V. Provoost and G. Pennings, 'Open-identity sperm donation: how does offering donor-identifying information relate to donor-conceived offspring's wishes and needs?', *Journal of Bioethical Inquiry* 2015, 503–509.

53 A. Indekeu, A.J.B.M. Maas, J. Benward, E. McCormick and J. Scheib, above n. 37.

54 A. Indekeu and K. Hens, above n. 47.

identity development but will also be helpful for their own children. Donor-conceived people are often not only interested in 'factual information'. To complete their own self-narrative and develop a consistent identity, they also want to learn more about their genetic origins, their ancestry.[55] It should be noted that, even though the major formative work of identity development is thought to be completed by adulthood, identity development is an ongoing process.

3.2. GENES AND RELATEDNESS

3.2.1. *Vertical Relatedness*

In contrast to the views of some (intending) parents, donor-conceived people perceive genes as *person-al:* they are wrapped up in a person, they are not detached material.[56] This is also reflected in the information that donor-conceived people are interested in. They not only wish for merely factual information, but are also interested in the donor's hobbies, personality, motives for donating, whether he/she wanted to be contacted, all of which bring the donor as a person more to the foreground.[57]

Sharing genes connects people. Donor-conceived people are still searching for a social meaning to give to their relationship with the donor. In the absence of social scripts, people fall back on the traditional notion that biogenetic connections are seen as kinship.[58] Consequently, sperm donor-conceived people will frequently use words referring to 'fatherhood' to describe the donor (genetic father, donor father, etc.). They are aware that the connotation of kin makes the genetic connection with the donor threatening for others. Donor-conceived people often experience a loyalty conflict if they are interested in the donor but do not want to hurt their non-genetic parent.[59] However, the word 'donor' does not feel accurate to all donor-conceived people, mainly because the donor did not donate to them but to their parents. In such cases, words referring to an 'ancestor' (such as 'genetic father') are preferred. Moreover, donor-conceived

---

55 E. Canzi, M. Accordini and F. Federica, '"Is blood thicker than water?" Donor conceived offspring's subjective experiences of the donor: A systematic narrative review', 38(5) *Reproductive Biomedicine Online* 2019, 797–807.

56 A. Indekeu and K. Hens, above n. 47.

57 E. Blyth, M. Crawshaw, L. Frith and C. Jones, 'Donor-conceived people's views and experiences of their genetic origins: a critical analysis of the research evidence', 19(4) *Journal of Law & Medicine* 2012, 769–789.

58 M. Klotz, 'Wayward relations: Novel searches of the donor-conceived for genetic kinship', 35(1) *Medical Anthropology* 2014, 45–57.

59 E. Canzi, M. Accordini and F. Federica, above n. 55; A.A. Indekeu, A.J.B.M. Maas, J. Benward, E. McCormick and J. Scheib, above n. 37.

people will often use multiple words to describe the donor, depending on the context, often carrying multiple meanings.[60] This demonstrates that assigning the donor a space and role in their life is a long process, in which internal reflection and negotiation with their own family is needed.[61]

For some donor-conceived people sharing genes is not enough to create a kinship relationship.[62] These donor-conceived people perceive the donor instead as a source of information about themselves; a way to learn more about their own personal identity. Others see the donor as an external individual who provided material, but who is not a family member. In this case, the genetic connection is described as a non-familial link ('an acquaintance'). Some experience genetic connections as associated with responsibilities and they want the donor to know them in order to take up his/her responsibilities. Others refer to the donor as a family member with whom they share genes but who is not an actual parent. Even when they are interested in personal contact, this is rarely driven by any desire for an ongoing 'parent-offspring' relationship.[63] Even those with a known donor and those with an identity-release donor do not necessarily assign the donor any closer relationship than that of an acquaintance.[64] Research has mainly focused on donor-conceived people's conceptualisation of the donor and his/her genetic contribution to their existence, and less on their (non)-genetic parents. This does not mean that donor-conceived people do not consider both nature and nurture elements when reflecting on who they are.[65] Moreover, research shows that donor-conceived people can acknowledge genetic and non-genetic connections simultaneously. It should not be seen as a case of 'either/or'; interest in the donor, their genetic ancestor, does not mean a rejection of the social parent.

Genes are also perceived as having the ability to place and situate people among their group of genetic relatives through sharing traits and recognising traits, as resemblance can create a feeling of belonging and fitting in.[66]

Notwithstanding that information about the donor is perceived as important in identity development, this information is legally often only available at 18 or 16 years of age, depending on the country, if the country allows access to

60 R. Hertz, M.K. Nelson and W. Kramer, 'Donor-conceived offspring conceive of the donor: The relevance of age, awareness, and family form', 86 *Social Science & Medicine* 2013, 52–65.

61 M.M. Harrigan, S. Dieter, J. Leinwohl and L. Marrin, '"It's just who I am ... I have brown hair. I have a mysterious father": An exploration of donor-conceived offspring's identity construction', *Journal of Fam. Comm.* 2015, 75–93.

62 E. Canzi, M. Accordini and F. Federica, above n. 55.

63 E. Blyth, M. Crawshaw, L. Frith and C. Jones, above n. 57.

64 A.S. Koh, G. Van Beusekom, N.K. Gartrell and H. Bos, 'Adult offspring of lesbian parents: how do they relate to their sperm donor?' 114(4) *Fertility & Sterility* 2020, 879–887.

65 E. Blyth, 'Genes r us? Making sense of genetic and non-genetic relationships following anonymous donor insemination', 24(7) *Reproductive Biomedicine Online* 2012, 719–726.

66 A. Indekeu and K. Hens, above n. 47.

donor information at all. Non-identifying information is often available earlier (at 12 or 16 years of age), but there is a huge variation in the extent of information which is made available. This means that identifying information is often only available at the end of identity development. Moreover, in the current digital age with an exponential growth in the use of direct-to consumer DNA testing, via which people have found donor-conceived relatives, we need to reflect on who becomes the owner or gatekeeper of the donor's information (the parents, donor-conceived people themselves, ...).[67]

3.2.2. *Horizontal Relatedness*

Donor-conceived people not only share a genetic tie with the donor, but are also genetically related to other offspring conceived by donation from the same donor – so called same-donor peers – and to the possible legal offspring of the donor. Research shows that many donor-conceived people are interested in same-donor peers.[68] Furthermore, in the last decade more and more services have been set up to facilitate contact between genetic relatives, such as through voluntary contact registries and direct-to-consumer DNA testing. These services make it possible for same-donor peers to find and contact each other.[69] While these genetic connections might be socially significant, they are not always legally recognised.[70] For example, the Flemish state-funded and professionally led contact service, with a DNA database attached, Vlaams Afstammingscentrum (Flemish Ancestry Centre), only allows searches regarding offspring–ancestor relatedness and does not allow searches on a sibling level. On the other hand, in 2020 in the Netherlands, a law amendment is proposed, amongst other things, entitling donor-conceived people to access identifying information about same-donor offspring.

Donor-conceived people's interest in same-donor peers appears to be mainly driven by two motives: same-donor peers are, like the donor, seen as a source of identity-relevant information, and seen as potential new relationships. Noticing traits that are shared (that may or may not be genetically based) and other traits that are unique to them and their context, offers an opportunity to explore

67 M. Klotz, above n. 58.

68 A. Indekeu, A.J.B.M. Maas, J. Benward, E. McCormick and J. Scheib, above n. 37; R. Hertz, 'Sociological Accounts of Donor Siblings' Experiences: Their Importance for Self-Identity and New Kinship Relations', 19(4) *International Journal of Environmental Research & Public Health* 2022, https://doi.org/10.3390/ijerph19042002.

69 M. Crawshaw, K. Daniels, D. Adams, K. Bourne, J.A.P. Van Hooff, W. Kramer, L. Pasch and P. Thorn, 'Emerging models for facilitating contact between people genetically related through donor conception: a preliminary analysis and discussion', 1(2) *Reproductive Biomedicine Online* 2015, 71–80.

70 N. Cahn, above n. 6, p. 33.

their identity.[71] Some are looking for medical information and/or want to avoid consanguineous relationships. Information from same-donor peers can also help in more deeply grasping what it means to be donor-conceived, as most friends of donor-conceived people are not familiar with the experience of being donor-conceived.[72]

Additionally, donor-conceived people show an interest in the potential to form new relationships and extend their family networks.[73] When contact with same donor-peers is made, donor-conceived people are challenged to give meaning to these unprecedented relationships. In a biogenetic culture that equates genetic connection with kinship, these bonds are often understood within a framework of '(half-) sibling relationships'. Experiences of similarities with same-donor peers can create a form of intimacy and consequently a bond. A huge variety is seen in the description of these bonds, ranging from acquaintances, to friends, to extended family, using elements of emotional intimacy as well as genetics to define the relationships between same-donor peers.[74] For most donor-conceived people, time and energy must be invested to make a genetic connection a socially significant one. Genes alone are not enough.[75] Some donor-conceived people meet their same-donor peers during adulthood, but others meet at a young age. Contacts at a young age are often initiated by the parents with the intention 'of creating extended kin'.[76] Getting to know each other at a young age resembles a sibling relationship more than meeting each other for the first time as an adult, as sibling relations are characterised by growing up together, living together and sharing experiences.

While contacts with same-donor peers are mainly described as positive, these meetings can be challenging when same-donor peers present in large numbers.[77] Donor-conceived people are once more impelled to reflect on the importance and social significance they want to give to these genetic connections with multiple same-donor peers. Moreover, they need to repeatedly manage and reframe these connections, as the network of same-donor peers often continues to expand.[78] Some see all same-donor peers as family, others would like to see all

---

71 R. Hertz, above n. 68.

72 R. Hertz, above n. 68; J.E. Scheib, E. McCormick, J. Benward and A. Ruby. 'Finding people like me: contact among young adults who share an open-identity sperm donor', *Human Reproduction Open* 2020/4 (Corrections Vol. 2021/1).

73 A. Indekeu, A.J.B.M. Maas, J. Benward, E. McCormick and J. Scheib, above n. 37.

74 N. Cahn, above n. 6, p. 37.

75 R. Hertz, above n. 68; S.H. Bolt, C. Notermans, A.C. van Brouwershaven, A.J.B.M. Maas and A. Indekeu, 'The ongoing work of kinship among donor half-siblings in The Netherlands', 18(4) *BioSocieties*, 2023, 156–173.

76 A. Indekeu, A.J.B.M. Maas, J. Benward, E. McCormick and J. Scheib, above n. 37.

77 A. Indekeu, S. Bolt and A.J.B.M. Maas, 'Meeting multiple same-donor offspring: psychosocial challenges', 25(4) *Human Fertility* 2021, 677–687.

78 Prior to laws regarding donor conception, there were often no national limits on the maximum number of donor-conceived offspring per donor. Even today large groups of

same-donor peers as family but find it difficult, given the number of connections and the limited time available to invest in these connections to 'make them kin'. Others will 'pick and choose',[79] whereby some genetic connections become close (earning the title of friends or extended family) and other same-donor offspring are merely acquaintances.

Lastly, donor-conceived people are not only genetically related to other offspring conceived by donation from the same donor, but also to the possible legal offspring of the donor. Some children of the donor have shown interest in the donor-conceived people with whom they share a genetic connection.[80] Psycho-social research on these connections is scarce. It should be noted that while the genetic connection between same-donor peers on the one hand, and between donor-conceived and legal offspring from the donor on the other hand, is the same, they are often regulated differently. For example, the UK-wide state-funded voluntary register Donor-Conceived Register (formerly known as UK Donor-Link until 2013) was set up to facilitate information exchange and/or direct contact between adults related to each other by donor conception (i.e. donors, donor-conceived adults and their genetic siblings). The UK Donor-Conceived Register thus includes legal offspring of the donor. In the Netherlands, the Fiom KID-DNA database is a nation-wide voluntary register to facilitate information exchange and/or contact between people who are genetically related *as a result* of donor-assisted reproduction. Legal offspring of the donor are not included in the Dutch scheme.

3.3. INFLUENCING FACTORS

Even although existing research is rather limited, donor-conceived people express a wide variety of experiences, meaning and weight given to genes, ranging from indifference, to curiosity, to a wish, need or right to have information about genetic relatives.[81] Some only want information; others want contact with the donor (their genetic ancestor) and/or genetic relatives. The importance given to genes can change over time, being linked to significant milestones in life when people become more interested in kinship and ancestry more generally (such as getting married, becoming a parent, being diagnosed with an illness, and/or the

same-donor peers are still possible due to the practice of international, commercial sperm banks and the possibility of online DNA testing (to identify same-donor peers).

79 R. Hertz, above n. 68; R. Hertz and M.K. Nelson, above n. 6.

80 K.R. Daniels, W. Kramer and M.V. Perez-y-Perez, 'Semen donors who are open to contact with their offspring: Issues and implications for them and their families', 25(7) *Reproductive Biomedicine Online* 2012, 670–677.

81 E. Canzi, M. Accordini and F. Federica, above n. 55; A. Indekeu, A.J.B.M. Maas, J. Benward, E. McCormick and J. Scheib, above n. 37.

process of aging) or situations that trigger questions about identity or genetic information on the part of the donor-conceived person or their children.[82] A literature review reveals several factors that might influence interest in genetic relatives (such as the donor-conceived person's gender, family type, family functioning, and the age of disclosure), but these are merely indications and need further research. It must be noted that most research concerns people conceived by anonymous sperm donation. People conceived by egg donation, surrogacy or with an identity-release donor might attribute different significance and meaning to genes and genetic and biological ties.[83]

4. DONORS: THEIR MEANING AND EXPERIENCES

4.1. GENES AND THE DONOR'S IDENTITY

At the outset of the practice of donor conception the sperm donor was made invisible through the very procedure of donation, by which 'material from an anonymous testis, a nonperson' was provided.[84] Later on, and until very recently, the donor was mainly seen as a means to an end.[85] The donor as a person with feelings and thoughts who lived within their own social network, merely existed. Any interest on the part of the donor in the outcome of his/her donation was seen as unhealthy. This view is also mirrored in laws concerning donor conception (such as the Belgian law) stating that donors should not be informed whether and when their semen is used for insemination; nor should they be informed of how many children are born as a result of their donation. The conceptualisation of the donor is slowly changing, partly due to the fact that more and more countries have abolished donor anonymity. The practices of identity-release donors, known donors and, more recently, online donors, make the donor as a person more alive.

As mentioned in the introduction to this chapter, experiences and meanings are always embedded in a certain socio-cultural, legal and organisational

---

82 T. Freeman, K. Bourne, V. Jadva and V. Smith, 'Making connections: contact between sperm donor relations' in T. Freeman, S. Graham, F. Ebtehaj and M. Richards (eds.), *Relatedness in Assisted Reproduction. Families, Origins and Identities*, Cambridge University Press, Cambridge 2014, pp. 1–18; A. Indekeu, A.J.B.M. Maas, J. Benward, E. McCormick and J. Scheib, above n. 37.

83 A. Indekeu, A.J.B.M. Maas, J. Benward, E. McCormick and J. Scheib, above n. 37.

84 M. Glezerman, 'Two hundred and seventy cases of artificial donor insemination: management and results', 35(2) *Fertility & Sterility* 1981, 180–187, p. 185.

85 U. Van den Broeck, M. Vandermeeren, D. Vanderschueren, P. Enzlin, K. Demyttenaere and T. D'Hooghe, 'A systematic review of sperm donors: demographic characteristics, attitudes, motives and experiences of the process of sperm donation', 19(1) *Human Reproduction* 2013, 37–51.

context. In the research consulted in this chapter, donors experience the same Euro-American socio-cultural norms as parents and donor-conceived people, in which biogenetic connections are automatically assigned social significance such as kinship and family values. In such a narrative, the genetic tie between donor and donor-conceived offspring is easily associated with a parental connection. The donor is seen as the genetic *father/mother* of the donor-conceived offspring. Moreover, in the donor's own social life and family, such a genetic connection makes him/her a parent with certain parental obligations and responsibilities. In contrast to these socio-cultural norms, national laws in various countries regarding donor conception and sperm bank practices – regardless of whether the donor donated in a system of anonymous, identity-release or known donation in a clinic – see these genetic connections as contractual relations, in which the donor renounces all parental rights and responsibilities towards the possible future child born as a result of his/her donation and in which the genetic connection to the donor-conceived child should be negated.[86] How do donors give meaning to their genetic donation and these genetic connections, in a context where the law and practice ensure that donors have no parental rights or responsibilities but the culture automatically appoints kinship to biogenetic ties?

In the limited research that exits on anonymous, identity-release, and known egg and sperm donors, donors typically do not assign themselves a parental role or identity in relation to the donor-conceived offspring. Donors often explicitly state that they are not the parents, and that those who receive the donated gametes (the recipient(s)) are undoubtedly the parent(s). The fact that they feel they need to make this explicit illustrates how engrained the ideology of biogenetic kinship is. Donors fear and experience that they could be 'mixed up' with the parents' position and they want to make clear they are not parents. They do this in various ways,[87] for example, through de-emphasising the significance of their genetic connection to donor offspring, emphasising that there was no conception history ('There were no emotions involved in the conception, so it is not my child'), or highlighting the importance of intention, gestation and caring practices ('I did not raise them, the parents did'). Some donors actively reject and avoid the term 'parent' ('I am a kind of uncle'); others *do* define themselves

86 S. Mohr, 'Living kinship trouble: Danish sperm donors' narratives of relatedness', 34(5) *Medical Anthropology* 2015, 470–484.

87 G. Orobitg and C. Salazar, 'The gift of motherhood: Egg donation in a Barcelona infertility clinic', 70(1) *Ethnos* 2005, 31–52; E. Blyth, Y. Samantha and A. Ka Tat Tsang, '"They were my eggs; they were her babies": known oocyte donors' conceptualizations of their reproductive material', 33(11) *Journal of Obstetrics & Gynaecology Canada* 2011, 1134–1140; S. Mohr, above n. 86; A. Wheatley, '"We're not related in any way, only by blood": Danish sperm donors and (imagined) relationships', 8(1) *Families, Relationships & Societies* 2019, 137–152; L. Gilman, 'Tracing pathways of relatedness: how identity-release gamete donors negotiate biological (non-)parenthood', *Families, Relationships & Societies* 2020, 235–251.

as fathers but make a definite distinction between social and biological 'fatherhood' (for example, 'biologically they are my children, yes. But I do not have any other affiliation with them besides that').[88] Identity-release donors have been known to essentially construct non-parental connections with (potential) donor offspring.[89] Known donors push their friendship or kinship with the *recipient* to the foreground ('I am an aunt/godmother, not a mother to her', 'I just helped my friend, I knew how much she longed for a child'). Other donors focus on the relationship between their own children and the donor-conceived children, on the '(half-)sibling relationships'. Relying on familiar non-parental relationships gives donors a language to talk about the genetic connection with the donor-conceived person that is often less emotionally loaded than the terms of father, mother, and parent. These familiar relationships also provide images of how such relationships can function. Moreover, such relationships (e.g. friends, aunts, etc.) do not have such an exclusive character as parental ones do; exclusivity is seen by some as a fundamental part of what it means to be a parent. Such an exclusive relationship belongs solely to parents.[90]

4.2. GENES AND RELATEDNESS

4.2.1. Donor's Genetic Relatedness to Donor-Conceived Offspring

In the beginning, when donation was mainly anonymous, the legal and organisational culture implied that donors 'just donate material', and interest in the offspring was seen as unhealthy; it was assumed that anonymous donors had no interest in the offspring resulting from their donation. However, it is not because organisational and legal frameworks erase any social significance of the genetic connection between donor and donor-conceived offspring that this is how donors experience this connection. There are sperm donors who were previously anonymous and later made themselves identifiable, who thought about the offspring born out of their donation, some from the moment they had donated, others when they became a parent themselves, or after reading donor-conceived peoples' life stories in the media.[91] Subsequently, these formerly

---

88 A. Wheatley, above n. 87, p. 142.

89 Badok II-study: 'Ontmoeting tussen donor en donorkind; wat zijn de behoeftes aan ondersteuning en een ethische beschouwing' (Meeting between donor and donor-conceived person; what are the needs for support and an ethical consideration). ZONMWProjectnumber 854020001. https://www.zonmw.nl/nl/onderzoek-resultaten/kwaliteit-van-zorg/programmas/project-detail/ethiek-en-gezondheid-3/ontmoeting-tussen-donor-en-donorkind-wat-zijn-de-behoeftes-aan-ondersteuning-en-een-ethische-bescho/verslagen/BADOK II.

90 M. Melhuus, *Problems of conception: Issues of law, biotechnology, individuals and kinship*, Berghahn Books, Oxford 2012.

91 J.M. Speirs. 'Semen donors' curiosity about donor offspring and the barriers to their knowing', 15(2) *Human Fertility* 2012, 89–93; M. Kirkman, K. Bourne, J. Fisher, L. Johnson and

anonymous sperm donors wanted to know whether any offspring had resulted from their donations and the number of genetic donor-conceived offspring, and some wished for some sort of contact. Research also shows that genetic connections seem to evoke feelings of responsibility.[92] Both egg and sperm donors have reported feelings of responsibility towards those born from their donations. For example, donors were worried that their 'biological child' might potentially be raised by someone who treated them badly, wondering 'How are they doing?'. Some anonymous donors stepped out of anonymity because they became aware of the need of (some) donor-conceived people for information and felt it to be their responsibility to respond to these needs.[93] On the other hand, sperm donors have also expressed fears of feeling emotionally or financially compelled to care for offspring born as a result of their donation if they were to be contacted by donor-conceived offspring.[94]

Times have changed and so has the socio-cultural-legal context of donor conception for at least some donors. Some countries have abolished donor anonymity and now only allow identity-release donation. These legal changes are situated within a change in culture in which openness regarding genetic parentage is promoted and expected, from both (intending) parents and donors. In this new context, donors are expected to be open to contact.[95]

Research shows that donors in an identity-release context acknowledge that they have contributed to the creation of another human being.[96] They also accept that information about one's genetic ancestry or one's genetic make-up could be important for offspring conceived by their donation, and that questions are to be expected. Consequently, donors see it as their responsibility as donor to 'be available' to the donor-conceived person to give information on who they are. Different views exist as to the age at which this information

K. Hammarberg. 'Gamete donors' expectations and experiences of contact with their donor offspring', 29(4) *Human Reproduction* 2014, 731–738; E. Blyth, M. Crawshaw, L. Frith and O. van den Akker, 'Gamete donors' reasons for, and expectations and experiences of, registration with a voluntary donor linking register', 20(4) *Human Fertility* 2017, 268–278; S. Bolt, D. Postema, A. van der Heij and A.J.B.M. Maas, 'Anonymous Dutch sperm donors releasing their identity', 24(1) *Human Fertility* 2019, 24–30.

92 M. Konrad, *Nameless relations: Anonymity, melanesia and reproductive gift exchange between British ova donors and recipients*, Berghahn Books, Oxford 2005; R. Almeling, *Sex cells: The medical market for eggs and sperm*, University of California Press, Berkeley 2011; K.R. Daniels, W. Kramer and M.V. Perez-y-Perez, above n. 80; A. Wheatley, above n. 87; Badok II study, above n. 89.

93 E. Blyth, M. Crawshaw, L. Frith and O. van den Akker, above n. 91; S. Bolt, D. Postema, A. van der Heij and A.J.B.M. Maas, above n. 91.

94 J.M. Speirs, above n. 91; A. Wheatley, above n. 87.

95 S. Graham, S. Mohr and K. Bourne, 'Regulating the "good" donor: The expectation and experiences of sperm donors in Denmark and Victoria, Australia' in S. Golombok, R. Scott, J.B. Appleby, M. Richards and S. Wilkinson (eds.), *Regulating reproductive donation*, Cambridge University Press, Cambridge 2016, pp. 207–231.

96 L. Gilman, above n. 87.

should best be given. In a system of identity-release this is often at the age of 18 (or 16). As identity development takes place throughout adolescence, some donors perceive the age of 18 as too late. This was for some donors the reason for donating as a known donor outside a clinic, so they would be available to the donor-conceived offspring at a younger age. Others who donated at a clinic think that 18 is about the right age. They believe that meeting the donor 'too young' would lead the child to over-emphasise the importance of genetics in their own sense of identity.

Besides being 'merely available'[97] to donor-offspring, donors may themselves have a need to connect with the donor-conceived person, or think about the relationship between them and the person born as a result of their donation. This is a challenge, as there are no cultural scripts for donors (or donor offspring) to make sense of their relationship to one another.[98] In the few studies which ask identity-release donors how they make sense of these unscripted connections, some envisage a socially meaningful relationship with their donor offspring, but find it difficult to articulate what this might involve (for example 'They are not my children, but they are my biology, if you can say it in that way – they are more connected to me than some random child').[99] These donors are only certain of the fact that it is a non-parental relationship. Furthermore, most of the interviewed donors had not yet had any contact with offspring conceived by their donation (some donors had possible offspring that were not yet old enough to make contact with them). Therefore, the relationships they describe are hypothetical relationships based on 'imagined' experiences, shaped by hopes and fears about the connection they (and their family) could have with the donor-conceived offspring. Sometimes such images are reassuring; having offspring born out of their donation can sometimes be an implicit validation of their virility and masculinity. Other images of the relationship between donor and donor-conceived offspring are perceived more negatively, as contact with the donor-conceived offspring could potentially threaten donor's own family stability. Positive and negative ideas can exist at the same time. In the absence of social scripts, pop culture and media can have an influence on the images that are created.[100] Donors have used the language of the sudden 'knock on the door' to describe meeting their offspring, which is often disruptive (in the

97 H. Burke, L. Gilman and P. Nordqvist, 'Being an egg or sperm donor: balancing "being available" with "knowing your place"?', University of Manchester, Morgan Centre for Research into Everyday Lives 2020, see: https://www.research.manchester.ac.uk/portal/files/176777689/Being_an_egg_or_sperm_donor_being_available_and_knowing_your_place.pdf.

98 M. Klotz, above n. 58.

99 L. Gilman, above n. 87; S. Mohr, above n. 86, p. 478.

100 A. Wheatley, above n. 87.

short or long term) for the donor's family functioning.[101] This is often how movies and sitcoms display contact between a donor and donor-offspring (e.g. the comedy film *Delivery Man*, Ken Scott, 2013). However, there is no evidence of donor-conceived persons stalking their donor or their donor-siblings.[102]

One small study reported on formerly anonymous donors' experiences of meeting the offspring conceived by their donation.[103] They started these meetings considering their role as 'being available' for the donor-conceived offspring, but had not anticipated the impact that such a meeting would have on themselves. Donors often experience strong feelings, such as surprise over the resemblances they share, pride, responsibility for the donor-conceived person, and concern. By focusing so much on their role of 'being available', they had blotted out their own feelings. In the absence of any social scripts, they struggle to find what role (if any) and position they (could) have in the donor-conceived person's life. They noticed that their meeting not only affected the donor-conceived person, but had an impact on their own family-system (partner, children) as well as the donor-conceived person's wider family-system (grandparents, siblings, etc.).

4.2.2. Donor's Genetic Relatedness to Own Family

Even when in recent years donors have been considered to be 'persons', they have mainly been seen as 'people on their own', detached of any social network.[104] They have been presented as 'merely' donors. However, donors do not live in a vacuum but within a social network where they fulfil different roles, such as partner, parent, son/daughter, brother/sister. Their decision to donate has repercussions for donors' everyday lives and relationships in various ways, and other people feel involved in the donation. Policy, research and practice have mainly focused on the relationships between donors, parents and donor-conceived people, or on individual experiences. The donor's wider social network has scarcely been addressed.

On the one hand, the donation of gametes is seen as an individual, autonomous decision; an adult man/woman deciding over their own body. On the other hand, gametes are linked to reproduction, which is seen as a

---

101 J.M. Speirs, above n. 91; M. Kirkman, K. Bourne, J. Fisher, L. Johnson and K. Hammarberg, above n. 91.

102 M. Klotz, above n. 58, p. 54.

103 Badok II study, above n. 89.

104 P. Nordqvist, 'Un/familiar connections: On the relevance of a sociology of personal life for exploring egg and sperm donation', 41(3) *Sociology of Health & Illness* 2018, 601–615; H. Burke, L. Gilman and P. Nordqvist, above n. 97.

joint decision. In pre-donation counselling, the partner of the potential donor is commonly not invited to take part and is considered only indirectly: a counsellor may ask if the potential donor has talked about donation with their partner. If a donor has a partner at the time of donation, studies show that 78 to 92 per cent of donors inform their partner, but less than 50 per cent of donors inform their children about their past donations.[105] The extent to which the partner was actually *involved* or how much they felt they had a say in the decision to donate, varies. The impact on the partner can become tangible many years later, when a meeting takes place between the donor, the donor's family and the donor-conceived offspring.[106] It can happen that a partner goes through a phase of 'feeling an outsider' as he/she is the only one not connected by genes in these new relationships. It takes time to rebalance the genetic and non-genetic relationships. Besides partners, the donation can also have an impact on the legal offspring of the donor. This impact is not always clear to the donor at the moment of donation, when some donors do not yet have children of their own. Later on, a donor may think differently anyway about their children's relationship to the offspring born out of their donation when their own children begin to comprehend the genetic connection between them and the donor-conceived person. Very little research exists about the legal offspring of the donor. Some have shown an interest in meeting the donor-conceived children they are genetically related to, while others have not, and opinions can change.[107] In addition to partners and own children, research shows that the donor's parents are also people who could be affected by their donation. Some donors do not inform their parents about the donation to prevent them from identifying the potential donor-conceived offspring as a grandchild.

Not only does donation affect the social network of donors, but these significant others can also attribute different social significance to their genetic connection with a donor-conceived offspring. These other views are not only observed and noticed by the donors; because these ideas are embedded in a specific relationship, the donor's relationships with these people (as partner, father/mother, son/daughter) affect how the donor relates to the donor-conceived offspring.[108] The donor's sense of who they are in relation to these

105 K. Daniels, A. Lalos, C. Gottlieb and O. Lalos, 'Semen providers and their three families', 26(1) *Journal of Psychosomatic Obstetrics & Gynaecology* 2005, 15–22. E. Blyth, M. Crawshaw, L. Frith and O. van den Akker, above n. 91; S. Bolt, D. Postema, A. van der Heij, and A.J.B.M. Maas, above n. 91; V. Jadva, T. Freeman, W. Kramer and S. Golombok, 'Sperm and oocyte donors' experiences of anonymous donation and subsequent contact with their donor offspring', 26(3) *Human Reproduction* 2011, 638–645.

106 These are examples of the donor-linking practice at Fiom, and at UK DonorLink, now Donor-Conceived Register.

107 K. Daniels, A. Lalos, C. Gottlieb and O. Lalos, above n. 105.

108 L. Gilman, above n. 87; J. Mason, 'Personal narratives, relational selves: Residential histories in the living and telling', 52(2) *The Sociological Review* 2004, 162–179.

others will co-define who they would like to be and think they should be in relation to the donor offspring. Furthermore, donors are often challenged in how to manage similar genetic connections in other contexts; on the one hand in their daily life (between the donor and their family-members), and on the other hand in the context of donor conception (towards the donor-conceived offspring), especially in relation to 'responsibilities' and 'boundaries'. 'I want to be responsible as donor and be available for information, but I also want to be a responsible partner and not burden my partner with my donation'. 'I want to be responsible as a donor and be available for questions, but I want to respect my children's wishes not to be involved'. Donor-conceived offspring can be seen as part of the family by the donor, but other family-members might prefer more distance, or vice versa. Boundary questions are not only raised in relation to the (intending) parents – such as how to respect their parental role – but also in relation to the donor's own family ('Do I involve them or not, or how far?').[109]

4.3. INFLUENCING FACTORS

4.3.1. Gender and Technology

Eggs and sperm are biologically comparable, as each cell provides half of the genetic material needed to create life. Despite the parallel, these cells are produced by differently sexed bodies (males and females), and eggs and sperm are produced in different ways (the female body has a limited supply of eggs, while the male body replenishes sperm). These two features seem to influence how society and donors give meaning to genes.

Different socio-cultural meanings are attributed to the male and female body. A women's reproductive body is strongly associated with socio-cultural norms of caring motherhood. An egg donor contributes to the motherhood project of another woman. In this sense, egg donation is often presented as a gift exchange.[110] Genes are conceptualised as a gift of motherhood to another woman, who carries the pregnancy and gives birth.[111] The fact that egg donors usually donate to just one intending parent, making it more personal, might enhance this image. In contrast, sperm donors view donation as a more general act to help people out or to do a good deed.[112]

---

109 S. Mohr, above n. 86.

110 See for example: G. Orobitg and C. Salazar, above n. 87; E. Blyth, Y. Samantha and A. Ka Tat Tsang, above n. 87.

111 R. Almeling, above n. 92.

112 H. Burke, L. Gilman and P. Nordqvist, above n. 97.

In contrast to the gift idea of egg donation, a review of the motivations of sperm donors found a number of secondary motives (besides altruism and financial motives) that may be just as, or even more, important to donors due to their intrinsic nature, such as 'procreation' and 'passing on genes'.[113] These secondary motivations are not seen among the motivators of egg donors.[114] There is little research on how sperm donors view their genetic contribution. One study on sperm donors showed that having 'good sperm' boosts the feeling of virility and masculinity, as 'sperm quality' is strongly related to the potential for producing children and passing on one's genes.[115] Also, in contrast to egg donors, sperm donors can in fact have numerous donor-conceived offspring. While some prolific donors may pursue this goal, other donors fear the consequences of a large number of offspring if they were to meet them.[116] Such a fear might be realistic for donors who donated prior to the introduction of legal regulations in the practice of donor conception. Currently many countries set limits on the number of donor-conceived offspring per donor. Still, donors who donate to commercial sperm banks, whose sperm is used internationally, can still be confronted with a large number of offspring.

4.3.2. Context of Donation

How a donor gives meaning to and experiences the donation of genetic material, and the genetic connections resulting from their donation, are often a combination of personal experiences and ideas and the organisational, legal and cultural context in which they donate.[117] The difference between an anonymous and identity-release context and how this can colour the meaning the donor gives to genes and genetics have been described above. More recently, online donation is emerging. Often donors choose to donate via the internet, as they feel their ideas about genes and genetic connection do not fit the organisational context of a clinic or sperm bank and the legal context of their country. Research indicates that online donors have different views of their role as a donor compared to that defined in their national laws. For example, they wanted to be more involved as a parent, wanted to make genetic information available

113 U. Van den Broeck, M. Vandermeeren, D. Vanderschueren, P. Enzlin, K. Demyttenaere and T. D'Hooghe, above n. 85.

114 S. Purewel and OB.A. van den Akker, 'Systematic review of oocyte donation: investigating attitudes, motivations and experiences', *Human Reproduction Update* 2009, 499515.

115 A. Wheatley, '"One of the good guys": sperm donor masculinity and the falling Danish sperm count discourse', 21(5) *Culture, Health & Sexuality*, 2019, 495–509; M.K. Nelson and R. Hertz, 'Pride and concern: differences between sperm and egg donors with respect to responsibility for their donor-conceived offspring', 36(2) *New Genetics & Society* 2017, 137–158.

116 S. Mohr, above n. 86; A. Wheatley, above n. 87.

117 R. Almeling, above n. 92; L. Gilman, above n. 87; A. Wheatley, above n. 87.

earlier for the child, or wanted to procreate and did not agree with the limits of offspring per donor.[118]

5. CONCLUSION

This chapter has described the experiences of and meaning given to genes and genetic connections by (intending) parents by donor conception, donor-conceived people, and donors themselves, based on research results. People do not live in a vacuum but in a specific societal context. In order to gain a comprehensive understanding of (intending) parents', donor-conceived people's and donors' experiences and meaning given, it is important to include the broader socio-cultural context, as the societal, professional and political discourse co-shape the meaning-making process. Moreover, as (health and legal) professionals we are not immune to the effect of the context in which we live and operate. We too have socialised and internalised views about genes, genetics, genetic relationships etc., and we need to be alert to our own views and any tendency to downplay, emphasise or hold contradictory thoughts and views (genes are relevant and irrelevant) on genes and genetics.

The findings illustrate that the term genetics appears to be the most incomprehensible, pervasive of all concepts within donor conception. The meaning of genes and genetics is multi-layered and changeable dependent on the context, and can even carry conflicting meanings within one individual despite the underlying essentialist rhetoric.[119] Meanings and experiences of all those involved are not static but often change throughout one's lifetime, as genes touch on many aspects of life.

Changeable must not be confused with unstable or unreasonable. Given the deeply rooted socio-cultural ideology of biogenetic kinship, people exert themselves and show great flexibility regarding whether or not particular aspects of 'biological' processes and substances matter in the construction of kinship, and creativity in relation to how such things are made meaningful. This creativity contradicts the criticism sometimes expressed that people over-emphasise the impact of genetic knowledge. If there is one thing that is common in all this variation and fluidity, it is that all those involved struggle with the deeply rooted socio-cultural ideology of biogenetic kinship.

The term genes not only carries multiple and fluid meanings but sometimes also conflicting meanings.[120] These conflicting meanings can occur within an

---

118 S. Graham, T. Freeman and V. Jadva, 'A comparison of the characteristics, motivations, preferences and expectations of men donating sperm online or through a sperm bank', 34 (11) *Human Reproduction* 2019, 2208–2218.

119 T. Freeman, above n. 7, p. 18.

120 T. Freeman, above n. 7, pp. 16–17.

individual as people can both emphasise and minimise the significance of genes or genetics. Genes can be simultaneously relevant and irrelevant. But conflicting meanings are easily presented as 'opposing' views between (intending) parents, donor-conceived people and donors. Some differences between the parties involved are to be expected, as each party looks upon and engages with genes and genetic connections from a different position. Moreover, the findings above have illustrated that a single experience and meaning given by parents, donor-conceived people and donors does not exist because neither '*the*' parent, *the* donor-conceived person, nor *the* donor exists. For reasons of readability, the groups have been described separately in this chapter, but it should be noted that each group is itself very heterogenous (in terms of gender, age, family context, sexuality, etc.), and each situation co-shapes the experience and meaning given.

More striking than the differences is that (intending) parents, donor-conceived people and donors seem to struggle with similar challenges. Genes and genetic connections are simultaneously emphasised and downplayed. Moreover, they all struggle to manage this new genetic relatedness. These 'genetic connections' resemble genetic ties in our traditional kinship view, but they cannot simply be represented by the traditional kinship view nor do they fit into ready-made kinship categories. In the absence of a specific social script, people fall back upon familiar scripts, using words from familiar scripts. A suitable vocabulary is missing, and people are uncertain about what can be expected and demanded from each other in these connections, what obligations they carry, etc. Each one involved in this field (personal or professional) should be given flexibility in the vocabulary that they use rather than having a specific vocabulary imposed upon them, or imposing a vocabulary on others. As this is pioneering work of doing relatedness, a lot of unknowns and various options will exist, and there should be space and an open mind for new plots to develop. Research shows that these new relationships are complementary rather than colonising.[121] They do not displace other ways of relating.

Lastly, in the debates about 'right to ancestry' and 'right to identity' in the context of donor conception the connection between donor-conceived people and the donor is given a central place. The findings presented here illustrate that in the search for information about ancestry and identity-building, (genetic) *networks* are created rather than merely connections between two genetically related individuals. Donor-conceived people not only show interest in the donor, but also in same donor-offspring (who again live in various families), and in the family of the donor. The donor's family may show interest in the people conceived by his/her donation, parents connect with same-donor families, and grandparents show an interest.

---

121 M. Klotz, above n. 58.

These constantly expanding connections were not anticipated at the start of the practice of donation, and as a society we are only beginning to explore them. The entrance angle to these genetic connections in the debates about 'right to ancestry' and 'right to identity' has always been the donor-conceived person. To be successful it might be necessary to start looking from and including other angles as well (e.g. the donor angle, same-donor offspring angle, ...). Not all genetic connections are given the same legal recognition in these debates. There is a difference between the genetic connection to the donor versus the genetic connection to same-donor peers, or non-donor-conceived children of the donor. There are also differences in who has a right to information, and the direction of that right. Genes connect, and such a connection is not limited to a genetic connection between two people. Donor conception creates especially complex networks. This should be mirrored in our reflections about genetics in donor conception.

COUNSELLING INTENDED PARENTS IN NEED OF DONOR GAMETES

Julie NEKKEBROECK

1. INTRODUCTION

Use of donor sperm has been a form of family building for perhaps more than a century in a clinical context; the use of donated oocytes, however, did not become feasible until the 1980s.[1] Counselling intended parents who consider use of donor gametes is still a relatively new field and has since the start been influenced by public attitudes towards the importance of genetics and kinship in parentage, moral and community standards and legal frameworks. One of the issues influenced by these attitudes is the disclosure of donor conception and identity to donor conceived children.

For decades, it was not an option to disclose donor conception to children so conceived and to the outside world.[2] Nowadays, under the influence of donor conceived offspring themselves and scientific evidence, promotion of greater openness of donor conception is supported by new policy frameworks in a number of countries. Evidence shows that openness is the better approach for parents and offspring[3] and the only realistic approach, given the growing curiosity towards ancestry information and the increased use of direct-to-consumer genetic testing.[4] However, even today donor conception is veiled in secrecy for many heterosexual families[5] and even homosexual families or single mothers do not always talk to their offspring about their conception with donated gametes.[6] Nevertheless, fertility centres who offer treatment with donor gametes have a responsibility to offer evidence-based counselling on the use of donor gametes including information provision, assessment of readiness to use donor gametes, guidance of patients on decision-making on (non-) disclosure of donor conception and psycho-education on the lifelong management of this topic.

Especially, the long-term follow-up provided by fertility centres and/or professional networks to ensure continuous support in management of donor conception is of great importance for the future well-being of parents, offspring and donors. In this chapter we aim to give an insight into the daily practice of counselling intended parents who consider use of donor gametes in Belgium's largest fertility clinic, Brussels IVF of the Universitair Ziekenhuis Brussel (UZ Brussel).

---

1 S.N. Covington and L.H. Burns, *Infertility Counselling: A Comprehensive Handbook for Clinicians*, 2nd edn., Cambridge University Press, 2006.

2 I. Raes, A. Ravelingien and G. Pennings, 'Donor conception disclosure: directive or non-directive counselling?', 13(3) *Journal of Bioethical Inquiry*, 2015, 369–379.

3 E. Ilioi, L. Blake, V. Jadva, G. Roman and S. Golombok, 'The role of age of disclosure of biological origins in the psychological wellbeing of adolescents conceived by reproductive donation: a longitudinal study from age 1 to age 14', 58(3) *Journal of Child Psychology & Psychiatry*, 2017, 315–324.

4 J.C. Harper, D. Kennett and D. Reisel, 'The end of donor anonymity: how genetic testing is likely to drive anonymous gamete donation out of business', 31(6) *Human Reproduction*, 2016, 1135–1140.

5 P. Nordqvist, 'The Drive for Openness in Donor Conception: Disclosure and The Trouble with Real Life', 28(3) *International Journal of Law, Policy and the Family*, 2014, 321–338.

6 V. Provoost, J. Bernaerdt, H. Van Parys, A. Buysse, P. De Sutter and G. Pennings, '"*No daddy*", "*A kind of daddy*": words used by donor conceived children and (aspiring) parents to refer to the sperm donor', 20(4) *Culture, Health & Sexuality*, 2017, 381–396.

2. THE POPULATION NEEDING DONOR GAMETES AND THE TYPES OF DONATION OFFERED AT BRUSSELS IVF

Since the '80s many fertility clinics worldwide have on a regular basis been treating (non-) heterosexual couples and individuals in need of donor gametes in order to reproduce. At Brussels IVF patients in need of donor gametes are most often single women, lesbian couples and, in a smaller number of cases, heterosexual couples where the male partner is infertile. Donor gametes are also used if a patient has a genetic condition that they want to avoid transmitting to the next generation.

Donation in Belgium can take the form of either 'anonymous donation' or 'known donation'. In case of 'known donation' the donor and the acceptor know each other and the acceptor him/herself brought the donor to the fertility centre with the explicit request to only use this donor's sperm or oocytes to reproduce.

As for who requests gametes for donation, we know that in 2019, 432 patients, including 232 lesbian couples, 138 single women and 62 heterosexual couples requested donor sperm for intra uterine insemination at Brussels IVF. Another 267 patients requested donor sperm to perform IVF, and 263 patients requested anonymous oocyte donation. These data show that lesbian couples and single women are the largest user-groups of donor semen. Since the implementation of intracytoplasmic sperm injection (ICSI)[7] and testicular sperm extraction (TESE) about 30 years ago, many men with a fertility problem have been able to genetically father a child without the use of donor sperm. Still, for a smaller proportion, there is no other option than to use donor semen to conceive a child. Furthermore, heterosexual women are the largest user-group of donor oocytes, especially due to advanced reproductive age. For lesbian couples there is the option of intra-relational oocyte donation, so they may be less likely to need donor oocytes.

3. WHAT IS COUNSELLING?

Before going into detail on counselling of intended parents in need of donor gametes, we will discuss what counselling in infertility entails. Three different types of counselling are commonly distinguished: patient-centred care, infertility

---

7 G. Palermo, H. Joris, P. Devroey and A.C. Van Steirteghem, 'Pregnancies after intracytoplasmic injection of single spermatozoa into an oocyte', 340 *The Lancet*, 1992, 17–18.

counselling and psychotherapy.[8] *Patient-centred care* consists of information provision and analysis, and guidance on decision-making and counselling on the implications of donor gamete use, for example. *Infertility counselling* is composed of the latter, including support and crisis counselling. At the next level of need, *psychotherapy* can be provided entailing crisis counselling and therapeutic counselling.[9]

Medical doctors and the staff of the fertility centre can offer patient-centred care, i.e. sufficient information about the pros and cons of medical treatment so that the patient knows enough about the treatment's implications to make informed decisions.

Infertility counselling is considered an entity that requires professional qualification and differs from patient-centred care. A key difference between patient-centred care and counselling is the counsellor's level of training. All staff can provide patient-centred care but only professionally trained mental health professionals can provide counselling.[10]

Mental health professionals and other qualified fertility counsellors can provide support counselling (e.g. grief work) and short-term crisis counselling, for instance, when people hear that conceiving a child with their own genetic material is no longer an option.

Mental health professionals can be involved in assessment and/or screening of patients for treatment and should address severe psychological problems (e.g. anxiety, depression, marital/sexual problems). They can work independently or within a clinic environment.[11]

Every fertility centre in Belgium is free to organise a counselling programme in accordance with their own standards. The mental health professionals involved in the counselling pathway at Brussels IVF are psychologists. In the counselling programme for intended parents in need of donor gametes a fixed minimum of consultations with the psychologist are obligatory.

For single women there are two consultations with a psychologist, before they go the gynaecologist specialised in fertility, followed by a consultation with the fertility counsellor – usually a nurse or midwife – who discusses the practical part of administering the treatment.

Heterosexual couples need to see the psychologist in the case of receiving oocyte and/or semen donation, before meeting with the gynaecologist for the prescription of the treatment and with the fertility counsellor. Lesbian couples need to see the psychologist only in the case of oocyte donation within the couple (intra relational oocyte donation) before proceeding to the consultation

---

8 B. Strauss and J. Boivin, 'Fundamental issues in counselling: Counselling within infertility' in *ESHRE Monographs: Guidelines for Counselling in Infertility*, Oxford University Press, 2002, 4–6.

9 Ibid.

10 Ibid.

11 Ibid.

with the gynaecologist and the fertility counsellor. They are not obliged to meet with the psychologist if they do not exchange oocytes.

4. COUNSELLING INTENDED PARENTS IN NEED OF DONOR GAMETES IN DAILY PRACTICE

In daily practice, during counselling, we evaluate whether patients can have access to treatment, and information is provided to stimulate well-informed decision-making. Readiness for treatment with donor material is assessed, guidance is given on decision-making about (non-)disclosure of the donor conception, and psycho-education is given regarding donor conceived families and children. Counselling on infertility typically occurs in a non-directive manner with respect for patients' autonomy.

4.1. PATIENT ACCESS TO TREATMENT?

Before embarking on treatment, patient evaluation occurs. This means that not everybody who applies for treatment gets access to treatment. Patient evaluation is thus at odds with patient-centred care and non-directive counselling since the patient himself does not ask to be evaluated and the fertility clinic experts will decide whether the patient will have access to treatment. The Brussels IVF team sees itself as (partially) responsible for the welfare of the resulting children, who would not be born without its help.

Patient evaluation occurs within a legal framework[12] and on the basis of a handbook that contains the internal guidelines of the fertility centre to ensure quality control. During patient evaluation the guiding principle is the perspective of 'the welfare of the future child'. Arguments in favour or against fertility treatment are evaluated from the perspective of the well-being of the future child, in the knowledge that the well-being of the child is a difficult concept to define. Three levels are distinguished[13,14] and help to define this guiding principle. There is the maximum threshold, which are the ideal circumstances for the child to be born, and there is the minimum threshold, when not living would be better for the child than living. The reasonable welfare

12 Belgian Act regarding medically assisted reproduction and the destination of supernumerary embryos and gametes of 6 July 2007, *Belgian Law Gazette (Belgisch Staatsblad)* 17 July 2007.

13 G. Pennings, 'Measuring the welfare of the child: in search of the appropriate evaluation principle', 14(5) *Human Reproduction*, 1999, 1146–1150.

14 G. Pennings, G. de Wert, F. Shenfield, J. Cohen, B. Tarlatzis and P. Devroey, 'ESHRE Task Force on Ethics and Law 13: the welfare of the child in medically assisted reproduction', 22(10) *Human Reproduction*, 2007, 2585–2588.

principle reflects an intermediate level wherein the future child should have the possibility to develop normal human interests and to achieve life goals, which are generally considered to make human life worthwhile.

We aim at achieving this reasonable welfare level for the child. When patient evaluation indicates that this level might not be achieved, the patient's request for treatment is discussed at an ad hoc internal ethical committee of Brussels IVF and the Centre for Medical Genetics of the UZ Brussel. This committee consists of a fixed multidisciplinary group of gynaecologists, psychologists, paediatricians, geneticists, ethicists, embryologists, and a child-psychiatrist. The case is presented and an evaluation occurs by these experts on the basis of the future child's best interest. Decisions are made sometimes by voting. Participants simply raise their hand if they are pro treatment. In the case of a negative response patients are referred to other fertility clinics where they can apply for treatment. Upon a positive advice, patients can start treatment, sometimes after complying with certain criteria.

Fortunately, during a consultation not only does patient evaluation occur but also a lot of information is given to enable patients to make well-informed decisions, for instance, on the use of donor material.

4.2. PROVISION OF INFORMATION

The different types of donation mentioned earlier are discussed with the patient during counselling. Do they prefer anonymous donation or a known donation? Further elaboration on the implications of each type of donation is given; the possible benefits and pitfalls are listed.

Medical information is provided on use of donor gametes, e.g. how many oocytes patients will receive, success rates, explanation of the (psychological) impact of an intrauterine insemination or IVF treatment.

Legal aspects of the use of donor gametes are addressed to ensure informed consent. For instance, patients should know that in Belgium the woman who gives birth is considered to be the mother of the child, even though the oocytes come from a donor, meaning there is no genetic link between birth-mother and offspring. The male or female partner of the woman using donor sperm is considered also to be the legal parent (automatically if the partner is married to the mother; by their recognising the child if the mother is not married) with all the accompanying parental rights and obligations. Furthermore, a donor who donates semen to a fertility clinic cannot claim paternity or legally pursue the parents who were treated with his sperm.[15]

---

[15] Article 27 and Article of the 56 Act regarding medically assisted reproduction and the destination of supernumerary embryos and gametes of 6 July 2007, *Belgian Law Gazette (Belgisch Staatsblad)* 17 July 2007.

Information is given on donor assessment and selection. How donors are screened, matched and selected is a question frequently asked by the intended parents during consultation. Already at a pre-conception stage we give information on (non-) disclosure practices after use of donor gametes. Intended parents themselves also often inquire whether it is recommended to be open with close family, friends and the child about the donor conception.[16]

4.3. GUIDANCE ON THE TRANSITION TO PARENTHOOD USING DONOR GAMETES

During counselling a lot of attention is paid to the fact that patients receiving donor gametes undergo an alternative way of transitioning to parenthood and family building. Unlike parents who conceive with their own genetic material, these future parents go through a change (and grieving) process, since the initial idea of procreating with own genetic material does not correspond with what is possible.

The 'five-stage change model of Virginia Satir'[17] offers a theoretical basis that guides counselling. The model describes the impact of change on feelings, thinking, performance, and physiology. It also includes the stages of grief during the process of change. In this model change starts with a stage or situation in which there is an 'old status quo'; then people encounter a 'foreign element'. In case of infertility this could be the knowledge that there is an inability to conceive a child with their own genetic material. It will often be the fertility specialist who has to pass on this difficult message.

The second stage is the 'resistance' stage. Patients may not want to hear that they are unable to conceive and sometimes extra treatments with their own gametes are needed – against all the odds – to make them realise that it is not going to work. This leads to 'chaos', the third stage in Satir's change model. The purpose of chaos is to generate a 'transforming idea': for instance, the possibility of building a family with the use of donor material. The transforming idea can be introduced in many ways, even prior to treatment it can be mentioned that donor gametes are an option, or this idea can slowly emerge through persistent hit-and-miss explorations of new ways to cope. Patients begin to see a way out of the 'chaos' into a paradigm shift (the fourth stage).

---

16 P. Nordqvist and C. Smart, *Relative Strangers: Family Life, Genes and Donor Conception*, Palgrave Macmillan, 2014.

17 W. Strider and E. Strider, *The Satir Change Process: a model for individuals, groups & organizations during a change process.* Adapted from the Virginia Satir Change Model (2019). https://satirglobal.org/wp-content/uploads/2020/04/Satir-Change-Model.pdf.

Mental health professionals in the area of reproduction need to aid people by guiding them through this change process, by helping them explore the possibilities and consequently allow them to internalise this idea which might bring them to a 'a new status quo'. In this last stage, donor conception becomes a valuable option to achieve their goal of creating a family.

Coming to terms with the fact that donor gametes are needed to conceive a child is a very different process for each type of patient. Same-sex couples have already dealt with this idea of having to use donor material when they discovered their sexual orientation. Single women opting to conceive a child on their own have often also already accepted the transforming idea of single parenthood and hence the need for donor semen.

Heterosexual couples, however, are usually encountered by the clinic in the phase of chaos, still grieving the loss of the possibility to procreate with their own genetic material. Time is a very important aspect in this change process; change does not happen overnight. Usually, heterosexual couples are able to take the next step when they are convinced that they have run out of treatment options with their own genetic material. One year can easily pass between the first moment that the consideration of use donor gametes was suggested to them and their actually requesting treatment. Sometimes additional treatments with their own genetic material are necessary to be able to close the chapter. Patients sometimes move back and forward in this process before they achieve a new status quo and the use of donor material is accepted as a valuable option.

Use of donor gametes and donor conception is a topic that needs to be managed not only prior to conception but also after conception and eventually for an entire life-time by parents as well as children.

Pursuing non-genetic parenthood requires prospective parents to reconfigure conceptualisations of parenthood and address the loss of their imagined genetically related child. At the same time prospective parents need to undertake emotional and intellectual work in order to gain a sense of entitlement to parent a genetically *un*related child. This process is also called 'Parental Claiming'.[18] In a study[19] where 85 women were interviewed who had conceived after egg donation and had a child between 6 and 18 months old, most mothers felt secure and confident in their position as the child's mother by the end of the first year. These mothers used a range of strategies across the transition to parenthood that enabled them to establish their identity as the child's mother and facilitated the process of feeling that the baby was theirs,

---

18 M. Sandelowski, B.G. Harris and D. Holditch-Davis, '"Somewhere out there": Parental claiming in the preadoption waiting period', 21 *Journal of Contemporary Ethnography*, 1993, 464–486. http://dx.doi.org/10.1177/089124193021004003.

19 S. Imrie, V. Jadva and S. Golombok, '"Making the child mine": Mothers' thoughts and feelings about the mother-infant relationship in egg donation families', 34 *Journal of Family Psychology*, 2020, 469–479. https://doi: 10.1037/fam0000619.

helping them to manage the ambivalence and uncertainties associated with non-genetic parenthood. Furthermore, the importance of pregnancy plays a role in parental claiming: the fact that the oocyte receptor gives birth and hence life plays a central role in the ownership of the child.

Already at a preconception level, strategies were observed in the narratives of the candidates for donor conception showing this parental claiming process. For instance, in this study most women had a preference for an unknown donor, thinking this would help them to establish their identity as the child's only mother, as opposed to known donation where the donor could have a stake in the child's upbringing and/or make the mother feel she is in their debt forever. On the other hand, for those opting for known donation it may feel comforting to have a genetic connection with the child in the case of intra family donation. Intended parents often try to minimise the role of the donor; the donor is not giving away a baby, she is providing the eggs.

Normalisation of this way of family building needs to be established. Prospective parents need to realise that nowadays there is a lot of family diversity (new recomposed families, lesbian families, single parenthood, etc.) and that hence, they do not form an exception.

After birth, confidence needs to be built and reassurance given that bonding with the child can occur, and hence that mothers have an influence beyond genetics. External reminders of the fact of egg donation need to be managed, e.g. comments on (lack of) physical resemblance. Eventually, the donor needs to be given a 'psychological place' with which parents feel comfortable. Often they succeed in describing the donor in ways that imply little or no threat.

All these important mental tasks need to be performed. However, patients leave the fertility clinic six weeks into their pregnancy when a foetal heartbeat is detected and when many of these important mental tasks in parental claiming still need to be built up. Although mental health professionals remain available, it is possible that a lot of couples miss out on important support during pregnancy and the first year post-partum, since no standard follow-up is installed by fertility centres.[20]

4.4. ASSESSMENT OF PATIENT READINESS FOR TREATMENT WITH DONOR GAMETES

When intended parents in need of donor gametes apply for treatment it is important that their readiness for use of donor gametes is assessed.

---

20 P. Nordqvist and C. Smart, *Relative Strangers: Family Life, Genes and Donor Conception*, Palgrave Macmillan, 2014.

4.4.1. Heterosexual Couples

During counselling of heterosexual couples for use of donor gametes, the infertility history of the couple is explored as well as their experience and their motivation/reason for using donor gametes. The grieving process associated with the couple's infertility and the inability to have a child biologically related to both intended parents is addressed.[21] How and when did they come to the decision to use donor gametes? For heterosexual couples it is important that before embarking on donor conception they feel they have tried everything and ran out of treatment options with their own genetic material.

The couple's feelings and comfort level with use of donor gametes (e.g. biological inequality, where one parent has a genetic link with the child and the other does not, and concerns about attachment) are explored. Can intended parents make the leap from dwelling on the fact that this is perhaps not their ideal way of making a child, to 'use of donor gametes can deliver us our ideal family'?[22]

We explore the meanings both partners attribute to the donor and their disclosure intentions for significant others and for the future child. How much time has gone by since the couple heard that donor material might be needed? Are they able to picture the child as their own even without a genetic bond? Are there fears and concerns? Is there coercion (from one of the partners?) to use donor gametes?[23]

For some couples it can be helpful to encourage or set a waiting period between receiving the diagnosis and commencing donor conception so that the grieving process and relational and psychosocial adjustment can take place. Additional counselling on the topic can be beneficial in creating a more open attitude towards discussing the issue within the couple and with significant others, and can promote the making of well-informed choices which patients feel at ease with.

Awareness needs to be created that the issue of the use of donor gametes will be present for the rest of their lives and the child's life. The conception of a child or achievement of a pregnancy is for many people an 'endpoint' of a difficult journey of fertility problems. However, another journey starts, namely, that of a family-building process which is a continuous process over a life-time period

---

21 S.N. Covington and L.H. Burns, *Infertility Counseling: A Comprehensive Handbook for Clinicians*, 2nd edn., Cambridge University Press, 2006, ISBN-10: 0521619491 ISBN-13: 978-0521619493.

22 K.R. Daniels, 'Telling donor insemination offspring about their conception: The nature of couples' decision-making', 40 *Social Science & Medicine*, 1995, 1213–1220. doi:10.1016/0277-9536(94)00251-N.

23 S.N. Covington and L.H. Burns, *Infertility Counseling: A Comprehensive Handbook for Clinicians*, 2nd edn., Cambridge University Press, 2006. ISBN-10: 0521619491 ISBN-13: 978-0521619493.

and over different generations. Before, donor conception was seen as something impacting the child and making the child 'different'; today, we point to the fact that donor conception impacts the entire family.[24]

4.4.2. *Lesbian Couples*

The adjustment to the idea that transition to parenthood is only possible with the use of donor gametes has usually already taken place a long time before lesbian couples present themselves at the fertility clinic. It is evident not only for the couple but also for the couple's family and social network that donor gametes will be used. Lesbian couples seemed to be less inclined to become a biological parent per se and/or to have a biologically related family than heterosexual couples, and therefore feel less threatened by use of donor material or by the donor as such.[25]

However, assessment of the stability of the relationship as well the desire for pregnancy and/or desire to donate eggs to the partner is mandatory. Also reflection on the type of donation and the position of the donor in the child's life needs to be stimulated. Although lesbian couples are open about donor conception towards offspring and children be given an active role in the co-construction of the donor conception narrative it also remains useful for lesbian parents to receive information and guidance on how and with what aids (e.g. booklets) the subject can be addressed.[26]

4.4.3. *Single Motherhood*

Likewise, for most single women the use of donor gametes is evidently required provided that they have given themselves enough time to conclude that single-parenting a child is the better option. For many single women the pivotal event that leads to single parenthood is the lack of a partner in combination with advanced reproductive age, giving them the feeling there was 'no other choice' if they wish to become a mother.[27] Ideally, the desire for

---

24 A. Indekeu, K. Dierickx, P. Schotsmans, K.R. Daniels, P. Rober and T. D'Hooghe, 'Factors contributing to parental decision-making in disclosing donor conception: a systematic review', 19 *Human Reproduction Update*, 2013, 714–733.

25 A.E. Goldberg, J.B. Downing and H.B. Richardson, 'The transition from infertility to adoption: Perceptions of lesbian and heterosexual couples', 26(6/7) *Journal of Social and Personal Relationships*, 2009, 938–963. http://dx.doi.org/10.1177/0265407509345652.

26 H. Van Parys, V. Provoost, E. Wyverkens, P. De Sutter, G. Pennings and A. Buysse, 'Family communication about the donor conception: a multi-perspective qualitative study with lesbian parents and their children', 26(14) *Qualitative Health Research*, 2016, 1998–2008.

27 S. Graham and A. Braverman, 'ARTs and the single parent', in M. Richards, G. Pennings and J.B. Appleby (eds.), *Reproductive donation: Practice, policy and bioethics*, Cambridge University Press, 2012, 189–210. http://dx.doi.org/10.1017/CBO9781139026390.011.

a child has overruled the desire for a partner and has become a clear priority. It is essential that significant others (family and friends) are aware of the patient's intention to become a single mother by choice and are supportive. The impact of single-parenthood for a child needs to be realistically appreciated. Emotional, professional and financial stability, as well as the quality of the social support network, need to be evaluated.[28] In counselling a lot of attention is paid to the assessment of resilience and stability as well as the provision of information on how to explain donor conception to the outside world and the future child.

4.5. GUIDANCE IN DECISION-MAKING AND PSYCHO-EDUCATION ON (NON-) DISCLOSURE OF DONOR CONCEPTION

4.5.1. *Disclosure Practices: Past and Present*

Disclosure versus non-disclosure in families has become a key issue in debates on donor conception. In the past parents of children conceived using donated eggs, sperm, or embryos were advised and encouraged to keep the donation a secret.[29] At that time, the dominant idea was that disclosure of donor conception was harmful and that this practice should be kept a secret for the child and the external world. Western societies highly value genetic ties and genes are seen as the primary basis for kinship.[30] A donor was considered a third party that entered the partner relationship, possibly posing a threat to family relations and especially challenging the father's role as a parent due to the latter's lack of genetic connectedness.[31]

This made people who used donor gametes potentially subject to stigmatisation. In the past the idea was promoted that when revealed to the external world and to the child, parents would have great difficulty in accepting the child as their own and that the child might reject them as parents. Legal

28 S.N. Covington and L.H. Burns, *Infertility Counselling: A Comprehensive Handbook for Clinicians*, 2nd edn., Cambridge University Press, 2006. ISBN-10: 0521619491 ISBN-13: 978-0521619493.

29 E. Blyth, L. Frith, C. Jones and J.M. Speirs, 'The role of birth certificates in relation to access to biographical and genetic history in donor conception', 17(2) *International Journal of Children's Rights*, 2009, 207–233.

30 I. Raes, A. Ravelingien and G. Pennings, 'Donor conception disclosure: directive or non-directive counselling?', 13(3) *Journal of Bioethical Inquiry*, 2015, 369–379.

31 A. Widbom, S. Isaksson, G. Sydsjo, A. Skoog Svanberg and C. Lampic, 'Positioning the donor in a new landscape – mothers' and fathers' experiences as their adult children obtained information about the identity-release sperm donor', 36(8) *Human Reproduction*, 2021, 2181–2188.

insecurities fed these ideas, and religious conviction and moral and behavioural codes (e.g. the sinfulness of masturbation) also played their part.[32]

Over the past decade there has been a significant shift towards disclosure, leading to a policy revision in this area. An important marker of this shift towards openness is the removal of donor anonymity in several countries, such as Sweden, Norway, Austria, New Zealand, Australia and the UK. Children conceived in clinics in these countries are able to access identifying details about their donor when reaching maturity.[33] Moreover, for instance in the Swedish context, all recipients of donor gametes are informed about their offspring's legal right to donor information and encouraged to share information about the donor conception from an early age.[34]

Not only have legal and policy frameworks changed in many countries, but stigmatisation is also decreasing and the number of parents intending to reveal donor conception is rising when compared to 30 years ago. Parents were found to be influenced by perceived values in their communities and are now inclined to greater openness.[35] There are reports of higher disclosure rates among parents who have undergone treatment in the past two decades than during earlier periods, reflecting a change in societal attitudes towards greater openness about donor conception, especially in Scandinavian countries. However, whilst the legal and policy frameworks support openness, there is evidence to suggest that openness might still not be a 'done deal' among parents of donor conceived children.[36]

A meta-analysis[37] showed that the willingness of parents to talk to a child about how the child was conceived is influenced by the existence of a genetic link with the child and/or the child's age. When comparing the percentages of parents who told their offspring about the ART versus those who were planning to tell, uncertain to tell or planning to not tell, there were no statistically significant

32 I. Raes, A. Ravelingien and G. Pennings, 'Donor conception disclosure: directive or non-directive counselling?', 13(3) *Journal of Bioethical Inquiry*, 2015, 369–379.

33 P. Nordqvist, 'The Drive for Openness in Donor Conception: Disclosure and The Trouble with Real Life', 28(3) *International Journal of Law, Policy and the Family*, 2014, 321–338. https://doi.org/10.1093/lawfam/ebu010.

34 J. Stoll, *Swedish Donor Offspring and Their Legal Right to Information*, Uppsala: Department of Law, Uppsala University, 2008.

35 D. Shehab, J. Duff, L.A. Pasch, K. MacDougall J.E. Scheib and R.D. Nachtigall, 'How parents whose children have been conceived with donor gametes make their disclosure decision: contexts, influences, and couple dynamics', 89 *Fertility & Sterility*, 2008, 179–187.

36 P. Nordqvist, 'The Drive for Openness in Donor Conception: Disclosure and The Trouble with Real Life', 28(3) *International Journal of Law, Policy and the Family*, 2014, 321–338. https://doi.org/10.1093/lawfam/ebu010.

37 M.A. Tallandini, L. Zanchettin, G. Gronchi and V. Morsan, 'Parental disclosure of assisted reproductive technology (ART) conception to their children: a systematic and meta-analytic review', 31(6) *Human Reproduction*, 2016, 1275–1287. https://doi:10.1093/humrep/dew068.

differences between autologous ART (IVF/ICSI with own material) and donor ART (IVF/ICSI with donor material) in the age group of children under 10. In both groups, autologous and donor ART, the probability of disclosure was less than 50 per cent.

Conversely, in the older age group (≥ 10 year-old children), a statistically significant difference was observed for autologous ART. Disclosure in the autologous ART group was more than 50 per cent and disclosure in the donor ART group was less than 50 per cent. Parents planning to tell featured higher in the plus 10 years age group for the autologous ART subsample, than in the donor ART subsample. Consequently, authors conclude that the use of donor material is linked to less openness about the mode of conception and that the decision to disclose may become more difficult over time as children grow older.

Results of a recent study concerning openness about donor conception in Sweden[38] are more promising. More than half of the parents using oocyte donation and sperm donation had already disclosed the donor conception to their 7–8 year-old child (oocyte donation 61 per cent, semen donation SD 58 per cent).

Still, today studies show that a significant proportion of parents do not make, or intend to make, their children aware of being donor conceived, which means that many families live with the possible burden of a secret.[39] It has been described that keeping a secret is cognitively and psychologically 'hard work'. Individuals and couples might get preoccupied with the secret as they have to suppress and manage intrusive thoughts, situations or conversations wherein topics related to the secret are raised. Furthermore, children's rights may not be given due consideration in view of the potentially hidden medical risks (genetic illnesses, inadvertent consanguinity), and many donor conceived children are not able to benefit from information being made available about their donor through the new policies in some countries.

4.5.2. Why do Parents Still Opt for Secrecy?

Some heterosexual couples might not feel the 'need' to tell because the mother gestated the child, as opposed to the situation where the child was adopted. Another argument people use is that this child will be 'ours anyway', applying the 'rejection of difference strategy' (rejection or denial of difference in being a parent of a donor conceived child) in order to gain some sense of entitlement

---

38 C. Lampic, A. Skoog Svanberg, K. Sorjonen and G. Sydsjo, 'Understanding parents' intention to disclose the donor conception to their child by application of the theory of planned behaviour', 36(2) Human Reproduction, 2021, 395–404.

39 D. Lane and M. Wegner, 'The cognitive consequences of secrecy', 69(2) *Journal of Personality and Social Psychology*, 1995, 237–253.

to be the legitimate parent of a genetically unrelated child. A concept also known to adoption research.[40]

It was found that once a family was formed with donor semen, couples avoided talking about the donor because it was perceived as disrupting men's growing confidence in their position as a father.[41] The fear exists that the child will reject them if they know, and/or that their relationship with the child will be undermined by this knowledge, or that the child's development will be disturbed. Heterosexual parents were found to be very much influenced by the societal norm, privileging the nuclear family based on genetic ties.

For many parents, donor conception is still considered a 'private' matter. Infertility still raises questions on masculinity and manhood in all cultures to some extent. Sometimes religious or cultural beliefs make disclosure 'impossible'. Fear that family and the social environment will 'reject' the child or that one – as a parent – will be judged for the choice to use donor gametes, supports non-disclosure. The use of donor gametes is not habitually accepted in Muslim culture, but contrasts with the fact that being a childless couple is still more of a stigma than the secretive use of donor material.[42]

Non-disclosure is a way to protect the child and oneself (as a parent) from potential stigmatisation and/or rejection, by limiting information about the donor conception to a small circle, e.g. the core family, depending on their assessment of the child's ability to control this information.[43,44]

4.5.3. Are Secrets Harmful?

Secrets can pull at the fabric of a family and are rooted in the shame of broken rules and taboo subjects. These secrets are often kept in order to prevent embarrassment, protect a family from judgement and avoid punishment (by being rejected or excluded from the family/network).

---

40 M. Sandelowski, B.G. Harris and D. Holditch-Davis, '"Somewhere out there": Parental claiming in the preadoption waiting period', 21(4) *Journal of Contemporary Ethnography*, 1993, 464–486. http://dx.doi.org/10.1177/089124193021004003.

41 E. Wyverkens, V. Provoost, A. Ravelingien, G. Pennings, P. De Sutter and A. Buysse, 'The meaning of the sperm donor for heterosexual couples: confirming the position of the father', 56(1) *Family Process*, 2017, 203–216. doi:10.1111/famp.12156.

42 I. Raes, A. Ravelingien and G. Pennings, 'Donor conception disclosure: directive or non-directive counselling?', 13(3) *Journal of Bioethical Inquiry*, 2015, 369–379.

43 J. Readings, L. Blake, P. Casey, V. Jadva and S. Golombok, 'Secrecy, disclosure and everything in-between: Decisions of parents of children conceived by donor insemination, egg donation and surrogacy', 22 *Reproductive BioMedicine Online*, 2011, 485–495. doi:10.1016/j.rbmo.2011.01.014.

44 S. Isaksson, A. Skoog-Svanberg, G. Sydsjo, L. Linell and C. Lampic, 'It takes two to tango: information-sharing with offspring among heterosexual parents following identity-release sperm donation', 31 *Human Reproduction*, 2016, 125–132.

Secrets tend to have a negative impact on family dynamics because they imply an unequal division of power leading to alliances and therefore 'distance' between those aware and the unaware. In case of donor conception, the child is excluded from the coalition between their parents on this particular topic. These secrets often lead to internal trust issues, increased anxiety, and shame. They give rise to tension when it comes to certain topics associated with the secret, e.g. questions from the child on how babies are made or how he/she was made?[45]

Research shows that the number of secrets that family members perceived their family to hold *in comparison to other families* was inversely correlated with family satisfaction. In addition, individuals' perception that some of their family members held secrets concerning taboo topics from other members was negatively related to satisfaction. Overall, results suggest an association between secrecy and family satisfaction. However, family satisfaction is influenced by the form, topic and function of the secret.[46] When the motivation to keep a secret is to protect a relationship (and not to harm someone) a diminishment of the association between avoidance and dissatisfaction (harm) is observed.

It remains hard to measure whether secrets are harmful, especially the revelation of secrets, since those aware can only be questioned retrospectively and it is difficult to compare this group with the unaware since this group is unlikely to be reached for participation in research.

4.5.4. *Is Non-Disclosure of Donor Conception Harmful?*

Intentional or unintentional late disclosure in anger or by inappropriate people, may lead to the development of psychological problems in children due to the feeling of betrayal. This feeling of betrayal by the parents may weigh more heavily than the donor conception itself. The impact of late disclosure may be severe and this revelation may lead to long and frustrating searches for the donor or for donor information.[47] Genealogical bewilderment and identity problems or frustration may occur when no information is available on the donor. Study participants reported experiences of genetic discontinuity, the shock of disclosure and feelings of deceit and mistrust in the family. There was a negative and ongoing effect of withholding secrets and a feeling that 'things were not

---

45 A.J. Turner and A. Coyle, 'What does it mean to be donor-offspring? The identity experiences of adults conceived by donor inseminations and the implications for counselling and therapy', 15(9) *Human Reproduction*, 2000, 2041–2051.

46 A.L. Vangelisti, 'Family Secrets: Forms, Functions and Correlates', 11(1) *Journal of Social and Personal Relationships*, 1994, 113–135. doi:10.1177/0265407594111007.

47 A. Lalos, C. Gottlieb and O. Lalos, 'Legislated right for donor-insemination children to know their genetic origin: A study of parental thinking', 22(6) *Human Reproduction*, 2007, 1759–1768.

quite right', suggesting that children pick-up hidden clues. Authors conclude that non-disclosure of donor conception can cause psychological damage.[48]

Then again, other authors[49] point to the fact that we have no idea of what proportion of donor-conceived children is at risk, since we do not know how many donor-conceived offspring find out about their conception method at a late age and consequently develop psychological problems. It is possible that many more people find out about their donor conception at a later age but do not have a problem with it. Current research on donor-conceived persons' attitudes towards disclosure of their donor conception only involves biased samples. Individuals who are aware of their donor conception but do not have a problem with it and did not have a problem with the method or timing of disclosure will probably remain under the radar. Also, donor-conceived people who are angry or discontent are more likely to contribute to websites, networks or internet forums and participate in studies, making the generalisation of the results difficult. However, not all donor children who remain silent are necessarily fine with their donor conception and not all angry and malcontent donor children will express these feelings in support groups and actively try to trace their donor.

Furthermore, revealing the donor conception, even at a later point in time, can also have positive effects on family relationships.[50] In a few cases of accidental discovery of non-paternity in a medical context, it was found that the (unintended) disclosure was appreciated by the parties involved and did not disrupt family relationships.

4.5.5. Why Promote Openness in Heterosexual Couples?

Because there is a possibility to hide the truth, the question of whether children of heterosexual couples should be told of their biological origins is one of the most controversial issues in the past decades regarding the birth of children through donated eggs, sperm and embryos.

Secrets and late disclosure can be harmful to child development, but this is not always the case, and drawing firm conclusions on this topic is not possible since it is hard to measure the impact of secrets in general and more precisely, of non-disclosure of donor conception.

---

48 A.J. Turner and A. Coyle, 'What does it mean to be donor-offspring? The identity experiences of adults conceived by donor inseminations and the implications for counselling and therapy', 15(9) *Human Reproduction*, 2000, 2041–2051.

49 I. Raes, A. Ravelingien and G. Pennings, 'Donor conception disclosure: directive or non-directive counselling?', 13(3) *Journal of Bioethical Inquiry*, 2015, 369–379.

50 A. Ravelingien and G. Pennings, 'The right to know your genetic parents: from open-identity gamete donation to routine paternity testing', 13(5) *American Journal of Bioethics*, 2013, 33–41.

On the other hand, openness has some advantages: it might alleviate the stress that secrets induce, it may prevent trust-issues that can emerge in case of (late) disclosure and it might avoid the (psychological) distance between those aware and the unaware.[51] These psychological advantages – along with the development in many countries that the right to know your (genetic) roots now overrules the anonymity of the donor – make non-disclosure in heterosexual families untenable.

Furthermore, (commercial) genetic testing means the end of donor anonymity and is likely to drive anonymous gamete donation out of business.[52] Over 3 million people have already used direct-to-consumer genetic testing to find information about their ancestry, and many are participating in international genetic genealogy databases that will match them with relatives. The increased prevalence of these technologies poses numerous challenges to the current practice of gamete donation and to counselling of intended parents as well as donors.

Parents using donor conception need to be fully informed that their children's DNA will identify that they are not the biological parents, and they should be encouraged to disclose the use of donor gametes to their children.[53] Donor-conceived adults who have not been informed of their status may find out by accident that they are donor-conceived. It is not only commercial genetic testing that poses a risk in this context; increasingly genetic testing takes place for all kinds of diseases, and problems with a sperm and egg donor's health may also reveal a donor conception, e.g. when parents are invited back to a fertility clinic to screen their child for a genetic condition possibly transmitted by the donor to their child. Donors themselves should be informed that their anonymity is not guaranteed, as they may be traced if their DNA, or that of a relative, is added to a database. All parties concerned in donor conception must be made aware that donor anonymity can no longer be guaranteed.[54]

Besides the risks of uncontrolled disclosure due to an increase in genetic testing and the changes in legal and policy frameworks in many countries as well as in societal attitudes in favour of greater openness, psycho-social factors are also taken into consideration when promoting disclosure in case

---

51 A.J. Turner and A. Coyle, 'What does it mean to be donor-offspring? The identity experiences of adults conceived by donor inseminations and the implications for counselling and therapy', 15(9) *Human Reproduction*, 2000, 2041–2051.

52 J.C. Harper, D. Kennett and D. Reisel, 'The end of donor anonymity: how genetic testing is likely to drive anonymous gamete donation out of business', 31(6) *Human Reproduction*, 2016, 1135–1140. https://doi.org/10.1093/humrep/dew065.

53 Ibid.

54 J.C. Harper, D. Kennett and D. Reisel, 'The end of donor anonymity: how genetic testing is likely to drive anonymous gamete donation out of business', 31(6) *Human Reproduction*, 2016, 1135–1140. https://doi.org/10.1093/humrep/dew065.

of donor conception. There is reassuring evidence on child adjustment and psychological well-being of the child and parents linked to disclosure of donor conception.

In case of early disclosure, children accept the information, integrate it into their life story and have positive reactions towards the disclosure decision of their parents.[55] Authors conclude that children have no problems with donor conception itself but *do* have problems with parents keeping secrets that involve them.

In a longitudinal study in the UK, family relationships and adolescent adjustment was examined in donor-conceived families with a 14-year-old.[56] There were no overall differences between disclosing families and either non-disclosing or natural conception families. However, within the disclosing families, more positive family relationships and higher levels of adolescent well-being were found for adolescents who had been told about their biological origins before the age of seven. The authors concluded that the earlier that children born through reproductive donation are told about their biological origins, the more positive are the outcomes in terms of the quality of family relationships and psychological well-being in adolescence.

Also, parents can be reassured that the majority of them (in case of egg donation) will be successful in the transition to parenthood and will be able to manage ambivalences and uncertainties associated with non-genetic parenthood.[57]

Counselling in infertility is typically non-directive with respect for the patient's autonomy.[58] It remains the patient's decision whether or not they will tell their child about the donor conception. Ideally, anxiety-driven disclosure should be avoided, with parents moving towards a conscious choice for disclosure.[59] Through counselling, heterosexual couples considering use of donor material should be made aware of the possible benefits and risks of (non-)disclosure. Use of donor material is a major life-event to be managed over an entire lifetime

55 V. Jadva, T. Freeman, W. Kramer and S. Golombok, 'The experiences of adolescents and adults conceived by sperm donation: Comparisons by age of disclosure and family type', 24 *Human Reproduction*, 2009, 1909–1919.

56 E. Ilioi, L. Blake, V. Jadva, G. Roman and S. Golombok, 'The role of age of disclosure of biological origins in the psychological wellbeing of adolescents conceived by reproductive donation: a longitudinal study from age 1 to age 14', 58 *Journal of Child Psychology & Psychiatry*, 2017, 315–324.

57 S. Imrie, V. Jadva and S. Golombok, '"Making the child mine": Mothers' thoughts and feelings about the mother-infant relationship in egg donation families', 34(4) *Journal of Family Psychology*, 2020, 469–479. https://doi: 10.1037/fam0000619.

58 B. Strauss and J. Boivin, 'Fundamental issues in counselling: Counselling within infertility', in *ESHRE Monographs: Guidelines for Counselling in Infertility*, Oxford University Press, 2002, 4–6.

59 S. Zadeh, 'Disclosure of donor conception in the era of nonanonymity: safeguarding and promoting the interests of donorconceived individuals?', 31 *Human Reproduction*, 2016, 2416–2420.

for the parents and the child, often in the context of an environment that is focused on genetic kinship and physical resemblance, leading to unintentional confrontations with the use of donor material.

4.5.6. *When is the Right Time to Tell?*

For lesbian couples and single women there is no choice; openness is mandatory in the absence of a male partner. In many lesbian families, use of donor semen is evident or a 'non-issue' to the extent that it may be perceived as unnecessary or even alienating to talk about the way parenthood was achieved.[60] The child will also more actively question the parents about the lack of a father; possibly from the moment when language development allows it.[61] Lesbian couples and single women will therefore be confronted much earlier with telling the donor conception story than heterosexual couples.

Compared to heterosexual couples, lesbian couples more easily provide information about their donor conception circumstances to offspring,[62] although maintaining the strength of the parent-child relationship and preventing relational deterioration might also be an important motive in lesbian couples for not (often) talking about the donor conception.[63] For instance, a study showed that lesbian parents too avoid using expressions that point to the lack of a genetic bond with the child, perhaps to protect the parent-child relationship.[64]

When heterosexual couples are asked (if and) when they will tell the child about their donor conception, all too often it is mentioned that the child should be 'old enough to understand', pointing to adolescence. The perception that the child is too young and needs to reach sufficient maturity to understand donor conception is a commonly reported reason to postpone disclosure.[65]

---

60 A. Perlesz, R. Brown, J. Lindsay, R. McNair, D. de Vause and M. Pittsf, 'Family in transition: Parents, children and grandparents in lesbian families give meaning to "doing family"', 28 *Journal of Family Therapy*, 2006, 175–199. doi:10.1111/j.1467-6427.2006.00345.x.

61 S. Zadeh, T. Freeman and S. Golombok, '"What does donor mean to a four-year-old?" Initial insights into young children's perspectives in solo mother families', 31 *Children & Society*, 2017, 194–205. http://dx.doi.org/10.1111/chso.12181.

62 A. Goldberg and K. Allen, 'Donor, dad, or ...? Young adults with lesbian parents' experiences with known donors', 52 *Family Process*, 2013, 338–350: doi:10.1111/famp.12029.

63 H. Van Parys, V. Provoost, E. Wyverkens, P. De Sutter, G. Pennings and A. Buysse, 'Family communication about the donor conception: a multi-perspective qualitative study with lesbian parents and their children', 26(4) *Qualitative Health Research*, 2016, 1998–2008.

64 A. Hequembourg, 'Unscripted motherhood: Lesbian mothers negotiating incompletely institutionalized family relationships', 21 *Journal of Social and Personal Relationships*, 2004, 739–762.

65 A. Indekeu, K. Dierickx, P. Schotsmans, K.R. Daniels, P. Rober and T. D'Hooghe, 'Factors contributing to parental decision-making in disclosing donor conception: a systematic review', 19(6) *Human Reproduction Update*, 2013, 714–733; P.E. Hershberger, M. Driessnack, K. Kavanaugh and S.C. Klock, 'Oocyte donation disclosure decisions: a longitudinal follow-up at middle childhood', 24(1) *Human Fertility*, 2019, 31–45. 10.1080/14647273.2019.1567945.

This 'right time strategy'[66] is in contrast with the message from fertility clinics that parents should start sharing information about the donor conception with the child from an early age. Furthermore, this strategy entails the risk that the envisioned optimal time-point for disclosure may never appear,[67] and sharing this information may become more difficult the longer parents wait.[68] Longitudinal studies also indicate that parents' intentions to disclose are only borne out in practice to a limited degree.[69]

Although children aged four in lesbian families were aware that they did not have a father and questioned their mothers about the reason for this, they showed little interest in their donor.[70] Not knowing the identity of their biological father did not seem to impair their psychological well-being. However, these children were too young to fully understand the circumstances of their conception.

It is not until middle childhood that children develop an understanding of biological inheritance.[71] By then they grasp what it means to be donor conceived[72] and understand the meaning and implications of the absence of a biological connection to their parents.[73]

66 K. Mac Dougall, G. Becker, J.E. Scheib and R.D. Nachtigall, 'Strategies for disclosure: How parents approach telling their children that they were conceived with donor gametes', 87 *Fertility & Sterility*, 2007, 524–533.

67 L.D. Applegarth, N.L. Kaufman, M. Josephs-Sohan, P.J. Christos and Z. Rosenwaks, 'Parental disclosure to offspring created with oocyte donation: intentions versus reality', 31 *Human Reproduction*, 2016, 1809–1815.

68 K.R. Daniels, V.M. Grace and W.R. Gillett, 'Factors associated with parents' decisions to tell their adult offspring about the offspring's donor conception', 26 *Human Reproduction*, 2011, 2783–2790.

69 J. Readings, L. Blake, P. Casey, V. Jadva and S. Golombok, 'Secrecy, disclosure and everything in-between: Decisions of parents of children conceived by donor insemination, egg donation and surrogacy', 22 *Reproductive BioMedicine Online*, 2011, 485–495. doi:10.1016/j.rbmo.2011.01.014; P.E. Hershberger, M. Driessnack, K. Kavanaugh and S.C. Klock, 'Oocyte donation disclosure decisions: a longitudinal follow-up at middle childhood', 24(1) *Human Fertility*, 2019, 31–45. 10.1080/14647273.2019.1567945.

70 S. Zadeh, T. Freeman and S. Golombok, '"What does donor mean to a four-year-old?" Initial insights into young children's perspectives in solo mother families', 31 *Children & Society*, 2017, 194–205. http://dx.doi.org/10.1111/chso.12181.

71 D.M. Brodzinsky, 'Children's understanding of adoption: Developmental and clinical implications', 42 *Professional Psychology: Research and Practice*, 2011, 200–207. http://dx.doi.org/10.1037/a0022415; G.E.A. Solomon, S.C. Johnson, D. Zaitchik and S. Carey, 'Like father, like son: Young children's understanding of how and why offspring resemble their parents', 67 *Child Development*, 1996, 151–171. http://dx.doi.org/10.2307/1131693; J.M. Williams and L.A. Smith, 'Concepts of kinship relations and inheritance in childhood and adolescence', 28 *British Journal of Developmental Psychology*, 2010, 523–546.

72 L. Blake, P. Casey, J. Readings, V. Jadva and S. Golombok, '"Daddy ran out of tadpoles": how parents tell their children that they are donor conceived, and what their 7-year-olds understand', 25 *Human Reproduction*, 2010, 2527–2534.

73 D.M. Brodzinsky, 'Children's understanding of adoption: Developmental and clinical implications', 42 *Professional Psychology: Research and Practice*, 2011, 200–207. http://dx.doi.org/10.1037/a0022415.

Therefore, the best age at which to give this information seems to be before age seven. Children need time to digest and internalise information about their donor conception. Waiting for the moment when they can fully understand might complicate the absorption of this information as children suddenly grasp all the implications of donor conception due to this cognitive progression that allows much more reflection.

When deciding to be open about donor conception, parents need to realise that this is a continuous process with several layers of information to be given regularly from a young age onwards (<7 years) and adapted to the child's age. Parents can already practice telling the story to their baby even before language development occurs and the child starts asking questions about conception, allowing them to grow in the narrative building and feel at ease with donor conception before the child is in middle childhood.

5. CONCLUSIONS

Practices in counselling intended parents who consider use of donor gametes have changed significantly over the past decades – from stressing the need for secrecy in the past century to more actively promoting openness nowadays.

In a growing number of jurisdictions, donor-conceived offspring have the legal right to information about their genetic origin and use of anonymous donors is no longer an option, based on the premise that this is in the best interest of the child. However, in Belgium the law only allows for anonymous donation (or known donation) and donor offspring do not have a right to obtain information on their donor. Nonetheless, many Belgian fertility centres discuss and even promote the option of being open with future offspring about their donor conception.

There is reassuring evidence on child adjustment and psychological well-being of the child and parents linked to disclosure of donor conception. These psychological advantages, along with societal changes removing the taboo surrounding donor conception, the development in many countries where the right to know your (genetic) roots overrules the anonymity of the donor, and the relativity of donor anonymity in the context of commercial DNA testing risking disclosure in adverse conditions, have all made non-disclosure of donor conception untenable.

Still, donor conception is veiled in secrecy for many heterosexual families and openness is not the obvious choice. Many patients requesting donor gametes seem unacquainted with how to handle donor conception and are very much unaware of the possible (psychological) implications for themselves and the child so conceived.

Fertility clinics in Belgium are participating in the discourse of openness and have adapted their counselling accordingly over the past decades. However, counselling in infertility is typically non-directive counselling.[74] It remains the patient's decision whether or not to tell their child about the donor conception. On the other hand, patients need to be able to make well-informed decisions. Through counselling, intended parents considering use of donor material should be made aware of the possible benefits (and risks) of (non-)disclosure so that a conscious choice towards (non-)disclosure can be made. Evidence-based counselling is necessary, as well as psycho-education on child well-being, psychological adjustment of children after disclosure of donor conception and parental adjustment and management after transition to parenthood with use of donor conception. It can help patients to increase their confidence in open communication within the family and later to offspring.

Counselling intended parents in need of donor gametes is very challenging; patients are seen at a moment in their lives where having and raising children is hypothetical, since there is no pregnancy or previous child. This makes estimating how prospective parents will cope with their donor-conceived offspring very difficult, and it is impossible to predict how offspring will manage the topic of their donor conception if and when they are told.

Counselling is considered a practice that requires professional qualification and therefore fertility clinics need to invest in well-trained mental health professionals to guarantee appropriate evidence-based counselling, provision of psycho-education, assessment and/or screening of patients for treatment. Most important during counselling is guiding decision-making about use of donor gametes and the patients' (non-)disclosure practices in the future. Initiation of a family-building process and creating awareness of the continuous and long-term character of this concept are key. With counselling, preparation for the construction of narratives on donor conception and of the third party involved can start and awareness can be created that the child will be an active co-constructor of these narratives on their conception.

Use of donor material is a major life-event to be managed across an entire life-time for the parents and the child in the context of an environment that is focused on genetic kinship and physical resemblance, often leading to (un)intentional confrontations with the use of donor material. For those opting for secrecy, awareness needs to be created that hiding the truth about donor conception will lead to actively lying to the child and, in the end, inventing stories about conception. Exploring the 'good' reasons for secrecy and offering support in dealing with living with a secret may be helpful. In a non-directive counselling approach, fear of stigmatisation or rejection of the child by the extended family or community (e.g. when religion does not allow this treatment)

74 B. Strauss and J. Boivin, 'Fundamental issues in counselling: Counselling within infertility' in *ESHRE Monographs: Guidelines for Counselling in Infertility*, Oxford University Press, 2002, 4–6.

is seen as a justification for non-disclosure, believing that parents will handle the issue in the best interest of the child.[75]

For many users of donor gametes the subject is for the first time addressed more in detail and put into a broader light when applying for treatment at a fertility clinic. If a fertility clinic does not offer this counselling as standard, patients may rush thoughtlessly and with emotional unease into parenthood with the use of donor gametes. Possibly, counselling may also lack uniformity across the Belgian centres. Furthermore, once patients achieve pregnancy, they leave the fertility clinic and further follow-up is not normally offered, while it is clear that managing this topic is a lifelong task for parents and children.

Also donors are being under-prioritised. Their anonymity is under pressure especially due to the rise of direct-to-consumer genetic testing, the growing public curiosity and ability to trace ancestries and relatives.[76] Existing donors might be concerned about the tenability of their anonymity, a concern that might also discourage potential donors. Classically in Belgium there is a shortage of semen donors. Perhaps by creating more openness and awareness on donor conception among the wider public, by addressing the legal implications of donation and offering reassurance on future offspring's intentions and expectations towards the donor, potential donors' willingness to donate might be positively influenced. Also, existing donors could benefit from more extensive counselling and information provision on these topics: a responsible role that might be taken up by the fertility centres.

Donor conception has a longstanding impact for all parties involved: parents, children and donors. Fertility clinics have the responsibility to provide not only counselling prior to and during treatment but also after treatment. Uniformity across the Belgian fertility centres in counselling from the perspective of the 'reasonable welfare of the future child' principle[77] seems indispensable, and co-operation by the fertility centres with professional networks should be encouraged to ensure families and donors have access to additional support and long-term follow-up.

---

75 I. Raes, A. Ravelingien and G. Pennings, 'Donor conception disclosure: directive or non-directive counselling?', 13(3) *Journal of Bioethical Inquiry*, 2015, 369–379.

76 J.C. Harper, D. Kennett and D. Reisel, 'The end of donor anonymity: how genetic testing is likely to drive anonymous gamete donation out of business', 31(6) *Human Reproduction*, 2016, 1135–1140. https://doi.org/10.1093/humrep/dew065.

77 G. Pennings, 'Measuring the welfare of the child: in search of the appropriate evaluation principle', 14(5) *Human Reproduction*, 1999, 1146–1150.

THE DUTCH ACT ON DATA OF DONORS IN ARTIFICIAL INSEMINATION IN REVIEW

Lessons for the Future

Jozef Dorscheidt*

1. INTRODUCTION

On 29 May 2019, the Dutch Minister of Health Care presented the results of the second review[1] of the (Dutch) Act on Donor Data in Artificial Insemination

* This chapter originates from the author's online presentation at the RETHINKIN_Expert Seminar 'The Right to Identity and Access to Information on Genetic Origin and Parentage' on 16 April 2021, Leuven, Belgium, and relates in part to J.H.H.M. Dorscheidt and M.H. Wissink, 'De Wet donorgegevens kunstmatige bevruchting in kinderrechtelijk perspectief: bevindingen naar aanleiding van de tweede wetsevaluatie', *Tijdschrift voor Familie- en Jeugdrecht* 2020/6, 154–164.

1 N.O.M. Woestenburg, B.J.M. Frederiks, J.H.H.M. Dorscheidt, T. Floor, C.E. Bloemhoff and H.B. Winter, *Tweede evaluatie Wet donorgegevens kunstmatige bevruchting*, Den Haag, ZonMW, April 2019.

(*Wet donorgegevens kunstmatige bevruchting* – WDKB) to the Dutch Parliament.[2] This review, performed by a multidisciplinary research team of the Universities of Groningen and Amsterdam, aimed at obtaining a clear view on the WDKB's efficiency, side effects and general application. Apart from several positive developments, the evaluation regrettably showed various shortcomings in the registration and provision of donor information, the guidance given to donor-conceived children, donors and intended parents after such information was shared, as well as deficiencies in specific education, for instance on the proper time to inform a child about its parental origin. Furthermore, the performance of the Foundation on Donor Information relating to Artificial Insemination (the Foundation), responsible for the adequate implementation of the WDKB, gave rise to serious concerns about achieving the Act's objectives, especially with regard to safeguarding the (donor) child's right to information about its biological descent.[3]

In contrast to the first evaluation of the WDKB in 2012, the WDKB's second review examined separately to what extent current WDKB-practice could be considered 'children's rights-proof'. A realistic view on this was believed to be imperative, because the working of the WDKB would be tested when the first donor-conceived children, born under the WDKB and reaching age 16, would start (as of Spring 2021) to request donor-identifying information from the Foundation. In the course of this examination several fundamental legal interests of the donor-conceived child recognised in the UN Convention on the Rights of the Child (CRC)[4] were studied. Subsequently, the performance practice of the WDKB was reviewed against these protected interests. Following this examination, several concerns have emerged. One of them involved the fact that the societal acceptance of donor anonymity in the Netherlands before 1 June 2004 (the day the WDKB entered into force) was fairly problematic, if not in breach of applicable CRC standards.

The goal of this chapter is to present and clarify various considerations and developments that can substantiate this conclusion. After a description of the WDKB's basic content (section 2) and an exposé on the first and second reviews of this Act (section 3), the drafting history and meaning of the child's right to know his genetic origin and parentage under Article 7 paragraph 1 CRC will be discussed (section 4). Then, the question is posed whether the guaranteed anonymity of Dutch donors who donated prior to June 2004 and those who chose anonymity under the WDKB is compatible with Article 7(1) CRC (section 5). Furthermore, developments in Dutch case law and in regulatory

---

2 *Parliamentary Papers II*, 2018-2019, 30486, nr. 23.

3 Woestenburg et al., n. 1 above, pp. 157–176.

4 Netherlands Treaty Series 1990, 46, Netherlands Treaty Series 1990, 170 and Netherlands Treaty Series 1997, 83. Last amended by Netherlands Treaty Series 2002, 233.

adaptations are addressed, followed by an account of recent reports on cases of 'fertility fraud' by unscrupulous practitioners in the Netherlands (section 6). The chapter concludes with some thoughts for the future (section 7).

2. ESSENCE OF THE WDKB

The main objective of the WDKB, effective as of 1 June 2004,[5] is to safeguard the right of the child, who knows or suspects that they originate from donor sperm, donor eggs or a donor embryo, to know the identity of their biological parents.[6] This aim corresponds with Article 7(1) CRC, which recognises a child's right to know its genetic origin. The Netherlands – as of 7 March 1995 a State Party to the CRC[7] – is required, according to Article 4 CRC to undertake all appropriate legal, administrative and otherwise necessary measures to protect and also implement this right.

Article 3(1)(b) WDKB states that a donor-conceived child, from the age of 12, is entitled to request non-identifying donor information from the Foundation. According to Article 2(1)(b) WDKB, this involves information about physical characteristics, education and profession, social background and some personal attributes.[8] The Foundation discloses these data on the donor to the child, after the child's status as a donor-conceived child was proven correct, and the child's (legal) parents are informed about this provision.[9] If the child has not reached the age of 12 the parents, under Article 3(1)(c) WDKB, can themselves request this information about the donor from the Foundation.[10]

Article 3(2) WDKB states that a donor-conceived child, from the age 16, can ask the Foundation to provide donor-identifying information. Such information includes the donor's family name, first name, date of birth, social security number and place of residence. In principle, this information is disclosed only if the donor consents. If the donor does not consent to disclosure, the requested information is not provided. However, this does not mean 'case closed'. A

5 *Bulletin of Acts and Decrees of the Kingdom of the Netherlands* 2002, 240.

6 *Parliamentary Papers II*, 1992-1993, 23207, nr. 3, p. 17.

7 The Dutch Instrument of Ratification was lodged at the Office of the Secretary-General of the United Nations on 6 February 1995. In consequence, the CRC took binding legal effect in the Netherlands as of 7 March 1995; see UN Doc. CRC/C/117/Add.1, p. 5.

8 See further Article 3 *Besluit donorgegevens kunstmatige bevruchting* (Decree on Donor Data on Artificial Fertilisation), https://wetten.overheid.nl/BWBR0015455/2004-01-01.

9 In this regard, the donor-conceived child is informed about the messages provided to the parents. From the moment the donor child is born, the parents themselves can request information as well; see Article 3(6) WDKB.

10 A donor-conceived child's general practitioner is also allowed – see Article 3(1)(a) WDKB – to request donor information from the Foundation, yet only if it concerns medical information relevant for the child's healthy development; see Article 2(1) WDKB and Article 2 Decree on Donor Data on Artificial Fertilisation.

16-year-old donor-conceived child's request can be rejected only if the donor has substantial interests, which then justifies the Foundation's refusal to comply with the child's request. When assessing a donor's appeal to such substantial interests, it is imperative – according to the second sentence of Article 3(2) WDKB – that the Foundation considers the possible implications for the child of withholding these identifying data from them.

All this does not apply to donor-conceived children born out of sperm donated before the WDKB entered into force. In this situation, the donor is allowed, under Article 12(2) WDKB, to issue a written declaration stating that his identifying information will not be handed over to an applicant child or his/her parents. Moreover, according to Article 12(3) WDKB, these personal data concerning a donor who has not issued such a written statement, may still not be provided without his consent.[11] With regard to the provision of medical information and of non-identifying donor information, Article 12(4) WDKB makes no distinction between disclosures before and after the WDKB came into effect.

Article 4 WDKB emphasises the Foundation's central role in all this. Statutorily, the Foundation is entrusted with the preservation[12] and management of donor information and of data on women who have undergone artificial fertilisation.[13] Furthermore, the Foundation, as mentioned above, deals with the provision of information in accordance with the WDKB. Practical matters regarding the provision of information to the Foundation or to third parties are included in the Foundation's Rules of Procedure, in order to clarify the responsibilities of those who perform artificial insemination.[14] Moreover, and in view of the second sentence in Article 3(2) WDKB, the Foundation is required to establish the procedure and the applicable criteria for the assessment of a donor's 'substantial interests' in non-disclosure. Finally, the Foundation counts as an 'independent administrative body' under Article 4(3) WDKB, so that it needs to apply a special procedure to deal with notices of objection and with complaints, and it must produce an annual report.[15] It goes without saying that the Health Care Inspectorate (Article 10 WDKB) as

---

11 In the upcoming adaptation of the WDKB, further nuances in this regard are proposed in a new Article 12a. For now, it remains to be seen to what extend these in the end will reverse the current spirit of Article 12(3) WDKB. See *Parliamentary Papers II*, 2021-2022, 35870, nr. 7 (Amending Letter of 19 May 2022).

12 According to Article 8 WDKB for as long as 80 years.

13 This involves data which in line with Article 2(1) WDKB are gathered by 'natural persons or corporate bodies who / which performed or made to perform artificial insemination.'

14 See the Foundation's Rules of Procedure, previously adopted in *Government Gazette* 2005, 21 (p. 79), revised in *Government Gazette* 2011, 14290. See https://wetten.overheid.nl/BWBR0033072/2021-05-07.

15 This is mandatory as of 1 January 2014. See Decree of 13 December 2013, *Bulletin of Acts and Decrees* 2013, 450; *Bulletin of Acts and Decrees* 2013, 564.

well as the Minister of Health Care (Article 20 Independent Administrative Bodies Framework Act)[16] have special duties in supervising the Foundation's operations.

3. FINDINGS OF THE SECOND WDKB REVIEW

Up to now, the WDKB has been evaluated twice. In essence, both evaluation studies aimed to examine the Act's practical effects and the extent to which it had realised its goals.

The core findings of the first WDKB evaluation reflected that many fertility clinics at the time – partly due to difficulties with the digital registration system, and in part because of a lack of knowledge[17] – rather reluctantly complied with their legal duties under Article 12(1) WDKB, which urges them to provide all their data on donors, including donor information from the period before the WDKB entered into force. Furthermore, several clinics kept no records of donations which occurred before June 2004.[18] Moreover, the Health Care Inspectorate did little to enforce the WDKB.[19] In addition, the evaluation revealed various problems and shortcomings with regard to the Foundation's performance of its duties.[20]

The results of the WDKB's second evaluation provided a mixed impression.[21] Since 2012, clinics have implemented several improvements, particularly with regard to the registration of donor information. This has resulted in more

16 Act of 2 November 2006, concerning regulations on independent administrative bodies, *Bulletin of Acts and Decrees* 2006, 587.

17 For instance, the statutory term 'donor' appeared to be unclear. As a consequence, some clinics interpreted this term too narrowly and found that it merely referred to the sperm donor in general and, therefore, did not include an 'own' donor (i.e. a family member or a friend) arranged by the prospective parents. This viewpoint, however, is contrary to the WDKB. See H.B. Winter, W.J. Dondorp, M.C. Ploem, N.O.M. Woestenburg, C.P.M. Akerboom, J. Legemaate and G.M.W.R. De Wert, *Evaluatie Embryowet en Wet donorgegevens kunstmatige bevruchting*, Den Haag, ZonMW, September 2012, p. 12 and pp. 246–247.

18 Some clinics believed that disclosing information was not required when it concerned data on anonymous donations, because the Foundation was not allowed to hand over this information anyway. Sometimes, clinics did not even proceed to register such information. In line with this, the evaluators concluded 'From the fact that the clinics involved were not mentioned in the Foundation's annual report, it may be deduced that these registrations did not occur.' See Winter et al., n. 17 above, pp. 125–126.

19 Winter et al., n. 17 above, pp. 12, 127, 248.

20 Winter et al., n. 17 above, pp. 243–257; M.C. Ploem and W.J. Dondorp, 'Wet donorgegevens kunstmatige bevruchting: van geslotenheid naar openheid', *Tijdschrift voor Gezondheidsrecht* 2013/5, 434–448.

21 An overview of the results is offered by H.B. Winter, N.O.M. Woestenburg, J.H.H.M. Dorscheidt and B.J.M. Frederiks, 'De Wet donorgegevens kunstmatige bevruchting geëvalueerd; nog steeds veel dorre grond', *Tijdschrift voor Gezondheidsrecht* 2020/1, 15–18.

registrations through the KIDS-registration system and more knowledge in clinics about the duty to register than before.[22] Yet, in relation to administration and the disclosure of donor information by the Foundation, various concerns remained. Several of these touch upon the fundamental legal interests of the child. The evaluation, for instance, has shown that clinics did not register non-identifying data concerning donors who signed a confidentiality statement as mentioned in Article 12(2) WDKB. In 2004, the Foundation – assumedly for practical reasons, but still in violation of Article 12(1) WDKB – allowed clinics to store such statements themselves and to refrain from handing over any related information to the Foundation. Consequently, the Foundation had no overview of who had issued such a statement. Furthermore, donors who donated before June 2004 were still permitted to sign a confidentiality statement, even though under Article 12(2) WDKB this was no longer permitted beyond this date. It is striking in this regard that in December 2018[23] the Dutch Minster of Health Care uncritically tolerated this practice and failed to put an end to it. Moreover, some clinics appeared to have allowed donors who, prior to June 2004, were registered as identifiable and therefore known donors (B-donors), to revise their earlier choice and to modify it to being an anonymous donor (A-donor).

Rather worrisome was the second evaluation's revelation that many of the bottlenecks and problems already signalled in 2012 had still not been tackled. For instance, the registrations of donors remained incomplete, since relevant information on donors involved in so-called 'home insemination' or in treatments abroad was not recorded, social security numbers and information on Danish donors were not documented until 2014, and the Foundation did not verify donor information upon receipt, but merely when interested persons requested a disclosure of such information. Other deficiencies in the work of the Foundation, previously noticed in 2012, were still unabatedly topical in 2019. As the second evaluation showed, the Foundation – despite being an independent administrative body – also neglected for several years to produce an annual report. This practice may explain why a number of problems relating to the Foundation's functioning remained hidden from public sight for quite some time. Besides, the lack of adequate responses from supervisory authorities, such as the Ministry of Health Care and the Health Care Inspectorate,[24] enabled the

---

22 Nevertheless, up to 2018, various clinics performed inseminations using an 'own' donor, without passing on the required registration to the Foundation. In addition, two hospitals were still unaware of the statutory obligation to register when prospective parents brought an 'own' donor for treatment. See Woestenburg et al., n. 1 above, pp. 8, 106 and 158.

23 This is apparent from letter 1455944-184934-PG of 19 December 2018 to Radboud UMC Nijmegen. See Annex of Agentschap CIBG of 15 October 2018, 2–3.

24 During the second WDKB evaluation, the Health Care Inspectorate reported that it did not supervise the Foundation. Instead, the Inspectorate closely monitored the clinics. The Ministry of Health Care largely failed to organise supervising duties concerning the Foundation.

Foundation to keep managing its duties without correction.[25] Another concern involved the fact that the Foundation had not yet issued details of the special procedure to assess a donor's 'substantial interests' in non-disclosure.[26] This caused ongoing uncertainty about the review process to be used, as well as the applicable standards of assessment. Without a clear proactive mission statement of the Foundation, the WDKB's future viability, according to the evaluators, would not be guaranteed. In its subsequent response to the recommendation[27] to further reflect on the apparent functioning of the Foundation, the Minister of Health Care announced that changes would be made in the Foundation's package of tasks and privileges.[28]

4. THE CHILD'S RIGHT TO KNOW ITS GENETIC ORIGIN AND PARENTAGE

4.1. THE CONTENT OF ARTICLE 7(1) CRC

As mentioned above, a separate objective of the second evaluation of the WDBK was to study to what extent current WDKB practice complies with binding international children's rights law. While it is a basic right of every human person to know their biological origin, with respect to children, the right to have access to this knowledge is, as mentioned, protected under Article 7(1) CRC. This provision's first paragraph states that every child shall be registered immediately after birth and shall have the right from birth to a name, the right to acquire a nationality and, as far as possible, the right to know and be cared

---

25 Coinciding with the government's viewpoint on the second WDKB evaluation, three missing annual reports were made available by the Foundation at the end of 2019.

26 As early as 2012, it was signalled (Winter et al., n. 17 above, p. 248) that Article 8(3) of the Foundation's Rules of Procedure did not comply with Article 3(2) WDKB. In 2019, this issue was not resolved, as the WDKB's second evaluation showed. See. Woestenburg et al., n. 1 above, p. 157 ff. Contrary to what the Rules of Procedure imply, a submitted request should not be dealt with by 'balancing interests' – as the Strasbourg case law on Article 8 ECHR seems to suggest. The Foundation's only concern must be to determine whether a donor has substantial interests which justify refraining from disclosing identifying information to the applicant. With regard to situations which reflect an equal balance of interests, the second sentence of Article 3(2) WDKB clarifies that a donor-conceived child's interest in being informed prevails.

27 Woestenburg et al., n. 1 above, p. 176.

28 These involve the Foundation's supervisory duties regarding the maximum number of children a donor is allowed to produce; the possibilities to put half-siblings in contact with each other if so desired; the provision for this special procedure to assess a donor's 'substantial interests'; the reorganisation of the Foundation's Board of Governors; and the Foundation's communication with clinics about donors who suffer from a genetic condition. See 'Reactie op de tweede evaluatie Wdkb', Letter 1576646-194828-PG of 26 September 2019 to Dutch Parliament, *Parliamentary Papers II*, 2019-2020, 30486, nr. 24, p. 2.

for by its parents.[29] The paragraph's last sentence refers to a child's right to knowledge about (the identity of) their parents and to be cared for by them (as far as possible).[30] Both privileges relate to the fundamental task of parents[31] to protect and improve the well-being and healthy development of their children. By enshrining the child's right to information about their parents, the drafters of the CRC intended[32] to define guarantees for a child's psychological stability; a circumstance as important as a child's physical and mental growth and the balanced development of their personality.[33]

In order to establish whether the working of the WDKB complies with the requirements of Article 7(1) CRC, knowledge of the genesis, nature and scope of the child's informational right covered by the CRC provision is crucial. A glance at the provision's drafting history shows that, due to national regulations on the right to 'secret adoptions', several national delegations at the time noted that an absolute right to know one's parents may not always be applicable.[34] This consideration led to the inclusion of the phrase 'as far as possible' in a new text proposal.[35] Later, however, this adaptation gave rise to doubts, because the phrase might evoke arbitrary interpretations of the provision.[36] After that, various proposals for further text changes were rejected.[37] Eventually, the current text of Article 7(1) CRC was presented and subsequently adopted.[38] This shows that, in the end, the wording 'as far as possible' was tacitly included in the CRC provision.[39]

---

29 Article 7(2) CRC addresses the States Parties' obligation to ensure the implementation of the rights mentioned in paragraph 1, and to do so in accordance with their national law and their obligations under the relevant international instruments in this field, in particular where the child would otherwise be stateless.

30 I. Ziemele, 'Article 7 – The Right to Birth Registration, Name and Nationality, and the Right to Know and to Be Cared for by Parents', in A. Alen, J. Vande Lanotte, E. Verhellen, F. Ang, E. Berghmans and M. Verheyde (eds.), *A Commentary on the United Nations Convention on the Rights of the Child*, Leiden/Boston, Martinus Nijhoff Publishers, 2007, p. 26.

31 Remarkably, the CRC does not define who counts as 'parents'. See S. Detrick, *A Commentary on the United Nations Convention on the Rights of the Child*, Den Haag, Martinus Nijhoff Publishers/Kluwer Law International, 1999, pp. 169–179. In relation to donor-conceived children this may lead to questions about the scope of this wording, but this could sufficiently be answered under applicable Dutch inheritance law. See Woestenburg et al., n. 1 above, pp. 45–47. In relation to the right of an adopted child (under Article 7(1) CRC) to know its own parents, the CRC Committee usually refers to this child's biological parents.

32 UN Doc. E/CN.4/1989/WG.1/WP.4. See also Office of the UNHCR, *Legislative History of the Convention on the Rights of the Child*, Vol. 1, United Nations, New York and Geneva, 2007, pp. 377–380.

33 UN Doc. E/CN.4/1989/48, para. 94.

34 UN Doc. E/CN.4/1989/48, para. 96.

35 UN Doc. E/CN.4/1989/WG.1/WP.26; UN Doc E/CN.4/1989/48, para. 104.

36 UN Doc. E/CN.4/1989/48, para. 107.

37 UN Doc. E/CN.4/1989/48, paras. 108–111.

38 UN Doc. E/CN.4/1989/48, paras. 112 and 114.

39 S. Detrick, *The United Nations Convention on the Rights of the Child. A Guide to the 'Travaux Préparatoires'*, Dordrecht, Martinus Nijhoff Publishers, 1992, pp. 128–131.

Nevertheless, the definitive wording provides no clue as to which acquisition of knowledge concerning a child's personal history of descent should be 'possible' and which impossibilities count as inevitable or reasonably justifiable in this regard. Besides this, the wording does not clarify whether it merely refers to factual circumstances that might impede the tracing of descent information[40] or to situations involving a justifiable interest of third parties as well. Certain practical barriers – such as the absence of a data collecting system containing descent information – can be dealt with through laws and regulations, and thus may be resolved by implementing appropriate measures. Actions which enforce the operation of such systems may therefore be considered 'possible' for CRC State Parties. However, if descent information cannot be traced or is simply unavailable, it is hardly 'possible' to ensure a child's right to information about his/her biological origin. Then, at the most, the question remains whether a State Party has played an imputable part in the non-existence of this possibility.[41]

With regard to whether measures are 'possible' even when the disclosure of descent information to a donor-conceived child touches upon legal interests of third parties, the Dutch Supreme Court ruled in 1994 that the child's right to information about its parentage is not absolute and that the protection of this right must sometimes be subordinated to substantial rights or freedoms of others.[42] The phrase 'as far as possible' in Article 7(1) CRC actually confirms this viewpoint, and makes it all the more plausible that the drafters of the CRC provision intended to emphasise this premise when they adopted the phrase concerned. This impression is supported by the fact that several States Parties to the CRC believe that the very same phrase permits the imposition of domestic statutory restrictions on the child's exercise of its right to knowledge of origins.[43] This, however, leads one to wonder about which legal consequences

---

40 For instance, with regard to children who are anonymously abandoned, it may be difficult to trace their parents' identity. The same applies in situations where parents are nowhere to be found.

41 It follows from Article 4 CRC that the Dutch government, as a State Party to the CRC, is not free to choose whether to fulfil its duty to undertake all appropriate measures for the implementation of the rights recognised in the CRC. See UN Doc. CRC/C/GC/19, para. 18. To undertake 'possible' measures in view of Article 7(1) CRC, for instance, cannot be postponed beyond a reasonable period. Furthermore, measures taken must comply with the demand of 'effectiveness' and bear proof of their effect on the realisation of the right involved. See UN Doc. CRC/C/GC/19, para. 24.

42 Dutch Supreme Court 15 April 1994, *NJ* 1994, 608 (*Valkenhorst I*), annotated (in Dutch) by W.C.E. Hammerstein-Schoonderwoerd. See in particular legal consideration 3.3.

43 See, for instance, the interpretative statement of the Czech Republic as well as the reservations of Luxembourg and Poland regarding Article 7(1) CRC. Later, the Polish reservation was withdrawn. See Woestenburg et al., n. 1 above, pp. 35–37. The Netherlands expressed no objections to the earlier interpretation of Article 7(1) CRC by Poland, which stipulated 'that the right of an adopted child to know its natural parents shall be subject to the limitations imposed by binding legal arrangements that enable adoptive parents to maintain the confidentiality of the child's origin'. See UN Doc. CRC/C/2/Rev. 8 (7 December 1999), p. 35.

of such legislative restrictions are still in conformity with the CRC. In the view of this author, at least, it is clear that national legislation which creates too far-reaching obstacles to securing the child's right is at odds with Article 7(1) CRC, maybe even with the nature and purpose of the CRC.[44] So, whether or not such restrictions are permissible not only depends on their foundation in national laws and regulations, but also on their compliance with international human rights law.[45] In essence,[46] therefore, the wording 'as far as possible' in Article 7(1) CRC limits the freedom of States Parties to impose restrictions on a child's right to information about their biological origin.

While the Netherlands have been legally bound by this limitation since 7 March 1995 – the day the Dutch ratification of the CRC took effect – the question is to what extent the Netherlands in the nine years prior to the WDKB respected the child's right to information about their origin 'as far as possible'. Specifically, one might ask, in view of the nature and purpose of the CRC, which interpretation of Article 7(1) CRC served as the basis for the Dutch lenience towards donor anonymity current before June 2004?[47]

4.2. DONOR ANONYMITY UNDER THE WDKB AND ITS COMPATIBILITY WITH ARTICLE 7(1) CRC

In the WDKB, the donor-conceived child's legal interest in knowledge about their biological origin is put first.[48] Still, some uncertainty remains with regard to this prioritisation. For instance, does this ranking suggest that balancing this children's rights interest against other interests, such as the interest of the

---

44 At an earlier point in time, the CRC Committee was concerned about British legislation reflecting such a far-reaching obstacle, and called upon the United Kingdom, with reference to Articles 3 and 7 CRC, to undertake appropriate action so as to enable children, regardless of their circumstances of birth, as much as possible to acquire information on the identities of their parents. See UN Doc. CRC/C/15/Add.188 (9 October 2002), paras. 31–32.

45 See also G. Van Bueren, *The International Law on the Rights of the Child*, Dordrecht-Boston-London, Martinus Nijhoff Publishers, 1995, pp. 120–127.

46 J. Tobin and F. Seow, 'Article 7. The Rights to Birth Registration, a Name, Nationality, and to Know and Be Cared for by Parents', in J. Tobin (ed.), *The UN Convention on the Rights of the Child. A Commentary*, Oxford-New York: Oxford University Press, 2019, pp. 241–242 and pp. 261–266.

47 During the CRC ratification process, the Dutch government observed with reference to the phrase 'as far as possible' in Article 7(1) CRC: 'The child's right to know his or her parents and to be care for by them bears the limitation "as far as possible". With regard to our laws and regulations this has significance only in case a child's parents are totally unknown (foundling) or when it may be preferred that a child has no access to descent information (i.e. AID*). As regards the accessibility of descent information, definitive decision-making will take place by the end of 1991, in view of expected results of recently initiated inquiries. (*Parliamentary Papers II*, 1990-1991, 21800 VI, nr. 40).' [* See n. 50 below.].

48 *Parliamentary Papers I* 2000-2001, 23207, 201b, p. 2.

donor in anonymity, will not be considered, even under specific circumstances? And if balancing should occur in a given situation, would this undermine the prioritisation mentioned?

During the genesis of the WDKB it was noted that the personal right of a child to know their origins is not absolute, and that this right can be opposed to the privacy rights of the donor or the future mother (and the legal father). Apart from which of these rights has precedence in given circumstances, other societal interests and consequences may supersede this 'vital interest' of the donor child. These involve:[49]

- the societal interest in preventing a decrease of donors, due to the growing awareness that donor-identifying information in particular circumstances can come out anyway;
- the risk of reduced openness of parents towards their child concerning its conception through AID;[50]
- a possible increase in the incidence of inseminations without involvement of a semen bank;
- the possible by-passing of the WDKB by future parents when making use of donations from abroad.

If a donor withholds consent to the disclosure of identifying information, according to the Ministers involved at the time, the donor's interest in non-disclosure must be weighed against the donor-conceived child's interest in obtaining these donor-identifying data. Yet, the outcome of this balancing may be difficult to predict, because much depends on case-specific circumstances. Therefore, it was believed that the future procedure under Article 3(2) WDKB (the procedure to assess a donor's substantial interest in non-disclosure) would safeguard an accountable assessment procedure.[51] Eventually, the passing of the WDKB[52] emphasises that in the Netherlands, as of June 2004, the donor-conceived child's legal interest in knowing their history of descent takes precedence over the donor's interest in maintaining anonymity,[53] whereas

49 *Parliamentary Papers II*, 1997-1998, 23207, nr. 9, pp. 3–4.

50 Artificial Insemination with semen of a Donor.

51 *Parliamentary Papers II*, 1997-1998, 23207, nr. 9, pp. 3-4. See also the remarks concerning Article 8(3) of the Foundation's Rules of Procedure in n. 26.

52 A 1999 study showed that the introduction of legislation which would permit the disclosure of identifying information against a donor's will would bear the risk of a further decline in the number of (available) donors. This gave rise to the question to what extent the introduction of an enforced waiver of donor anonymity would be acceptable in broad society. Nevertheless, the related part of the then forthcoming Act, eventually, was not deleted, because the Ministers involved considered the donor-conceived child's right to descent information to be a greater good. See *Parliamentary Papers II*, 1997-1998, 23207, nr. 13, pp. 1–4.

53 *Parliamentary Papers I*, 2000-2001, 23207, 201b, p. 2.

Article 3(2) WDKB leaves room for another prioritisation if there is evidence of substantial interests of a donor.

But note: the above comments related only to the situation after the WDKB became effective; that is to say, only to conception with donor material after June 2004. Cases of donor-conceived children born as a result of semen donations before that date were not covered by the new Act. For such cases, nothing changed, at least as far as sharing donor-identifying information was concerned, according to the WDKB's transitional regime codified in Articles 12(2) and 12(3). Whereas Article 12(2) WDKB states that a donor, until June 2004, could issue a declaration to the Foundation on their preference for maintaining anonymity, Article 12(3) WDKB provides that without such a declaration, requested donor-identifying information is only to be revealed to an applicant if the donor agrees to this being done. According to the legislative history of the WDKB, any possible weighing of interests in this context was not required.[54]

On the one hand, the WDKB's transitional regime provides legal certainty, as it indicates the last point in time when anonymity as part of the donation agreement between the donor and a fertility clinic is statutorily safeguarded. On the other hand, during the WDKB's parliamentary genesis hardly any attention was paid to how this transitional regime would relate to, let alone be compatible with, Article 7(1) CRC. The willingness to uphold donor anonymity until June 2004 was probably motivated by apparently unsolvable problems going hand in hand with a too generous respect for a donor-conceived child's entitlement to origin information. In addition, societal considerations concerned with not too rigorously weaken the protection of a donor's privacy may have been deemed relevant. But either way, eventually, in codifying this transitional WDKB regime the Dutch legislator had considerable appreciation for the semen donor's interest in maintaining anonymity, and preferred not to subordinate this to the donor-conceived child's fundamental interest in knowing the identity of their biological parents. Still, this statutory policy is problematical, since it implies that both the written declaration under Article 12(2) WDKB and the space for non-approval by the donor under Article 12(3) WDKB, reflecting a legitimate impediment to a donor child's entitlement to information, were of no relevance for the anonymity of donors operating in the Netherlands before June 2004. At issue is whether or not the Dutch legislator was sufficiently aware of this constellation when Article 12(2) and Article 12(3) WDKB were introduced.

---

54 *Parliamentary Papers II*, 1992-1993, 23207, nr. 3, pp. 13–14; *Parliamentary Papers II*, 1997-1998, 23207, nr. 10, p. 2; *Parliamentary Papers II*, 1999-2000, 23207, nr. 14, p. 8; *Parliamentary Papers I*, 2000-2001, 23207, nr. 201b, p. 8.

In adopting the WDKB, the Netherlands created a certain 'cut-off' point in time. This 'cut-off' marks the moment from which a donor child's claim to information about origin has legal weight. However, unavoidable as such a 'cut-off' may seem, with regard to the Netherlands and seen from the context of children's rights, this author believes this 'cut-off' should not fall on 1 June 2004, the day the WDKB entered into force, but instead on 7 March 1995, the day the Netherlands became legally bound to implement the CRC.[55] Legally, this means that donor children conceived with donated semen (or eggs) before 1 June 2004 were not merely entitled to recognition by the Dutch state of their right under Article 7(1) CRC as of June 2004, but 'as far as possible' from a far back as 7 March 1995.[56] Yet, practice shows that these children actually enjoy their right to descent information only if their donor was a B-donor (a known donor), whereas donor children conceived with sperm from an A-donor (anonymous donor) who donated prior to the WDKB but after 7 March 1995, are likely to remain deprived of donor-identifying information, even though no assessment of this donor's 'substantial interests' in withholding this information has occurred. This situation causes a legal disparity between donor-conceived children born out of a donation made before June 2004 and those conceived from a donation made after that date. From a children's rights perspective, as of 7 March 1995, this inequality is important and evident indeed by the different standards by which a donor-conceived child's treaty-based claim to information on parental origin is now being assessed. Consequently, it shows that donor-conceived children born out of an anonymous donation before June 2004 will rarely receive such information, due to the then prevalent anonymity guarantee and not because the donor demonstrated any 'substantial interests' in non-disclosure. The question to be resolved, therefore, is to what extent the WDKB legislator, when creating this legal effect, adequately took the meaning of Article 7(1) CRC into account.

5. CASE LAW SINCE THE SECOND WDKB REVIEW

Now, what does this mean for a donor-conceived child born from a donation before 2004, who requests a clinic – be it directly or through the Foundation – to disclose available donor-identifying information? Recently, such requests were debated in two court cases, which will be addressed below. In the literature,

---

55 See n. 7.

56 Obviously, a State Party to the CRC must be granted a reasonable period of time in which to adopt effective legislation or otherwise suitable measures. See Dutch Supreme Court 10 October 2014, ECLI:NL:HR:2014:2928, *NJ* 2015, 12 annotated by E.A. Alkema; Dutch Supreme Court 27 September 2019, ECLI:NL:HR:2019:1449, *NJ* 2019, 377 (both cases concerned the prohibition on smoking). Yet, this period of time is limited. See n. 41.

an argumentative framework with regard to this debate was presented[57] and, in effect, this framework appears to have guided the requesting parties as well as the courts. The bottom-line of this framework is, as was signalled in the second evaluation of the WDKB, that before 2004 fertility care institutions upheld strict anonymity[58] for their semen donors, due to a standard confidentiality clause in the donation agreement[59] between the clinic and the donor.

In 2021 the District Court Gelderland[60] dismissed a donor-conceived child's request to reveal the identity of the anonymous sperm donor, her genetic father. In 1997, the child's mother entered into an insemination agreement with a hospital, knowing that the donor – registered as 'K34' – involved in the insemination procedure was a B-donor (a known donor), and who, therefore, was willing to disclose his identity to their future child. In 2017, this child asks the hospital to share the donor-identifying information with her, yet the hospital regrets to report that, in the meantime, this former B-donor has reconsidered and decided to withdraw his earlier willingness to provide identifying information to the child, and hence to remain anonymous. The donor justifies his change of heart by referring to Article 12(3) WDKB. Ultimately, the donor child's request is refused by the hospital. In court, the mother and the donor child claim that the hospital, in doing so, has acted contrary to the earlier insemination agreement and should be ordered to reveal the requested information about K34. Additionally, mother and child seek compensation for damages. The District Court considers itself to be unable to weigh the donor's interests, because he is unknown to the Court and not a party in this legal conflict. The District Court rules that the hospital cannot be held accountable for the donor's choice to reconsider his earlier viewpoint. The Court expresses understanding of the donor-conceived child's request, but holds that action by the legislator is required to provide for an opportunity for the Court to weigh

---

57 J.H.H.M. Dorscheidt and M.H. Wissink, 'De Wet donorgegevens kunstmatige bevruchting in kinderrechtelijk perspectief: bevindingen naar aanleiding van de tweede wetsevaluatie', *Tijdschrift voor Familie- en Jeugdrecht* 2020/6, pp. 154–164.

58 See also *Parliamentary Papers II* 1992-1993, 23207, nr. 3, p. 6. Similarly, G. van Overbeeke, '*In-Vitro-Fertilisatie.* De introductie van reageerbuisbevruchting in Nederland', (diss.), Amsterdam, VU-Huisdrukkerij, 1992, p. 191, who refers to an earlier Dutch Health Council's advice (*Advies inzake Kunstmatige Voorplanting*,' s-Gravenhage, 1986) in which it was considered 'desirable' to uphold donor anonymity.

59 This agreement counts as an agreement covered by the Medical Treatment Agreement Act of 1995 in Book 7 of the Dutch Civil Code. Under this statutory Act, such an agreement includes a care provider's obligation to observe medical confidentiality. If the legal relation between a clinic and a donor was not contractual but rather non-contractual, this would not alter the legal outcome of the analysis here. In that case, the clinic would have to account for its choice to uphold the donor's anonymity and how doing so legally relates to 'due diligence' standards applicable in the legal relationship between the clinic and the donor child.

60 District Court Gelderland 24 March 2021, ECLI:NL:RBGEL:2021:1388, *JA* 2021/79, *GJ* 2021/65 annotated by M.A. Fijnheer, M.A., *JPF* 2021/90 annotated by P. Vlaardingerbroek, *JIN* 2021/81 annotated by G.M.B.R. Niellissen.

both persons' interests rather than to allow a donor's choice for anonymity under Article 12(3) WDKB to be decisive in all circumstances.[61]

This ruling was quite different from the outcome in a second case, shortly after the Gelderland decision. In this case,[62] the Foundation as well as a fertility clinic had not complied with requests to disclose identifying information about 'donor 605'. At the time of his donation – which occurred before 2004 – this donor had assured the clinic that he was willing to share this information with future mothers and their children who might be born out of his donation. Yet, when some of these children at age 16 (joined by their mothers) requested that information, it became clear that after 2004 – and thus contrary to the WDKB – donor 605 had been permitted to reconsider his earlier choice and to opt for anonymity. The Foundation regretted that this had happened, but claimed not to be a party to this conflict and therefore to be unable to comply with the requests. The clinic argued it was legally bound by the changed viewpoint and, with reference to Article 12(3) WDKB, had no choice but to respect donor 605's altered preference. The District Court' s-Gravenhage, however, found these standpoints to be unlawful and asserted that a refusal to disclose donor-identifying information is only justifiable under the WDKB if the donor, prior to June 2004, declared they did not consent to such a disclosure, or if substantial interests on his part after that date would prevent such disclosure. Yet, no clear evidence was presented that either of these conditions was met. Hence, the Court found that applying Article 12(3) WDKB would lead to withholding the requested information from the donor-conceived child, which would constitute an inadmissible violation of the applicants' right to information about the identity of donor 605, as recognised under Article 7(1) CRC and Article 8(1) ECHR. Therefore, the court decided not to apply this provision. Furthermore, the Court ruled that the Foundation was obliged to review the requests in line with Article 3(2) WDKB, to establish whether donor 605 had substantial interests in maintaining his anonymity. In addition, the clinic, which was in possession of the requested identifying information, was ordered to contact donor 605 to grant him the opportunity to present relevant facts and circumstances, thus to enable the Foundation in view of Article 3(2) WDKB to examine whether these amounted to substantial interests which

---

61 While the donor-conceived child in the District Court Gelderland case disagreed with the Court's conclusion and therefore filed an appeal, K34 wised up and decided not to oppose disclosure of his identity any longer. Meanwhile, K34 and the donor-conceived child have met. See 'Na jarenlange juridische strijd ontmoet Maria (23) donorvader die anoniem wilde blijven', *NOS Nieuws*, 1 February 2022, https://nos.nl/artikel/2415303-na-jarenlange-juridische-strijd-ontmoet-maria-23-donorvader-die-anoniem-wilde-blijven; and 'Maria weet eindelijk wie haar donorvader is: "Een geweldige opluchting"', https://www.gld.nl/nieuws/7550727/maria-weet-eindelijk-wie-haar-donorvader-is-een-geweldige-opluchting.

62 District Court' s-Gravenhage 2 June 2021, ECLI:NL:RBDHA:2021:5461, *GJ* 2021/81, *JPF* 2021/93 annotated by P. Vlaardingerbroek.

can justify non-disclosure. The Foundation was then able to examine donor 605's reasoning. Subsequently, the Foundation decided to share the requested identifying information with the applicant children.[63]

Recently, the Dutch Supreme Court ruled on whether a possible biological parent can be obliged to undergo a DNA test in order to verify suspected biological fatherhood. In this particular case,[64] the Supreme Court held that the man involved, who was unwilling to undergo a DNA test, could be forced to do so. According to the Supreme Court, the child's fundamental right to know his genetic parents outweighs the possible father's interests in confidentiality and in refusing to cooperate with DNA testing. At the outset of the case, the District Court Amsterdam, ruling as the court of first instance, in essence for reasons of proportionality, had come to a similar conclusion. Yet, the Court of Appeal ruled that there could be an exception to the rule that knowing one's parental origin prevails over a possible biological parent's privacy interest. This Court believed that such an exception was present in this case, since there was no evident need for the applicant – born in 1968 – to know this genetic origin in view of possible hereditary illnesses. Besides, he had no intention to seek contact with the possible father, while there was a possibility that the health and wellbeing of the possible biological father would be compromised if he were forced to cooperate. The Supreme Court, however, dismissed the Court of Appeal's reasoning and considered that the circumstances mentioned to be insufficient deviated from the line that a child's interest in knowing his father, even if it takes a DNA test to confirm this, outweighs a possible parent's interest in preventing this from being established. Of special significance to the Supreme Court was the fact that the child's interest in information about parentage is widely believed to be essential to the development of a person's identity and personality. Eventually, the Supreme Court referred the case to the Court of Appeal in The Hague for further review and conclusion.

6. FURTHER DEVELOPMENTS

6.1. AMENDMENTS TO THE WDKB

In June 2021, the Dutch Government presented plans to Parliament for several adjustments of the WDKB.[65] According to the Explanatory Memorandum,[66]

---

63 The author is grateful to Tim Bueters (https://www.rex-advocaten.nl/advocaten/tim-bueters/) who represented the applicants in this case, for sharing this outcome.

64 Dutch Supreme Court 11 March 2022, ECLI:NL:HR:2022:349, *JIN* 2022/82 annotated by E.A.C. van Dijk, *NJ* 2022/169 annotated by S.F.M. Wortmann.

65 *Parliamentary Papers II*, 2020-2021, 35870, nr. 2.

66 *Parliamentary Papers II*, 2020-2021, 35870, nr. 3, pp. 1-2.

these adjustments include the creation of an advisory committee,[67] in order to support the Foundation[68] in its assessment of the substantial interests of donors who are not willing to share their identity with a donor-conceived child. Furthermore, it covers the cancellation of a fertility care provider's duty to register medical data of donors with the Foundation, and the codification of a legal basis for the Foundation to share information on donors' genetic disorders with other fertility care providers if they, too, have used semen of this donor. As a follow-up to the aforementioned decisions by the District Courts Gelderland and The Hague in 2021, in May 2022 a Letter of Amendment summarised further refinements.[69] This Letter adds a special regime for donor children who are born from B-donors who donated before June 2004, in order to align the position of these B-donors with that of B-donors who donated after 2004. This means that B-donors' identifying information will be shared, unless they can demonstrate substantial interests which justify non-disclosure. It also means that a donor who previously chose to be a B-donor can no longer become an A-donor. If a request to the Foundation to disclose donor-identifying information – as reported by the clinic involved – concerns an A-donor, and there is no clear evidence to assume that this donor might be open to reconsidering his viewpoint, then disclosure seems beyond what is achievable. Furthermore, the Letter mentions that the amended WDKB scheme will cover an arrangement involving substituted consent in case a donor has passed away. As a result, a donor who donated before 2004 will be able to appoint a particular person who, after his death, can give consent for disclosure of donor-identifying information on the donor's behalf, since, currently, no such information is provided when such a donor has died. Other refinements relate to central supervision of the maximum number of procreations per donor allowed in Dutch fertility clinics and to the Foundation's future registration of certain specified genetic disorders of a donor. While medical details on such disorders will remain at the fertility clinic, a donor-conceived child may request the Foundation to share information if its donor would appear to suffer from a genetic disorder.

In May 2023, Dutch Parliament (House of Commons) voted on several motions concerning the planned amendments to the WDKB.[70] Some of these were adopted, among which a motion urging the Dutch government to issue guidelines at European level to monitor the maximum number of donor-conceived children fathered by donors,[71] and the exchange of identifying

[67] Meanwhile, this committee is operational. See https://www.donorgegevens.nl/over-donorgegevens/bestuur-en-adviescommissie.

[68] Under the amended WDKB the Foundation will be renamed 'College on Donor Information relating to Artificial Insemination'.

[69] *Parliamentary Papers II*, 2021-2022, 35870, nr. 7.

[70] *Parliamentary Proceedings II*, 9 May 2023, TK 78-9-1.

[71] See in this regard a ruling by the District Court The Hague of 28 April 2023, ECLI:NL:RBDHA:2023:6047, *GJ* 2023/85. The Court ordered a sperm donor to refrain from

personal data.[72] Despite all these developments, it seems as if there is no hurry to process and implement these amendments to the WDKB. After all, the WDKB's second review was published back in April 2019. Unfortunately, further delay has followed from the collapse of the Dutch coalition government in July 2023 and the formation of a new government after the elections in November 2023. Taking all this into consideration, one would hope greater efforts are made to manage these amendments with appropriate urgency, especially since a new issue in Dutch fertility care requires attention.

6.2. CASES OF 'FERTILITY FRAUD' IN THE NETHERLANDS

In recent years, another phenomenon has gained public attention in the Netherlands. This phenomenon involves the practice of fertility fraud by several reproductive physicians. At first, this seemed just the bizarre conduct of a medical loner, who clearly lost his sense of decency and professionalism to give an evidently weird interpretation of aiding women who strongly wished for a child, by using his own sperm for inseminations without these women's consent. Yet, in the course of 2021 new such cases have come to light, and these raise serious concerns, not only among women who underwent artificial insemination in the early days of fertility care, but among donor-conceived children as well. The latter are now confronted not just with the lingering fact of not knowing their donor's identity, but also with the idea of possibly being the offspring of semen their mother would not have wanted to be inseminated with, if she had known of this semen's origin.[73]

---

further donations to new prospective parents, as he – according to his own calculations – had fathered some 550 to 600 donor-conceived children. The Dutch Donor Child Foundation issued a complaint about this practice, which eventually was upheld.

72 *Parliamentary Papers II*, 2022-2023, 35870, nr. 25.

73 On 1 July 2022, another case was made public. Investigative searches show that this is the 10th Dutch case, whereas six of these have now been addressed in the Dutch media. In this recent case, gynaecologist Henk Ruis appears to have inseminated clients using his own sperm between 1988 and 1992, thus producing at least three donor-conceived children. See 'Brabantse gynaecoloog verwekte kinderen bij vrouwen die hij behandelde', *De Volkskrant*, 1 July 2022, https://www.omroepbrabant.nl/nieuws/4111157/brabantse-gynaecoloog-verwekte-kinderen-bij-vrouwen-die-hij-behandelde. Other Dutch cases, quite recently revealed, involved gynaecologists Jan Wildschut (produced some 47 donor-conceived children), Jos Beek (some 22 donor children) and Henk Nagel (at least one child). Wildschut, as well as Karbaat, have also used their sperm in circumstances were the women involved were assured they would be inseminated with their partner's semen. Regarding Wildschut, see D.D.M. Braat et al., *Van kinderwens naar kind van de rekening* (Report of an independent investigative commission on the fertility practices of gynaecologist Wildschut in Sophia Hospital Zwolle in the period 1980–1994) Zwolle, Netherlands, 3 November 2021.

These reports bring to mind the notorious case involving Dutch general practitioner Jan Karbaat in Barendrecht, who in the mid-'80s used his own sperm to fertilise woman who visited him for artificial insemination. The women involved were unaware of this. In 2004, the WDKB urged fertility practitioners to carefully register donor data. In 2009, Karbaat's practice was shut down due to serious deficiencies apparent in his registration records. Then, offspring of Karbaat's inseminations learned about the possibility that the physician's semen might have led to their mother's pregnancy. A donor-conceived child approached Karbaat in 2011. During their meeting he admitted to sometimes having used his own sperm. Later, Karbaat was requested to voluntarily provide DNA to establish possible parentages, but he refused. In 2017, Karbaat died. Shortly after that, groups of donor-conceived children filed for a court order to collect Karbaat's DNA, only to learn that his widow refused to cooperate. Ultimately, the District Courts permitted these applicants to collect this DNA and to use it for this particular purpose. Subsequent tests confirmed that Karbaat, according to latest reports, has produced some 90 children using his own sperm.[74]

In other countries (in the USA some 44 cases,[75] in Germany at least three cases,[76] some in Belgium[77]) similar practices of fertility fraud have occurred and become public. All things considered, it seems as if these cases are merely scratching the surface of a once not uncommon practice in reproductive medicine. It may be asserted that these cases not only reflect an evident disrespect for women's reproductive autonomy, but also show that it becomes even more complex for donor-conceived children (wanting) to find out about their genetic origin.

7. FINAL REMARKS

The aim of this chapter was to address and discuss the problematic content as well as the worrisome workings of the WDKB shown by the second review of the Act. This review, in particular, has revealed serious deficiencies in the registration

74 See District Court Rotterdam 2 June 2017, ECLI:NL:RBROT:2017:4250, *GJ* 2017/99, annotated by R.A.C. Hoksbergen; District Court Rotterdam 13 February 2019, ECLI:NL:RBROT:2019:1050, *GJ* 2019/91 annotated by J.C.J. Dute; Court of Appeal The Hague 24 November 2020, ECLI:NL:GHDHA:2020:2185 (dismissed appeal by Karbaat's widow). In 2021, a majority of these children were denied claims for compensation (emotional and financial), because of expiry of the limitation period. See District Court Rotterdam 17 February 2021, ECLI:NL:RBROT:2021:1380, *GJ* 2021/41.

75 For further reading, see J. Lyneé Madeira, 'Understanding illicit insemination and fertility fraud, from patient experience to legal reform', 39(1) *Columbia Journal of Gender and Law* 2020, pp. 110–204. See https://doi.org/10.7916/cjgl.v39i1.4559.

76 See https://www.spenderkinder.de/zeit-dossier-die-macht-der-gene/.

77 See https://donorkind.eu/west-vlaamse-arts-bevruchtte-vrouwen-mogelijk-met-eigen-sperma-hij-beloofde-donor-maar-stond-zelf-te-masturberen/.

and disclosure of donor data on artificial insemination, some still ongoing in fertility clinics, others almost persistent, especially within public bodies (the Foundation, the Health Care Inspectorate, the Ministry of Health Care) who bear responsibility for the WDKB's proper implementation. The examination as to whether current WDKB practice would be 'children's rights-proof' was initially believed to be no more than a formality and merely a favour towards the evaluators to equip the review with a reflective assessment. However, the findings concerning the compatibility of this practice – 'as far as possible' – with the child's fundamental right to information about its parental origins, raised unexpected concerns. Apart from that, the serious indications that the WDKB's transitional regime codified in Articles 12(2) and 12(3) would in fact be invalid under Article 7(1) CRC – as has in the meantime been affirmed by Dutch case law – have even pointed at less than careful deliberation by the legislator while drafting the WDKB. In a way, all this indicates that it is still a long path to the realisation of a truly appropriate legal position of the donor-conceived child, at least under Dutch law. Besides, some new grave issues seem to be ahead, as the revelation of (previous) fertility fraud practices in the Netherlands may show. Nevertheless, recent initiatives in the area of information,[78] policy and legislation create high hopes for the better protection of the identity and personality-development interests of donor-conceived children in the future.

---

[78] For instance, as of March 2021, the National Information Center Donor Conception (LIDC – www.donorconceptie.nl) has been established. The Center aims to provide accountable information, narratives, and references to relevant organisations and specialised care providers for all those involved in donor conception.

THE FIOM KID-DNA DATABASE

A Decade of Experience in Facilitating Contact between Donor-Conceived People and Donors

Astrid INDEKEU and A. Janneke B.M. MAAS

1. INTRODUCTION

Insemination with donor sperm is 'the oldest technique in the new technologies of reproduction'.[1] It was first successfully practised in 1884.[2] Since WWII the number of donor insemination treatments has slowly increased. At its onset donor insemination was met with hostility and not socially accepted. As a result,

---

1 E. HAIMES and K. DANIELS, 'International social sciences perspectives on donor insemination' in K. DANIELS and E. HAIMES (eds.), *Donor insemination. International social sciences perspectives*, Cambridge University Press, Cambridge 1998, pp. 1, 6.

2 A.T. GREGOIRE and R.C. MAYER, 'The impregnators', 16(1) *Fertility & Sterility* 1965, 130–134.

non-disclosure and donor anonymity were the primary organising principles of the practice and it remained hidden from public view.[3] Linked with these principles were particular representations regarding those involved that co-constructed the practice of donor insemination. For example, donor-conceived people were represented as purely the end-product of a donor insemination treatment, a successful outcome of a medical procedure.[4] Policy-makers and practitioners talked *about* the donor-conceived children and it was decided for them that it was in their best interest not to know about their donor-conceived status. During the 1970s and the years following, laws were passed in some jurisdictions to ensure legal certainty regarding the status of the donor-conceived child. And in the '80s – after the birth of Louise Brown, the first IVF baby – discussions were raised about if and how assisted reproductive technologies should be regulated. These debates included whether or not donor-conceived people should have access to donor information.[5] Meanwhile, donor-conceived children had grown into adults and gained a voice of their own, expressing their needs and interests.[6] And societal views on the role of genes in identity development, the meaning of genes in relationships, and the importance for donor-conceived people of gaining access to genetic and biographical data were re-evaluated.

The first laws worldwide regarding access to identifying information were passed in the '80s and '90s. The majority of laws on accessing donor identity information, however, were only passed in the early 2000s.[7] Over the years a growing number of countries have recognised donor-conceived people's right to such information by abolishing donor anonymity and facilitating access to this information.[8] In the last five years alone, four additional countries have made

---

3 S. Bateman Novaes, 'The medical management of donor insemination' in K. Daniels and E. Haimes (eds.), *Donor insemination. International social sciences perspectives*, Cambridge University Press, Cambridge 1998, pp. 105–130.

4 E. Haimes, 'The making of the "DI child": changing representations of people conceived through donor insemination' in K. Daniels and E. Haimes (eds.), *Donor insemination. International social sciences perspectives*, Cambridge University Press, Cambridge 1998, pp. 53–75.

5 S. Allan, *Donor conception and the search for information. From secrecy and anonymity to openness*, Routledge, New York 2018, p. 22.

6 S. Bateman Novaes, 'The making of "the DI child": changing representations of people conceived through donor insemination' in K. Daniels and E. Haimes (eds.), *Donor insemination. International social sciences perspectives*, Cambridge University Press, Cambridge 1998, pp. 53–75.

7 S. Allan, above n. 5, pp. 23, 24.

8 E. Blyth and L. Frith, 'Donor-conceived people's access to genetic and biographical history: an analysis of provisions in different jurisdictions permitting disclosure of donor identity', 23(2) *International Journal of Law, Policy Family* 2009, 174–191; For an overview until 2015 see S. Allan, above n. 5, pp. 79, 80; E. Blyth and L. Frith, 'Access to genetic and biographical history in donor conception: an analysis of recent trend and future possibilities' in K. Horsey (ed.), *Revisiting the regulation of Human Fertilisation and Embryology*, Routledge, New York 2015, pp. 136–152.

such changes: Portugal (2018), Germany (2018), Ireland (2020) and France (2021). Even when all these jurisdictions facilitate access to donor information, it should be noted that this is often arranged in different ways (for example, how and where the information should be requested, variation in required length of retention of the data, etc.). Except for the Australian state of Victoria, which introduced retrospective access to information about the donor, all of these laws are prospective, allowing only those conceived after the legal change to access donor information.[9]

For donor-conceived people who were conceived prior to these legal changes, several voluntary-contact services have been developed in the last two decades that facilitate contact between people who are genetically related through donor conception.[10] Some of these services are publicly funded by central governments or states and are independent of treatment centres, such as for example the Voluntary Registers in Victoria State, Australia (established in 2001), the Donor Conceived Register (DCR) in the United Kingdom (established in 2004) or the Fiom KID-DNA database in the Netherlands (established in 2010). In other cases, services are provided through fertility treatment or gamete bank services (e.g. The Sperm Bank of California was the first to offer open-identity donors in 1982), provided privately by independent practitioners or through offspring-led and/or recipient parent-led initiatives (e.g. the US-based Donor Sibling Registry, established in 2000). Each has different possibilities and limitations that impact the likelihood of success.[11] Most of these voluntary-contact services rely on written records (for example, the state-funded Central Register at the Victorian Assisted Reproductive Treatment Authority (VARTA) established in 1988, and VARTA's Voluntary Register, established in 2001). But for those donor-conceived people who have no or incorrect written records, the only way to search for genetic relatives as a result of donor conception is via registers that rely on DNA tests. Worldwide, only three registers use DNA tests to enable contact between donor-conceived people and donors. The first, UK DonorLink (UKDL), was established in the United Kingdom in 2004 and then transferred to the DCR in 2013;[12] a second, the Dutch Fiom KID-DNA database, was launched

---

9 E. Decorte, *Recht op kennis van afstammingsinformatie bij medisch begeleide voortplanting*, die Keure, Brugge 2022, p. 630; with the limitation that such a law is only 'relevant' for those who know; see below in section 4.1.

10 M. Crawshaw, K. Daniels, D. Adams, K. Bourne, J.A.P. van Hooff, W. Kramer, L. Pasch and P. Thorn, 'Emerging models for facilitating contact between people genetically related through donor conception: a preliminary analysis and discussion', 1(2) *Reproductive Biomedine & Society Online* 2015, 71–80.

11 For full descriptions see M. Crawshaw, K. Daniels, D. Adams, K. Bourne, J.A.P. van Hooff, W. Kramer, L. Pasch and P. Thorn, above n. 10; J. Millbank, 'Identity disclosure and information sharing in donor conception regimes: the unfulfilled potential of voluntary registers', 28 *International Journal of Law, Policy & Family* 2014, 223–256.

12 E. Blyth and L. Frith, above n. 8.

in 2010.[13] A third state-funded service that relies on a DNA database was recently established in Belgium in April 2021 (Vlaams Afstammingscentrum (Flemish Ancestry Centre); www.afstammingscentrum.be).

Besides specific societal and legal changes directly applying to donor conception, general technological developments in society also impacted the field of donor conception, such as the widespread integration of and access to the internet, social media, and the development of 'direct-to-consumer-genetic-testing' (DTCGT).[14] DNA databases such as the DCR and the Fiom KID-DNA database were set up more than a decade ago specifically to enable contact between donor-relatives. Today they exist in an era of exponential growth of DTCGT testing, available through companies such as MyHeritage, Ancestry, 23andMe, and FamilyTreeDNA.[15] While these DTCGT companies are set up with different purposes (to find ancestry and health information), they are also used by donor-conceived people to search for donors and/or donor-relatives.[16] This has resulted in success, but also in unforeseen consequences such as the accidental discovery of being donor-conceived.[17] So the practices of state-funded registers and DTC DNA databases intertwine. While both types of databases rely on DNA testing, there are considerable differences in the technology used and support offered.[18] Moreover, DTCGT companies introduce a commercialisation aspect into the field of donor conception and consequently change the position of donor-conceived people (and parents) from a rather passive one (waiting until the age limit is reached to request information, or waiting for a link in a state-funded DNA database) to an active one (choosing when to start searching, actively

[13] A. Indekeu, C.F.M. Prinsen and A.J.B.M. Maas, 'Lessons from 10 years' experience running the Fiom KID-DNA database, a voluntary DNA-linking register for donor-conceived people and donors in the Netherlands', *Human Fertility* 2022, doi/full/10.1080/14647273.2022.2144772.

[14] J.T. Woodward, 'Third-party reproduction in the internet age: the new patient-centered landscape', 104(3) *Fertility & Sterility* 2015, 525–530; A.M. Braverman, 'How the internet is reshaping assisted reproduction: from donor offspring registries to Direct-to-Consumer Genetic testing', 11(2) *Minnesota Journal of Law, Science & Technology* 2010, 477–496.

[15] A. Regalado, '2017 was the year consumer DNA testing blew up: More people took genetic ancestry tests last year than in all previous years combined', *MIT Technology Review*, 12 February 2018, https://www.technologyreview.com/s/610233/2017-was-theyear-consumer-dna-testing-blew-up/.

[16] See e.g. the research project ConnecteDNA https://sites.manchester.ac.uk/connecte-d-n-a/ which investigates how donors, parents through donor conception and donor-conceived people experience online DNA testing as well as how the laws and information management systems interact with the use of DTCGT to access information about donor conception.

[17] J.C. Harper, D. Kennett and D. Reisel, 'The end of donor anonymity: how genetic testing is likely to drive anonymous gamete donation out of business', 31(6) *Human Reproduction* 2016, 1135–1140; M. Crawshaw, 'Direct-to-consumer DNA testing: the fallout for individuals and their families unexpectedly learning of their donor conception origins', 21(4) *HumanFertility* 2018, 225–228.

[18] D. Adams and C. Lorbach, 'Accessing donor conception information in Australia: A call for retrospective access', 19(4) *Journal of Law & Medicine* 2012, 707–721.

'unravelling' the ancestry-tree), with consequences for the legal framework of donor conception (e.g. donor anonymity can no longer be guaranteed).[19]

This chapter reports on what has been learned from running the Fiom KID-DNA database – a DNA database for donor-conceived people and donors in the Netherlands – for more than 10 years. The chapter will discuss the database's registrants, the links identified within the database and the contact experiences between donor-conceived people and donors, as well as the questions that arise from this knowledge. Fiom is a Dutch organisation, established in 1930, that provides amongst other things independent information and support to adoptees and donor-conceived people who are searching for their birth and biographical origins. The DNA database of Fiom is unique in the sense that is characterised by stability and continuity. It is the only donor conception DNA database that has been under unchanged management (Fiom), in collaboration with the same genetic laboratory (the Canisius-Wilhelmina Hospital, Nijmegen) and stable funding for more than 10 years. This creates a unique dataset.[20]

2. DONOR CONCEPTION IN THE NETHERLANDS

Donor conception has been practised in the Netherlands since 1948, but until the 1970s few doctors were willing to treat couples via donor insemination.[21] From 1970 onwards, donor insemination as a path to parenthood became more accepted due to societal changes (legalisation of abortion leading to fewer children available for adoption, attitude changes, the right to self-determination, more acceptance of social parenthood). As donor conception was shrouded in secrecy, no exact data are available on the number of people conceived by donor conception in the Netherlands prior to the introduction of the Artificial Insemination Donor Data Law (*Wet donorgegevens kunstmatige bevruchting*) in 2004. It is estimated that 700 children have been born annually through sperm donation since the end of the 1970s.[22] In other words, it is estimated that between 1948 and 2004, 40,000 children were born through sperm donation. In those

---

19 J.C. Harper, D. Kennett and D. Reisel, above n. 17; P. Borry, O. Rusu and H.C. Howard, 'Anonymity of sperm donors under threat', 496 *Nature* 2013, 169.

20 In contrast, UK DonorLink (UKDL) was established in the United Kingdom in 2004 and in 2013 the service transferred to the Donor Conceived Register (DCR) under different management and with different data-processing. The previously collected data at UKDL were not transferred to DCR.

21 J. Kremer and H.J.J. Leenen, 'De anonimiteit van de donor bij kunstmatige inseminatie met donorsperma in historisch perspectief', 135(33) *Nederlands Tijdschrift voor Geneeskunde*, 1991, 1476–1478.

22 P.M.W. Janssens, G.A. Dunselman, A.H.M. Simons and M.D. Kloosterman, 'Wet Donorgegevens Kunstmatige bevruchting: inhoud en gevolgen', 149 *Nederlands Tijdschrift voor Geneeskunde* 2005, 1412–1416.

days parents were advised by professionals not to talk to others, including their child, about donor conception, as it was believed there was no need to inform the child.[23] Research shows that the majority of Dutch parents via donor conception followed this advice and did not disclose the donor conception to their child.[24] Consequently, most donor-conceived children who grew up in this era did not know about their donor-conceived status. But by 1996, research showed some change: while most parents still did not disclose the donor conception to their child, more did disclose it to others (family, friends), thereby increasing the risk that their child might find out about the donor conception from others.[25] At this time, donors were anonymous. Consequently, donor-conceived people born during this era have no access to information about their own ancestry. Donors themselves were also not expected to have an interest in the outcome of their donation.[26] Sperm donation was medically constructed as a transaction with a clear beginning and end: donors were given money for their sperm. For this reason, donors prior to 2004 were not informed about the number of offspring conceived through their donation(s).[27] From 1992 to 2019, a national Dutch guideline recommended 25 as the maximum permitted number of offspring per donor.[28] But until today no central register exists, making it impossible to check whether the guideline is followed. In 2023 preparations for a register are being made.

In the 1990s things started to change and debates began about whether donor-conceived people should have access to (non-identifying or identifying) information about the donor. It would take 15 years before the law was changed so that only non-anonymous donation was allowed.[29] Between 1989 and 2004 a dual system was introduced, giving parents a choice between an anonymous donor (A-donor) and a donor who could be traced if the child requested

---

23 L.H. Levie, *Kunstmatige inseminatie bij de mens*, Stafleu, Leiden 1975.

24 S. Golombok, A. Brewaeys, R. Cook, M.T. Giavazzi, D. Guerra, A. Mantivani, E. van Hall, P.G. Crosignani and S. Dexeus, 'The European study of assisted reproduction families: family functioning and child development', 11 *Human Reproduction* 1996, 2324–2331; A. Brewaeys, S. Golombok, N. Naaktgeboren, J.K. de Bruyn and E.V. van Hall, 'Donor insemination: Dutch parents' opinions about confidentiality and donor anonymity and the emotional adjustment of their children', 12 *Human Reproduction* 1997, 1591–1597.

25 D. van Berkel, L. van der Veen, I. Kimmel and E. te Velde, 'Differences in the attitudes of couples whose children were conceived through artificial insemination by donor in 1980 and in 1996', 71 *Fertility & Sterility* 1999, 226–231.

26 K. Daniels, 'The semen providers' in K. Daniels and E. Haimes (eds.), *Donor insemination. International social sciences perspectives*, Cambridge University Press, Cambridge 1998, pp. 76–104.

27 S. Bolt, D. Postema, A. van der Heij and A.J.B.M. Maas, 'Anonymous Dutch sperm donors releasing their identity', 24 *Human Fertility* 2019, 24–30.

28 Centraal Begeleidingsorgaan voor de Intercollegiale Toetsing (CBO). *Advies medisch technische aspekten van kunstmatige donorinseminatie*, CBO, Utrecht 1992.

29 P.M.W. Janssens, G.A. Dunselman, A.H.M. Simons and M.D. Kloosterman, above n. 22.

identifying information about them (B-donor). Thus, donors could opt to donate anonymously or non-anonymously, but most donated anonymously.[30] In addition, advice regarding non-disclosure or disclosure of the donor conception changed: previously non-disclosure had been advised, but in the 1990s parents were advised to exercise their own judgement.[31]

In 2004, the Artificial Insemination Donor Data Law (*Wet donorgegevens kunstmatige bevruchting*) was introduced in the Netherlands, giving people conceived after June 2004 access to identifying information about the donor once they reach the age of 16. Non-identifying information, such as physical and social information, can be accessed from the age of 12.[32] Information about donors whose gametes are used after June 2004 is held in a government-funded national register under the authority of the *Stichting donorgegevens kunstmatige bevruchting* (Sdkb translated as 'The Artificial Insemination Donor Data Foundation'; www.donorgegevens.nl); this register also holds the information of donors who donated non-anonymously prior to 2004. The Dutch law further states that people should be supported by counselling and intermediary services. When a request for information is made, the Sdkb engages Fiom for psycho-social support for those involved. In 2020, a law reform proposal was put forward that would entitle donor-conceived people to access identifying information about same-donor offspring with mutual agreement. The proposal was accepted in 2023. This amended law would apply to all donor-conceived people conceived after June 2004. In 2023, the Dutch Minister of Health, Welfare and Sport proposed a change in the law to release the age limits in the Artificial Insemination Donor Data Law.[33] The expectation is that the change will be enacted into law in the summer of 2024.

People conceived prior to 2004 with an anonymous donor previously had no possibilities to access ancestry information. In 2006, *Stichting Donorkind* (Donor Child Foundation), an organisation of donor-conceived people and donors, started a voluntary register for donor-conceived people and donors, using written records to enable contact between them. In 2007, *Stichting Donorkind* contacted Fiom for guidance on the searches and contacts between donor-conceived people and donors, given Fiom's longstanding experience

---

30 M. Visser, M.H. Mochtar, A.A. De Melker, F. Van Der Veen, S. Repping and T. Gerrits, 'Psychosocial counselling of identifiable sperm donors', 31 *Human Reproduction* 2016, 1066–1074; S. Allan, above n. 5, p. 106.

31 D. van berkel, L. van der Veen, I. Kimmel and E. te Velde, above n. 25.

32 P.M.W. Janssens, A.H.M. Simons, R.J. Van Kooij, E. Blokzijl and G.A.J. Dunselman, 'A new Dutch Law regulating provision of identifying information of donors to offspring: background, content and impact', 21 *Human Reproduction* 2006, 852–856.

33 E. Kuipers, Reactie Onderzoeksrapport 'Zorgvuldigheid in de omgang met leeftijdsgrenzen in de Wet donorgegevens kunstmatige bevruchting', Ministerie van Volksgezondheid, Welzijn en Sport, January 2023. https://open.overheid.nl/documenten/66051e9b-19ce-4e0d-953b-2780d396b397/file.

with ancestry information requests and family reunions in the field of adoption. When *Stichting Donorkind* closed their register in 2007, Fiom started its own register for donor-conceived people and donors, also initially based on written records. In many cases, however, incorrect information and a lack of clinical records made the linking process unreliable, which confirmed the need for DNA tests to determine genetic connectedness, especially for people conceived prior to 2004. In 2010, Fiom launched the KID-DNA database in collaboration with the Canisius-Wilhelmina Hospital in Nijmegen, which oversees the DNA analysis and matching process. In 2018, Fiom closed the written records register.

3. THE FIOM KID-DNA DATABASE

3.1. RUNNING THE FIOM KID-DNA DATABASE[34]

3.1.1. Technology

The Fiom KID-DNA database is a nationwide voluntary register that facilitates the exchange of information and contact between people who are genetically related as a result of anonymous donor-assisted conception through Dutch fertility clinics prior to 2004. Initially, the DNA database was set up to identify genetic links between donors and donor-conceived people using three Short Tandem Repeat (STR) techniques (autosomal, X-chromosomal and Y-chromosomal). The autosomal STR testing is used for forensics and for legal paternity/kinship testing. The STR techniques also have the potential to identify relationships between donor-conceived people of the same sex, but are less suited to identifying donor-conceived half-siblings of the opposite sex. To do this additional DNA samples from close relatives (e.g. mother) are needed. In contrast, commercial DTC DNA databases, not bound to the same legal framework as the Fiom KID-DNA database, use a different technology based on single nucleotide polymorphism (SNP) analysis. This technique appears more powerful for detecting half-siblings, in particular those of the opposite sex, depending on related individuals present in the database. Because half-sibling links could not always be established by the Fiom KID-DNA database due to the technology used, in 2018 Fiom put forth a clear statement that its database mainly focuses on the relationship between donor and donor-conceived people. Donor-conceived people who are looking for siblings are referred to the Fiom

34 For a detailed description of the running of the Fiom KID-DNA database, see: A. Indekeu, C.F.M. Prinsen and A.J.B.M. Maas, above n. 13.

website where information on the various DTC DNA databases is presented so people can make their own choice. The word 'linking' and not 'matches' will be used here when referring to genetic connections between registrants of the DNA database, as 'matches' are associated with 100 per cent certainty while DNA testing always implies a certain probability level.[35]

3.1.2. *Financial Support and Public Awareness*

Fiom's KID-DNA database is funded by the Dutch Ministry of Health, Welfare and Sport. From its inception in 2010, 'working costs', including the wages of the technical and counselling staff, have been covered by government funding. Costs for DNA analysis in the first years were at the expense of donor-conceived people (250 €) and donors (150 €) themselves. The difference in cost is due to the higher number of STR tests used for donor-conceived people versus for donors. In June 2017, the Dutch Minister of Health, Welfare and Sport publicly called upon anonymous donors to 'perform a second good deed' by registering in the Fiom KID-DNA database, pointing out the importance of ancestry information for donor-conceived individuals. In addition, the minister announced that donors' registration costs would be reimbursed by the government, not only from June 2017 onwards but also retroactively. Consequently, donors were given the opportunity to register free of charge with the Fiom KID-DNA database.[36] All of this was part of a public campaign set up by the Ministry in collaboration with interest groups to increase the number of donors registered, making it more likely that donor-conceived people would be able to access their ancestry information. Since December 2018 the registration fees for donor-conceived people have also been (retroactively) reimbursed by the government, so donor-conceived people can also register at no cost. Accordingly, registration of donors and donor-conceived people is currently at no cost.

3.1.3. *Operating Procedures*

We will describe the operating procedures here briefly, as a detailed description is published elsewhere.[37] When people want to search for the donor, or make themselves available for donor-conceived people, they can register online on

---

35 M. Crawshaw, C. Gunter, C. Tidy and F. Atherton, 'Working with previously anonymous gamete donors and donor-conceived adults: recent practice experiences of running the DNA-based voluntary information exchange and contact register, UK DonorLink', 16 *Human Fertility* 2013, 26–30.

36 E. Schippers, *Kamerbrief Actieplan ondersteuning donorkinderen*. Ministerie van Volksgezondheid, Welzijn en Sport 2017, https://www.rijksoverheid.nl/documenten/kamerstukken/2017/07/04/kamerbriefover-actieplan-ondersteuning-donorkinderen.

37 A. Indekeu, C.F.M. Prinsen and A.J.B.M. Maas, above n. 13.

the Fiom website and subsequently receive a saliva swab DNA collection kit at home. They send the saliva sample back to the laboratory at the Canisius-Wilhelmina Hospital, and the identification form, which declares their identity and that their DNA has been collected, is returned to Fiom. Next, DNA is extracted from the sample, and a DNA profile is created in the laboratory and uploaded to the DNA database. A weekly run of the database is performed for linking purposes. It can take up to 14 weeks after the DNA arrives at the laboratory before a genetic link, if present, is reported to Fiom. If a link is made, a Fiom counsellor contacts the individuals involved after receiving the result.

3.1.4. Professional Psychosocial Support

A voluntary DNA-based information exchange and contact service can offer different kinds of services and supports such as professional psychosocial support, intermediary and therapeutic counselling.[38] From the start of the KID-DNA database, professional psychosocial support has been included; this support is optional and free of charge to registrants through funding from the Dutch government. Fiom offers professional psychosocial support for registrants or those considering registration by helping them consider the implications of searching for genetic relatives through donor conception using a DNA test. Fiom also offers intermediary services, such as expectation management, to everyone in the DNA database who has a genetic link identified with one or more other registrants and who wants support during the process of exchanging information and/or making contact. Fiom does not offer therapeutic counselling for those wanting in-depth help with psychological, emotional or relationship issues arising from their involvement in donor conception. Due to limited financial resources, support is focused on the moment a genetic connection is identified between registrants. Support is available for donor-conceived people, donors, as well as their relatives (if needed). Fiom's counsellors are professionally qualified social workers with experience in adoption reunions, as Fiom has a longstanding history in providing information and support to adoptees who are searching for birth and biographical origins. There are differences but also similarities between post-adoption work and donor-linking, and the experience of adoption reunions forms a good foundation for donor-linking.[39]

---

[38] M. Crawshaw, L. Frith, O. van den Akker and E. Blyth, 'Voluntary DNA-based information exchange and contact services following donor conception: an analysis of service users' needs', 35 *New Genetics & Society* 2016, 372–392.

[39] M. Crawshaw and L. Marshall, 'Practice experiences of running UK DonorLink, a voluntary information exchange register for adults related through donor conception', 11 *Human Fertility* 2008, 231–237.

3.2. OUTCOMES OF THE FIOM KID-DNA DATABASE

As of June 2023, a total of 3,754 people were registered in the Fiom KID-DNA database. In comparison, only 581 people were registered in the UK's DCR, of which 341 were in the DCR DNA database in November 2022.[40] This difference in number of registrations may firstly be explained by the support from the Dutch Ministry, not only financially but also by publicly calling on donors to register. Secondly, a nationwide alert as well as Fiom's communication department raised public awareness of donor conception. And thirdly, the continuity of management of the Fiom KID-DNA database has made a positive contribution to the number of registrations. Due to the fact that almost no data on donor-conceived adults conceived prior to 2004 exists in the Netherlands, let alone data on those people who know about their donor-conceived status, it is impossible to know what percentage is interested in finding genetic relatives as a result of donor conception and whether the DNA database also reaches these people. Another way of assessing the DNA database is to see if it fulfils its potential: does it facilitate contact between people who are genetically related through anonymous donor conception?[41] In the past eight years, the database has almost quintupled in size, which has led to an increase in the number of identified genetic links. Comparing data from the first five years (period 1) of the Fiom KID-DNA database with the last eight years (period 2) shows that when more people register the chance increases of finding a genetic connection between a donor-conceived person and a donor. In period 1, only 12 per cent of donor-conceived registrants were connected to a donor profile, while in period 2 this increased to 49 per cent. Similarly, in period 1, 14 per cent of the donors found a genetic connection with one or more donor-conceived persons. This increased to 31 per cent in period 2. This shows that a voluntary DNA database – generally speaking – has the possibility of fulfilling its potential when there are enough registrants. But a voluntary register is limited by its 'passive character': people register and have to passively wait until a link is identified with another registrant.[42] Possibilities to further 'activate' the register are discussed below (section 4.1).

3.2.1. Donors

Of 915 donors on the database, 906 were sperm donors and 9 were oocyte donors. Again, no proportionate take-up rate can be calculated, as numbers of anonymous donors do not exist. What these numbers do show is that past

40 Personal communication with DCR administrator.
41 J. Millbank, above n. 11.
42 J. Millbank, above n. 11.

donors do not necessarily wish to remain anonymous, as was often assumed.[43] Moreover, a survey conducted with the donors in the Fiom KID-DNA database showed that donors were not only moved by child-oriented motivations (e.g. donors believed that their offspring are entitled to their physical and social details and/or they want to give their offspring the chance to contact them) but also by donor-oriented motivations (such as curiosity about the number of offspring, their well-being and the desire to establish contact).[44] Furthermore, research observations at Fiom show that media attention and the removal of financial burdens encourages registration.[45] Between 2010 and 2023 donor conception has received significant publicity in the Netherlands. Political statements and personal stories, both positive and negative, have led to increased public awareness about both the importance of ancestry information for donor-conceived people and the existence of the Fiom KID-DNA database.[46]

As of June 2023, donors' mean age in the Fiom KID-DNA database ($n = 915$) is 68, ranging from 36 to 94 years of age. These numbers show that the donation of semen can have a life-long impact, even when at their time of donation it was seen as a transaction with a clear beginning and end. It was perceived negative (even 'unhealthy') when donors were interested in the outcome of their donation. It was assumed that they would forget about their donation. Research from the Fiom KID-DNA database donors shows that some donors (14.7 per cent) did think about the outcome of their donation from the start, while for others this grew over the years (2.3 per cent), or was triggered by the birth of own children (9 per cent) or by media stories explaining the importance of ancestry information for donor-conceived people.[47] Furthermore, the mean age is around retirement age. There are some findings in which donors

---

43 S. Allan, above n. 5, p. 48, 49; see for example E. Blyth, M. Crawshaw, L. Frith and O. van den Akker, 'Gamete donors' reasons for, and expectations and experiences of, registration with a voluntary donor linking register', 20 *Human Fertility* 2017, 268–278.; S. Bolt, D. Postema, A. van der Heij and A.J.B.M. Maas, above n. 27; M. Kirkman, K. Bourne, J. Fisher, L. Johnson and K. Hammarberg, 'Gamete donors' expectations and experiences of contact with their donor offspring', 29 *Human Reproduction* 2014, 731–738; J.M. Speirs, 'Semen donors' curiosity about donor offspring and the barriers to their knowing', 15 *Human Fertility* 2012, 89–93; M.A. Crawshaw, E.D. Blyth and K.D. Daniels, 'Past semen donors' views about the use of a voluntary contact register', 14 *Reproductive Biomedicine Online* 2007, 411–417; K.R. Daniels, W. Kramer and M.V. Perez-y-Perez, 'Semen donors who are open to contact with their offspring: issues and implications for them and their families', 25 *Reproductive Biomedicine Online* 2012, 670–677.

44 S. Bolt, D. Postema, A. van der Heij and A.J.B.M. Maas, above n. 27.

45 M. Crawshaw, L. Frith, O. van den Akker and E. Blyth, n. 38; S. Bolt, D. Postema, A. van der Heij and A.J.B.M. Maas, above n. 27. Fiom's communication department keeps systematic records of Dutch media reports on donor conception, making it possible to link publicity data to the number of subsequent registrations.

46 S. Bolt, D. Postema, A. van der Heij and A.J.B.M. Maas, above n. 27; A. Indekeu, C.F.M. Prinsen and A.J.B.M. Maas, above n. 13.

47 S. Bolt, D. Postema, A. van der Heij and A.J.B.M. Maas, above n. 27.

address the fact that retirement was a good time to make themselves available for questions and/or contact: in this period in their life they have more free time and energy to meet donor-conceived people. They imagined it would be more challenging when they were professionally active and their own family included young children.[48] Lastly, the mean age of donors in the Fiom KID-DNA database has increased over the years. Some donors are now more than 90 years old, and Fiom has faced situations in which the donor has passed away. Firstly, to preserve information for those donor-conceived offspring who are identified after a donor passes away, or when a physical meeting is not possible anymore, the option of making a video portrait was established.[49] Both information and images of the donor are recorded for donor-conceived offspring who are identified in the future. Secondly, this has also created ethical and privacy concerns (Is a family aware of a donor's past donations? Can donor data be released posthumously without prior consent?). While the law of 2004 explicitly states that the information of donors who donated post-June 2004 should be retained for 80 years, there is no legal guideline regarding the preservation of donor information in a voluntary DNA database. Fiom now asks donors to explicitly state how they want their data to be handled in the event of their death. They can choose to: a) share their information with future genetic connections; b) permit their relatives to decide what should happen; c) allow their DNA to remain in the database but not allow information to be shared; or d) remove their DNA from the database and not allow any information to be shared. In the first two cases, the donor's next of kin will be contacted when a genetic connection is identified.

Eighty-one per cent of the donors who have a genetic connection identified with a registrant are linked to between one and three donor-conceived people, and 19 per cent have a genetic link with four or more donor-conceived people, with a maximum of 84. This maximum clearly exceeds the guideline established between 1992 and 2019 of a maximum of 25 donor-conceived offspring per donor.[50] Note that these numbers include *only* DNA connections identified within the Fiom KID-DNA database, and that additional DNA links via online

48 BADOK II-study: 'Ontmoeting tussen donor en donorkind; wat zijn de behoeftes aan ondersteuning en een ethische beschouwing' (Meeting between donor and donor-conceived person; what are the needs for support and an ethical consideration). ZONMWProjectnumber 854020001, https://www.zonmw.nl/nl/onderzoek-resultaten/kwaliteit-van-zorg/programmas/project-detail/ethiek-en-gezondheid-3/ontmoeting-tussen-donor-en-donorkind-wat-zijn-de-behoeftes-aan-ondersteuning-en-een-ethische-bescho/verslagen/.

49 For more info on the video-portraits, see A. Indekeu, C.F.M. Prinsen and A.J.B.M. Maas, above n. 13. See also the Varta Donor legacy project: https://www.varta.org.au/about/projects/donor-legacy-project.

50 Centraal Begeleidingsorgaan voor de Intercollegiale Toetsing (CBO), above n. 28.

commercial databases may exist. As mentioned earlier, donors prior to 2004 were usually not informed about the number of offspring conceived through their donation.[51] Even though they consciously decided to make themselves available for offspring conceived through their donation, and thought about the implications, they might be confronted with entirely unforeseen outcomes and consequences such as having many more donor-conceived offspring than they expected. Another possible scenario is that donor-conceived offspring might prefer contact amongst their multiple donor-conceived half-siblings over contact with the donor, making the donor, who made the effort to step out of anonymity, feel left out. A first, small study on donors from the Fiom KID-DNA database shows that first contact with offspring conceived through their donation was experienced as very positive, and meetings often impacted them more than expected.[52] They experienced often unexpectedly strong feelings such as surprise about resemblance, happiness, and pride, but also feelings of responsibility and concern. Donors felt that the needs of the donor-conceived offspring should regulate the contact. This might be influenced by societal changes in which the interest of the donor-conceived offspring became guiding principles of changes in the law. But by focusing on the donor-conceived offspring's needs, donors often overlooked their own needs (e.g. mode and pace of contact). Finding the right role as donor towards the donor-conceived offspring without any framework for these new relationships was challenging. And lastly, this study indicated that meetings with donor-conceived offspring did not only influence donors, but often impacted other family members as well.

3.2.2. *Donor-Conceived People*

Of the 2,839 donor-conceived people, 965 (34 per cent) were men and 1,874 (66 per cent) women. As of June 2023, the mean age of donor-conceived people in the Fiom KID-DNA database (n = 2,839) was 33, ranging from 12 to 68 years of age, meaning that most donor-conceived registrants were born at a time when non-disclosure was still the norm. No recorded data is available on the time window between learning about their donor-conceived status and registration (starting to search for genetic relatives as a result of donor-assisted conception), but for some this is shortly after disclosure. This might make the experience of searching even more stressful, as two major life events and emotional processes come together. A literature review showed that several elements influence the decision of donor-conceived people to start searching, such as psychosocial, sociodemographic, relational, and environmental variables. Personal life events

51 S. Bolt, D. Postema, A. van der Heij and A.J.B.M. Maas, above n. 27.
52 BADOK II-study, above n. 48.

such as starting college, leaving home, starting a relationship, and starting a family can also trigger a search.[53] In the Fiom KID-DNA database more female than male donor-conceived people are registered. This sex ratio is similar to that in the field of adoption where more female adoptees than male adoptees tend to search for their biological parents.[54] It is suggested that women may be more emotionally engaged in linking and are the custodians of family knowledge.[55] We have no statistical data on family status of registrants, but the age distribution shows that most registrants are between 24 and 42 – an age when people often start (or have already started) their own family and are more independent from the family they were raised in.

An initial small study asking donor-conceived people from the Fiom KID-DNA database how they experienced contact with the donor shows that the first meeting was stressful but for most it went well. Often donor-conceived people felt relief or other positive emotions, especially in cases where they experienced recognition of traits/physical resemblance. The majority did not expect the donor to have a major ongoing involvement in their life, but they found it important to know who he was.[56] Observations at Fiom show a wide variation in contacts between donor-conceived people and donors: no contact (just wanting a name or information), one-time meeting, or some form of ongoing contact. We observe more ongoing relationships between donor-conceived half-siblings than with the donor.

In formal registers, participants define by default who they seek (for example the donor, or donor-conceived half-siblings).[57] But in informal voluntary registries (or online ancestry services) this cannot be specified upfront. There are cases of donor-conceived people searching for genetic relatives other than the donor as a result of donor-assisted conception, but there are also cases where they have not thought about these other relatives when registering at a DNA database and consequently are suddenly and

---

53 A. Indekeu, A.J.M.B. Maas, E. McCormick, J. Benward and J. Scheib, 'Factors associated with searching for people related through donor conception among donor-conceived people, parents and donors: a systematic review', 2 *Fertility & Sterility Review* 2021, 93–119.

54 D. Howe and J. Feast, *Adoption, search and reunion: the long term experience of adopted adults*, The Children's Society, London 2000.

55 E. Blyth, M. Crawshaw, L. Frith and C. Jones, 'Donor-conceived people's views and experiences of their genetic origins: a critical analysis of the research evidence', 19 *Journal of Law & Medicine* 2012, 769–789; D. Dempsey, F. Kelly, B. Horsfall, K. Hammarberg, K. Bourne and L. Johnson, 'Applications to statutory donor registers in Victoria, Australia: information sought and expectations of contact', 9 *Reproductive Biomedicine & Society Online* 2019, 28–36.

56 BADOK II-study, above n. 48.

57 F. Kelly, D. Dempsey, J. Power, K. Bourne, K. Hammarberg and L. Johnson. 'From stranger to family or something in between: donor linking in an era of retrospective access to anonymous sperm donor records in Victoria, Australia', 33 *International Journal of Law, Policy & Family* 2019, 277–297.

unexpectedly confronted with a link or multiple links.[58] Donor-conceived registrants who share a genetic link with a donor profile form a network of donor-conceived half-siblings.

Table 1. Growth of large (>20) networks of donor-conceived half-siblings in the Fiom KID-DNA database over time

	Year of identification in Fiom KID-DNA database	Network size at time of identification in Fiom KID-DNA database	Network size as of June 2023	Growth of network (%)
D1	2011	7	52	643%
D2	2017	18	84	367%
D3	2017	19	48	153%
D4	2017	12	25	108%
D5	2017	27	59	119%
D6	2017	11	26	136%
D7	2018	22	53	141%
D8	2019	12	23	92%
D9	2020	14	57	307%
D10	2020	26	34	31%
D11	2022	13	42	223%
D12	2013	3	23	667%

Source: Compiled by the authors.

As of June 2023, there were 75 networks in the Fiom KID-DNA database. A network was defined as a group of at least four donor-conceived half-siblings. The largest network consists of 84 donor-conceived half-siblings. These numbers reflect only DNA connections identified using the Fiom KID-DNA database. These authors' personal communications with members from different networks of donor-conceived half-siblings show that the total number of links may be twice as large. Some network sizes increase rapidly (e.g. 223 per cent growth in a year), while others expand over a longer period of time (e.g. 667 per cent growth in 10 years) (see Table 1). We have noticed at Fiom that donor-conceived people may find it challenging to meet multiple donor-conceived half-siblings and to be part of a large network.[59] Specific professional support is often appreciated

[58] A. Indekeu, S.H. Bolt and A.J.B.M. Maas, 'Meeting multiple same-donor offspring: psychosocial challenges', 12 *Human Fertility* 2021, 1–16; A. Indekeu, A.J.M.B. Maas, E. McCormick, J. Benward and J. Scheib, above n. 53.

[59] S.H. Bolt, C. Notermans, A.C. van Brouwershaven, A.J.B.M. Maas and A. Indekeu, 'The ongoing work of kinship among donor half-siblings in The Netherlands', *Biosocieties* 2021, 10.1057/s41292-021-00259-z.

to help manage these multiple new contacts and work through how to give meaning to these new connections.[60] These challenges notwithstanding, establishing relationships between donor half-siblings is often experienced as easier and more beneficial than connecting with a donor.[61] The benefit of donor-conceived half-sibling contacts not only entails identity-relevant information (through shared traits and experiences) but also includes relationships with and support from people who understand the unique experience of being donor-conceived.

3.3. PROFESSIONAL PSYCHOSOCIAL SUPPORT

Most registrants in the Fiom KID-DNA database take up the offer of professional support prior to or during a meeting between donor-conceived person and donor. In the BADOK II study,[62] the majority of the donors ($n = 21$) and donor-conceived-offspring ($n = 23$), all registered in the Fiom KID-DNA database, also positively evaluated the support received. The presence of professional support is perceived as positive and can be an influencing factor when registering with a voluntary register.[63] Both professional counselling (helping to decide whether to register, to prepare for a meeting in case of a link, and to manage expectations and emotions) as well as the intermediary services during the meeting were valued. Counsellors' familiarity and experience with donor conception and more specifically donor-linking was experienced as very positive by those involved (BADOK II study) and is essential to delivering quality support.[64] Knowledge about the history of donor conception (donor anonymity, non-disclosure, no limits to offspring per donor), the implications of past practices, as well as knowledge about genetics and the impact of current DTCGT on donors and donor-conceived people's lives, is essential for all (front desk staff, counsellors, geneticists) active in this field due to the sensitivity of the issues and possible high impact on people's lives.

More than a decade of professional support has also revealed shortcomings and challenges. An inquiry into users' needs, conducted in 2018 at Fiom, revealed that support was not only vital around the moment of an identified

---

60 A. Indekeu, S.H. Bolt and A.J.B.M. Maas, above n. 58.

61 T. Freeman, K. Bourne, V. Jadva and V. Smith, 'Making connections: contact between sperm donor relations' in T. Freeman, S. Graham, F. Ebtehaj and M. Richards (eds.), *Relatedness in assisted reproduction. Families, Origins and Identities*, Cambridge University Press, Cambridge 2014, pp. 270–295; J.E. Scheib, E. McCormick, J. Benward and A. Ruby, 'Finding people like me: contact among young adults who share an open-identity sperm donor', *Human Reproduction Open* 2020/4, https://doi.org/10.1093/hropen/hoaa057.

62 BADOK II-study, above n. 48.

63 M. Crawshaw, L. Frith, O. van den Akker and E. Blyth, above n. 38.

64 M. Crawshaw and L. Marshall, above n. 39.

genetic link but also at other moments during the search process: deciding whether to register at all, deciding whether to register with the Fiom KID-DNA database or a DTC DNA database, discussing implications, seeking practical help with registration, coping with the waiting time, preparing for a possible meeting, managing emotions after a meeting, etc.). As expansion of the counselling team was not possible due to limited financial resources, extensive psycho-educative material was made available online in 2020 (including accessible information, questions readers could ask themselves or discuss with others, stories of experiences and stories of how other registrants coped, etc.) to give people tools to gain more control over their own search process. Also, since 2018, Fiom registrants receive a newsletter four times a year to update them on the number of new registrants, the latest 'matching' run and results, and other developments, as well as to inform them about related (inter)national news and developments in the field.

A remaining existing limitation is the lack of post-meeting support. Donor-linking is more of a process than a one-off experience. A follow-up call is made a few weeks after a meeting between donor-linked people, but defining what these new relationships mean for those involved and integrating these new relationships into their existing network takes time, and issues can arise long after a meeting or over a longer period. In addition, referrals to professional psychosocial care are not possible due to the lack of knowledge about donor conception issues in Dutch general psychosocial healthcare.

A meeting between genetic relatives as a result of donor-assisted conception is not only challenging for those directly involved, but also creates (new) challenges for professionals offering support. It is increasingly recognised that donor-linking is not about two individuals meeting but about the networks that are created and constantly evolving.[65] Therefore, a counsellor in the field of donor-linking will need specific skills such as a systemic approach rather than an individual approach. Moreover, new questions continuously arise in the field. For example, as values regarding openness have changed in society (openness is now encouraged, and possibilities exist to request or search for information about the donor) and the risk of accidentally finding out has increased due to online DNA testing, parents might rethink their past choice of non-disclosure and now desire to inform their adult children about donor conception. But this is often felt to be a daunting process in which parents appreciate professional support. In other cases we have seen multiple donor-conceived half-siblings who are linked and would like to meet each other in a group meeting and would like to have support during this first meeting.[66] Counsellors in the field of

---

65 ESHRE Campus Course (2020), *Moving on from individual connections to networks: new challenges in donor conception*, https://www.focusonreproduction.eu/article/Blogs-Donor-conception.

66 A. Indekeu, S.H. Bolt and A.J.B.M. Maas, above n. 58.

donor-linking need specific skills and knowledge that are distinct from those of fertility counsellors who work with people at the start of a fertility trajectory or donation. Thus, a new specialisation in the area of donor conception seems to have emerged.

4. PAST, PRESENT AND FUTURE

4.1. CHALLENGES FROM THE PAST

In different ways we are nowadays confronted with the consequences of past practice. First, there are the consequences of the practice of donor anonymity. By introducing a new law that merely allows non-anonymous donors to be identified, we are confronted with an imbalance in access to donor information between those who were conceived before and after the new law. As the outcomes of the Fiom KID-DNA database show, a voluntary register has the potential of facilitating contact between genetic relatives as a result of previous anonymous donor-assisted conception. But Millbank points to the unfulfilled potential of voluntary registers due to their 'passive' character and argues for a more active, flexible and responsive system.[67] For example, Millbank discusses the possibility that donor-conceived people could send a request for donor information to a central registry (e.g. the Sdkb) which would then actively approach the anonymous donor and invite them to register consensually. Policy and professional organisations have argued against this as it raises concerns about breaching confidentiality due to the contracts of anonymity in the past.[68] Yet, in a changing world of the exponential successes of DTCGT in which donor anonymity can no longer be guaranteed, it could also be seen as 'taking care' of former donors rather than 'breaching confidentiality' (see below section 4.2). Another consequence related to anonymity/non-anonymity is more specific to the Dutch context. The Artificial Insemination Donor Data Law of 2004 does not distinguish between A (anonymous) or B (identifiable) donors. In preparation for the law of 2004, Dutch fertility clinics had asked their donors from prior to 2004 if they wanted to maintain their initial donor status or change it. As a result, some B-donors from the past changed to being an A-donor. This led to two court cases when, later on, donor-conceived people who had a B-donor at the moment of conception were denied access to the information as the donor had changed his status.[69] The two courts decided differently (respectively

67 J. MILLBANK, above n. 11.

68 J. MILLBANK, above n. 11.

69 Rechtbank Den Haag 2 June 2021, ECLI:NL:RBDHA:2021:5461 and Rechtbank Gelderland 24 March 2021, ECLI:NL:RBGEL:2021:1388.

not granting and granting access to the donor information). A proposal for a legislative amendment was made in 2022 in which the procedure for information requests for donor-conceived people with a B-donor will be equalised with the procedure for donor-conceived people with a donor from 2004 and later.[70]

Another challenge from the past is the consequences of the practice of non-disclosure. As long as donor-conceived people are not informed about their donor-conceived status, they cannot exercise their right to access information about the donor. Along with law reform, an active approach that prioritises, encourages and facilitates openness of parents to their children is necessary (see for example the 'Time to Tell' campaign by VARTA).[71] Similar support should be developed for parents and donors who, in the past, were advised not to disclose, in order to help them learn how to disclose the donor conception or donation to their (now adult) children. This is important not only because it enables parents to reflect on their earlier decision due to changing societal values about openness, but also because, in an era of DTCGT, the risk of accidental and unprepared disclosure increases.[72]

A final challenge from the past is the fact that DNA analysis (be it via a state-funded DNA register such as the Fiom KID-DNA database or via a commercial DTCGT company) not only identifies genetic connections but also reveals (mal) practices of the past. These can include a gynaecologist himself being the donor, clinics not adhering to guidelines that limit the number of donor-conceived offspring per donor, siblings not sharing the same donor despite a clinic's earlier commitment, and using a donor's semen more often and over a longer period of time than agreed. The clinics involved should take responsibility for examining these mistakes of the past even when they were caused by former staff members. It is also the responsibility of the government to prevent such situations by designing control mechanisms to oversee the proper execution of the law or guidelines. Moreover, support should be made available to deal with the emotions associated with these revelations.

4.2. CHALLENGES FROM THE PRESENT

The internet, social media, technological developments in DNA analysis, and commercial DTC DNA companies are strongly reshaping the field of donor

---

70 'Wijziging van de Wet donorgegevens kunstmatige bevruchting in verband met de tweede evaluatie van de wet, het actieplan ter ondersteuning van donorkinderen en de omvorming van de Stichting donorgegevens kunstmatige bevruchting tot publiekrechtelijk zelfstandig bestuursorgaan'. (*Kamerstukken II* 2021/2022, 35870, nr. 7).

71 L. Johnson, K, Bourne and K. Hammarberg, 'Donor conception legalization in Victoria, Australia: The "Time to Tell"-campaign, donor-linking and implications for clinical practice', 19 *Journal of Law & Medicine* 2012, 803–819.

72 M. Crawshaw, above n. 17.

conception.[73] In the past, clinics were the gatekeepers of donor information. But due to the exponential successes of DTCGT, donor anonymity can no longer be guaranteed.[74] In the past, donor-conceived people, parents and donors were rather passive actors in the field of donor conception. DTCGT and the internet give them the possibility to become more active. It is known that donor-conceived people as well as parents use DTCGT to search for donors and/or donor-relatives with success.[75] Clinics could actively inform donors who donated anonymously in the past about the changing context, and consequently possibly prevent them being unprepared and unexpectedly confronted with a contact request via a DCT DNA company. These donors donated at a time when a donation was seen as a transaction with no lifelong consequences, and now their past donation has consequences not only for themselves but also for their families. Clinics could inform past donors about what guided release of information would look like and what support is available to help them in this process; they could also help donors inform their own family about the donation in case they are not yet aware, and let donors know if information about the number of offspring conceived through their donation(s) is available. Not knowing (or knowing) how many donor-conceived people you are connected to can be daunting; this support can help donors to feel in control of an information-release process.[76]

The development of commercial DTCGT companies also has implications for donor-conceived people. While it may lead to successful searches, it can also lead to unforeseen consequences such as accidental discovery of being donor-conceived.[77] Moreover, while the plethora of possibilities within DNA analysis enhances opportunities to search, it can also make the search process more complex. The state-funded and the commercial DTC DNA databases use different technologies that bring about different opportunities and restrictions. Also, regulations with respect to handling privacy rules and the confidence level of DNA analyses differ. But both types of databases rely on DNA testing and refer to 'finding ancestry/relatives'. This often blurs the underlying differences for many users, and sometimes leads to confusion and frustration amongst registrants in the Fiom KID-DNA database as to why outcomes may differ

---

73 J.T. Woodward, above n. 14; A.M. Braverman, above n. 14; research project ConnecteDNA, above n. 16.

74 J.T. Woodward, above n. 14.

75 J.C. Harper, D. Kennett and D. Reisel, above n. 17; M. Crawshaw, above n. 17.

76 For example; The Sperm Bank of California (TSBC) programme, before a donor-conceived offspring makes a request, attempts to contact a donor to inform him that his oldest offspring would soon be age 18 years and be eligible to request his identity, and to provide him (and possible partner) with resources, including for support See J.E. Scheib, A. Ruby and J. Benward, 'Who requests their sperm donor's identity? The first ten years of information releases to adults with open-identity donors', 107 *Fertility & Sterility* 2017, 483–493.

77 M. Crawshaw, above n. 17.

between registries. As noted above, technological differences and the sizes of the databases make a DTC DNA database more suitable for finding donor-conceived half-siblings. Our experience is that people particularly value the professional support of Fiom throughout the process of registering, finding a donor-conceived relative, and contact.

4.3. CHALLENGES FOR THE FUTURE

Until now, studies have focused on the interest of genetic relatives as a result of donor conception in searching for each other, as well as the first contact moments. Initial results already point to the fact that this involves more than a meeting of individuals – it entails the formation of new networks. These networks might grow even bigger in the future when donor-conceived offspring from an international commercial sperm bank donor find each other via DTCGT sites. Moreover, it is not yet known how those involved give meaning to these new relationships and these expanding networks, and how they are integrated into the existing social network. It is also not yet known how society will value or respond to these new relationships. The future will tell us.

As technologies further develop and become more and more integrated into society, it remains to be seen whether the law is still adapted to this new societal context.[78] For example, the internet and DTC DNA commercial companies have made it possible for donor-conceived people and parents (before and after the legal change) to take a more active role. These technologies give them the opportunity to be independent from a governmental register and to start their search at a moment they choose, which might be earlier than set out in the law. In addition, as anonymity can no longer be guaranteed, it is important to evaluate how this should be legally framed.

---

[78] See for example: https://www.progress.org.uk/donor-anonymity/ 'HFEA considers proposing donor anonymity law': The Human Fertilisation and Embryology Authority is considering ways gamete donor anonymity laws could be changed, as the advent of straight-to-consumer genetic testing has 'thrown into question' the assumption of anonymity.

European Family Law Series

1. *Legal Recognition of Same-Sex Couples in Europe*, K. Boele-Woelki and A. Fuchs (eds.)
2. *European Family Law in Action Volume I: Grounds for Divorce*, K. Boele-Woelki, B. Braat and I. Sumner (eds.)
3. *European Family Law in Action Volume II: Maintenance Between Former Spouses*, K. Boele-Woelki, B. Braat and I. Sumner (eds.)
4. *Perspectives for the Unification and Harmonisation of Family Law in Europe*, K. Boele-Woelki (ed.)
5. *Family Law Legislation of the Netherlands*, I. Sumner and H. Warendorf
6. *Indépendance et interdépendance patrimoniales des époux dans le régime matrimonial légal des droits néerlandais, français et suisse*, B. Braat
7. *Principles of European Family Law Regarding Divorce and Maintenance Between Former Spouses*, K. Boele-Woelki, F. Ferrand, C. González Beilfuss, M. Jänterä-Jareborg, N. Lowe, D. Martiny and W. Pintens
8. *Inheritance Law Legislation of the Netherlands*, I. Sumner and H. Warendorf
9. *European Family Law in Action Volume III: Parental Responsibilities*, K. Boele-Woelki, B. Braat and I. Curry-Sumner (eds.)
10. *Common Core and Better Law in European Family Law*, K. Boele-Woelki (ed.)
11. *All's well that ends registered?*, I. Curry-Sumner
12. *Model Family Code – From a global perspective*, I. Schwenzer and M. Dimsey
13. *Harmonisation of Family Law in Europe. A Historical Perspective*, M. Antokolskaia
14. *Brussels II bis: Its Impact and Application in the Member States*, K. Boele-Woelki and C. González Beilfuss (eds.)
15. *Tensions between Legal, Biological and Social Conceptions of Parentage*, I. Schwenzer (ed.)
16. *Principles of European Family Law Regarding Parental Responsibilities*, K. Boele-Woelki, F. Ferrand, C. González Beilfuss, M. Jänterä-Jareborg, N. Lowe, D. Martiny and W. Pintens
17. *Juxtaposing Legal Systems and the Principles of European Family Law on Divorce and Maintenance*, E. Örücü and J. Mair (eds.)
18. *Convergence and Divergence of Family Law in Europe*, M. Antokolskaia (ed.)
19. *European Challenges in Contemporary Family Law*, K. Boele-Woelki and T. Sverdrup (eds.)
20. *Children and their parents*, M. Vonk
21. *La capacité de l'enfant dans les droits français, anglais et écossais*, L. Francoz Terminal
22. *Joint Parental Authority*, C.G. Jeppesen de Boer
23. *Debates in Family Law around the Globe at the Dawn of the 21st Century*, K. Boele-Woelki (ed.)
24. *European Family Law in Action Volume IV: Property Relations between Spouses*, K. Boele-Woelki, B. Braat and I. Curry-Sumner (eds.)

25. *Foundational Facts, Relative Truths. A Comparative Law Study on Children's Right to Know Their Genetic Origins*, R. Blauwhoff
26. *Imperative Inheritance Law in a Late-Modern Society. Five Perspectives*, C. Castelein, R. Foqué and A. Verbeke (eds.)
27. *Juxtaposing Legal Systems and the Principles of European Family Law on Parental Responsibilities*, E. Örücü and J. Mair (eds.)
28. *La justice des mineurs en Europe*, Y. Favier and F. Ferrand (eds.)
29. *The Future of Family Property in Europe*, K. Boele-Woelki, J. Miles and J. M. Scherpe (eds.)
30. *The Place of Religion in Family Law: A Comparative Search*, J. Mair and E. Örücü (eds.)
31. *Reconstructing Marriage. The Legal Status of Relationships in a Changing Society*, C. Sörgjerd
32. *Legal Recognition of Same-Sex Relationships in Europe*, K. Boele-Woelki and A. Fuchs (eds.)
33. *Principles of European Family Law Regarding Property Relations Between Spouses*, K. Boele-Woelki, F. Ferrand, C. González Beilfuss, M. Jänterä-Jareborg, N. Lowe, D. Martiny and W. Pintens
34. *Der nacheheliche Unterhalt: Grundlagen und Ausgestaltung im deutschen Unterhaltsrecht und in den Prinzipien der Commission on European Family Law*, P. Beuermann
35. *Family Law and Culture in Europe: Developments, Challenges and Opportunities*, K. Boele-Woelki, N. Dethloff and W. Gephart
36. *Children's Rights in Intercountry Adoption. A European Perspective*, C. Fenton-Glynn
37. *Nordic Cohabitation Law*, J. Asland, M. Brattström, G. Lind, I. Lund-Andersen, A. Singer and T. Sverdrup
38. *European Family Law in Action Volume V: Informal Relationships*, K. Boele-Woelki, C. Mol and E. van Gelder (eds.)
39. *Divided Parents, Shared Children. Legal Aspects of Residential Co-Parenting in England, the Netherlands and Belgium*, N. Nikolina
40. *Family Forms and Parenthood. Theory and Practice of Article 8 ECHR in Europe*, A. Büchler and H. Keller (eds.)
41. *The Child's Interests in Conflict. The Intersections between Society, Family, Faith and Culture*, M. Jänterä-Jareborg (ed.)
42. *Same-Sex Relationships and Beyond. Gender Matters in the EU*, K. Boele-Woelki and A. Fuchs (eds.)
43. *Nacheheliche Verantwortung in Frankreich und Deutschland*, K. Kaesling
44. *The Future of Registered Partnerships: Family Recognition Beyond Marriage?*, J.M. Scherpe and A. Hayward
45. *Plurality and Diversity of Family Relations in Europe*, K. Boele-Woelki and D. Martiny (eds.)
46. *Principles of European Family Law Regarding Property, Maintenance and Succession Rights of Couples in* de facto *Unions*, K. Boele-Woelki, F. Ferrand, C. González Beilfuss, M. Jänterä-Jareborg, N. Lowe, D. Martiny and V. Todorova
47. *Die Familienschiedsgerichtsbarkeit in Recht und Praxis: Eine Rechtsvergleichende Untersuchung des Deutschen und Englischen Rechts*, S.C. Zellerhoff
48. *Elderly Care and Upwards Solidarity: Historical, Sociological and Legal Perspectives*, E. Alofs and W. Schrama (eds.)

49. *Party Autonomy in EU Private International Law: Choice of Court and Choice of Law in Family Matters and Succession*, J. Gray
50. *The Interaction between Family Law, Succession Law and Private International Law: Adapting to Change*, J.M. Scherpe and E. Bargelli (eds.)
51. *International Handbook on Child Participation in Family Law*, W. Schrama, M. Freeman, N. Taylor and M. Bruning (eds.)
52. *The Child's Right to Participate in Family Law Proceedings: Represented, Heard or Silenced?*, C. Mol
53. *Cross-Border Recognition of Formalized Same-Sex Relationships: The Role of* Ordre Public, L. Vaigė
54. *Between Sexuality, Gender and Reproduction: On the Pluralisation of Family Forms*, N. Dethloff and K. Kaesling (eds.)
55. *Changing Families, Changing Family Law in Europe*, K. Duden and D. Wiedemann (eds.)
56. *The Principles of European Family Law Revisited*, K. Boele-Woelki, F. Ferrand, C. González Beilfuss, M. Jänterä-Jareborg, N. Lowe, D. Martiny and V. Todorova

www.ingramcontent.com/pod-product-compliance
Ingram Content Group UK Ltd.
Pitfield, Milton Keynes, MK11 3LW, UK
UKHW051927100926
8556IPUK00022B/1424

9 781839 704376